To Ted

With many thanks for
your friendship and
Support.

Kenneth

APOCALYPSE AND MILLENNIUM
Studies in Biblical Eisegesis

This book is about the various ways in which the Book of Revelation (the Apocalypse) has been interpreted over the last 300 years. It examines in detail Methodist, Baptist, English Anglican, and Roman Catholic uses of Revelation from 1600 to 1800, and then American and Seventh-day Adventist uses from 1800 on.

Apocalypse and Millennium argues that far from being a random sequence of bizarre statements, millennial schemes (including the setting of dates for the second coming of Christ) are more often characterised by highly complex and internally consistent interpretations of scripture. Such interpretations do not always result in positive outcomes. As an example, the work of David Koresh is examined at length. Koresh, styled by some the 'Wacko from Waco', clearly had views which some would find odd. However, his interpretation of scripture did not lack system or context, and to see him in that light is to begin to understand why his message had appeal, particularly to those of the Seventh-day Adventist tradition. The final three chapters in this book outline Koresh's thinking on end-time events and trace the line of his interpretative tradition from nineteenth-century Millerism through Seventh-day Adventism and Davidianism (which began in 1929).

KENNETH G. C. NEWPORT is Reader in Christian Thought at Liverpool Hope University College and serves on the board of the Charles Wesley Society. He is a regular presenter of papers at meetings of the Society of Biblical Literature and the American Academy of Religion, and his publications include *The Sources and 'Sitz im Leben' of Matthew 23* (1995) and numerous papers in the *Bulletin of the John Rylands University of Manchester*, *Methodist History*, the *Baptist Quarterly* and the *Wesleyan Theological Journal*.

APOCALYPSE AND MILLENNIUM

Studies in Biblical Eisegesis

KENNETH G. C. NEWPORT

Liverpool Hope University College

CAMBRIDGE
UNIVERSITY PRESS

PUBLISHED BY THE PRESS SYNDICATE OF THE UNIVERSITY OF CAMBRIDGE
The Pitt Building, Trumpington Street, Cambridge, United Kingdom

CAMBRIDGE UNIVERSITY PRESS
The Edinburgh Building, Cambridge CB2 2RU, UK   www.cup.cam.ac.uk
40 West 20th Street, New York, NY 10011–4211, USA   www.cup.org
10 Stamford Road, Oakleigh, Melbourne 3166, Australia
Ruiz de Alarcón 13, 28014 Madrid, Spain

First published 2000

Printed in the United Kingdom at the University Press, Cambridge

Typeset in Baskerville 11/12.5 pt [VN]

A catalogue record for this book is available from the British Library

Library of Congress Cataloguing in Publication data

Newport, Kenneth G. C.
Apocalypse and millennium: studies in biblical eisegesis/Kenneth G. C. Newport.
p.   cm.
Includes bibliographical references and index.
ISBN 0 521 77334 2
1. Bible. N.T. Revelation – Criticism, interpretation, etc. – History. I. Title.

BS2825.2.N485 2000
228'.06'0903–dc21
99–051375

ISBN 0 521 77334 2 hardback

For Rose-Marie, a true companion and friend

Contents

Illustrations

Illustrations 1, 2, 3, 5 and 6 are reproduced by courtesy of the Director and University Librarian, the John Rylands University of Manchester.

Preface

The writing of any book is in practice a team effort. The members of my team include Ursula Leahy, my former student and now research assistant, who has put in many hours preparing this book for publication. Her seemingly inexhaustible goodwill, hard work and eye for detail have left their mark on virtually every page. Other co-workers include Malcolm Bull, whose friendship and support over many years have been a source of great encouragement. Chapter 9 could not have been completed without the assistance of Mark Swett, an individual to whom all Waco researchers will be indebted. The reason for that indebtedness will quickly become apparent to the reader. Particular thanks are due also to Livingstone Fagan, a Branch Davidian and survivor of the Waco siege, who, despite his difficult circumstances, has been generous in answering my questions and providing me with some insight into the centrality of the biblical text in the tradition to which he belongs. Chapter 8 owes much to the kind assistance of Lynda Baildam of Newbold College in Berkshire, who generously gave of her time in locating some of the more obscure Millerite and early Seventh-day Adventist literature. Earlier chapters reflect the similar goodwill of librarians and archivists across the United Kingdom. These include Gareth Lloyd at the John Rylands University Library of Manchester and the staff at the Gradwell Library in Upholland, at Ushaw College in Durham and at St Deiniol's, Hawarden.

My colleague Professor Ian Markham is due particular mention for encouraging me to write this book in the first place. As a friend he has supported, as a scholar he has criticised, and as a line manager he has enabled. At Liverpool Hope University College I have been provided with ideal working conditions. These include superlative office space and computer provision, and the award of several generous travel grants which have enabled me to present some of my findings to the broader scholarly community at conferences overseas. Sue Harwood first transformed my old and poorly formatted computer files into something approaching the state-of-the-art electronic text required by the publisher.

The two anonymous readers for Cambridge University Press provided a mass of stylistic improvement, factual detail and theoretical insight, most of which has been incorporated. Kevin Taylor at Cambridge University Press first encouraged me to submit the typescript and to say that he has been understanding in extending the original intended limit by some 35,000 words is nothing if not an understatement.

My wife Rose-Marie and children Matthew, Stephen and Sarah have supported me throughout.

CHAPTER I

Introduction: texts, eisegesis and millennial expectation

On 19 April 1993 the now infamous siege of the headquarters of the Branch Davidians in Waco, Texas came to a fiery and dramatic close. As the dust settled and the smoke dispersed, the horror of what had happened became clear. Not only had David Koresh, the self-styled prophet and leader of the movement, perished, but so too had some eighty[1] of his followers. The count included a large number of children.

While the disturbing events in Waco have now slipped from general view, in academic circles at least interest in the Branch Davidians (and their successors) lives on. Already a considerable amount of work has been completed on the broader reasons for the tragedy, much of it conducted from a social-scientific perspective.[2] There has also been intense debate regarding the actual nature and sequence of events that took place during the Waco siege and the relative roles of the Bureau of Alcohol, Tobacco and Firearms (BATF), the FBI and the Branch Davidians themselves in bringing them about.[3]

There is, however, another aspect of this case that deserves much more attention than it has been given to date. An important part of the Branch Davidians' understanding of the world in which they lived was the belief that it was in that tradition, and now specifically through David Koresh, that the 'real' meaning of the scriptures had been made known. In particular the book of Revelation, they believed, was now fully understandable because David Koresh, at God's instruction and in

[1] There is some debate about the precise number of deaths. This number is based upon the list found in Stuart A. Wright (ed.), *Armageddon in Waco: Critical Perspectives on the Branch Davidian Conflict* (London: University of Chicago Press, 1995), pp. 379–81.
[2] The main sources are James R. Lewis (ed.), *From the Ashes: Making Sense of Waco* (Lanham, MD: Rowman & Littlefield, 1994); Wright (ed.), *Armageddon in Waco*; and James D. Tabor and Eugene V. Gallagher, *Why Waco? Cults and the Battle for Religious Freedom in America* (Berkeley, CA: University of California Press, 1995).
[3] See, for example, Dick J. Reavis, *The Ashes of Waco: An Investigation* (New York: Simon & Schuster, 1995); the video 'Waco: The Rules of Engagement' (Fifth Estate productions, 1997) has also been influential in the debate.

God's good time, had come to unpack this most mysterious of codes. The 'Apocalypse' was now just that: a 'revelation'[4] of God's purposes in and through history.

The text of Revelation, which, as we shall see, was understood by Koresh as a code-breaker for the rest of the Bible, was a central part of the structure of Branch Davidian beliefs and expectations. To be sure, Koresh did claim prophetic authority and was thereby able to make what he considered to be divinely inspired pronouncements and offer some 'new light' independent of the biblical text. However, from documents and other sources that have become available,[5] it is clear that he saw his primary task as interpretative. It was, he claimed, his God-given responsibility in these last days to interpret the book of Revelation, especially the seven seals of Revelation 6–8, and it was this task above all others that dominated his theological agenda. In Revelation's symbols he saw reflected a picture of his own apocalyptic world, and in its words he found the voice of God. Similarly it was his claim to be *the* divinely appointed interpreter of the book that gave him status and authority among his followers. As is argued extensively in chapter 9, Koresh's interpretation, based upon and extending the broader Seventh-day Adventist tradition to which he was heir, was a significant factor in the events of February to April 1993.

To most people, and certainly biblical scholars, Koresh's interpretation of Revelation appears at best bizarre. However, the interpretations given to biblical texts by individuals such as Koresh, even if they do appear to the outsider as strange, are surely important in themselves. They may not tell us much about the authorial intentions of the people who wrote the original texts, and historical-critical scholars will find little in such interpretations of any value or credibility at all. However, to view the process by which interpreters such as Koresh came to their conclusions and to bring sharply into focus the end result of that process is to gain entry to the thought world and thought processes of the interpreter. This in itself is a valid exercise. It might even be important and beneficial. Regrettably it is too late to test the latter claim in the context of Waco itself.

In this book a plea is made for more attention to be paid to this area.

---

4 The word 'Apocalypse' (ἀποκάλυψις) means an 'unveiling'.
5 The principal sources of information upon which this remark is based come in three forms. First, transcripts and tapes of David Koresh's own teachings; second, personal correspondence with survivors of Waco; and third, a set of nine audio tapes which record a series of Branch Davidian recruitment meetings held in Manchester, England in early 1990. See chapter 9 for precise details and locations.

It is argued here that much more work is needed in assessing the way in which texts are understood in a non-critical context, for it is primarily in this setting and not in a critical one that texts have the most significant impact. For example, few lives will have been changed by J. Massyngberde Ford's detailed and very scholarly presentation of the view that most of the book of Revelation was written by a non-Christian writer.[6] By contrast, the history of millennialism in general bears adequate testimony to the way in which non-critical interpretations of the same text have affected the lives of millions. There are more Jehovah's Witnesses and Seventh-day Adventists than there are members of the Society of Biblical Literature, and while the members of the latter society surely take their discipline seriously, the willingness of a Jehovah's Witness to die rather than have a blood transfusion is a more powerful statement of the centrality of the biblical text to this individual's world view than are any number of Pentateuchal commentaries or source-critical analyses.

This, then, is not a book concerned with the discipline generally known in biblical studies as *Auslegungsgeschichte* (the history of (biblical) interpretation) or with its close companion *Forschungsgeschichte* (the history of (biblical) research). Rather, we are concerned here with the history of *popular* exegesis and the interaction between the biblical text and the *non*-critical interpreter of it. This is an area that has been much neglected, but its potential significance in the field of social and religious history suggests that it is worthy of considerable further research.[7] The fact that it now has its own German word, *Wirkungsgeschichte* (always a good sign in biblical studies), is encouraging.

The majority of these studies focus upon the period c. 1550–1900 and are therefore almost by chronological definition non-critical interpretations of the text. Isaac Newton (1642–1727), John Gill (1697–1771), Charles Wesley (1707–88), Joseph Priestley (1733–1804) and a host of others were all very much a part of the scholarly elite of their days. They were academics. However, the scholarly elite to which they belonged was one that had not as yet imbibed the spirit of rationalism in the area of biblical studies. The text was assumed to be of supernatural origin, faultless and timeless in its message. Such views continue to live on in the present day in the form of non-critical Christian communities, some of which are discussed here in a little detail.

---

[6] J. Massyngberde Ford, *Revelation* (Garden City, NY: Doubleday, 1975).
[7] See especially Heikki Räisänen, 'The Effective "History" of the Bible: A Challenge to Biblical Scholarship?', *Scottish Journal of Theology* 45(1992): 303–24.

Throughout this book the main (though not the only) focus is upon the book of Revelation. This is particularly appropriate since it is this book more than any other in the Bible that has enlivened the interpretative imagination, and it is in the unpacking of Revelation's strange symbols that the process referred to here as 'eisegesis' (the art of reading into a text more or less whatever one wishes to find) is so clearly seen. As is demonstrated here, the book of Revelation is often central to highly imaginative schemes involving papal plots, Antichrists, demon armies, God's eschatological punishments, the return of Christ and the end of the world. It is perhaps not surprising, therefore, that some have judged the strange contents of that book to be so hazardous that they have felt it necessary to warn others 'beware of the Apocalypse which, when studied, almost always either finds a man mad, or makes him so'.[8]

This is not, however, the kind of warning to which many have given heed. In the present day, especially as we turn the millennium, highly imaginative interpretations of the book of Revelation abound. Some of these are discussed in chapter 9 and even the shallowest trawl of the World Wide Web (WWW) will quickly bring to light countless more. But this willingness to find in the text of Revelation warnings of eschatological battles and descriptions of present-day natural disasters and political intrigues (not to mention the unmasking of Antichrist) is by no means a new phenomenon. While it is true that the ancients had some difficulties with the text and it entered into the Christian canon only after some considerable dispute,[9] once it was in, the Apocalypse commanded considerable respect and attention. This seems particularly to have been the case in post-Reformation England, where people from across the denominational spectrum devoted themselves to a careful study of the prophecies held in that book, convinced that the words in Rev. 1.1 ('The Revelation of Jesus Christ, which God gave unto him, to shew unto his servants things which must shortly come to pass')[10] were to be taken literally and with absolute seriousness.

The very considerable interest in the book of Revelation which existed in post-Reformation England is easy to document. Ever since

---

[8] *Rainbow: A Magazine of Christian Literature, with Special Reference to the Revealed Future of the Church and the World* (24 vols., 1864–87), vol. III, p. 55. I owe this reference to Jeanette Sears, 'The Interpretation of Prophecy and Expectations of the End in Britain, 1845–1883', Ph.D. thesis, University of Manchester (1984), p. 7.

[9] For a brief summary see Robert H. Mounce, *The Book of Revelation*, rev. edn (Grand Rapids, MI: Eerdman's, 1998), pp. 21–4.

[10] Unless otherwise indicated, all scriptural quotations given in this volume are from the KJV since it is this translation with which the majority of interpreters discussed here are principally concerned.

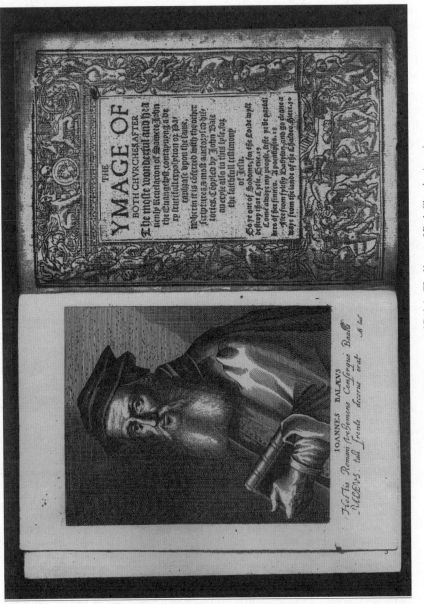

Figure 1   Title page of Bale's *The Ymage of Both Churches* (1550)

the publication of John Bale's book, *The Ymage of Bothe Churches after the Moste Wonderfull and Heavenly Revelacion of Sainct John the Evangelist* (1548), the title page of which is reproduced as Figure 1, a constant stream of works devoted to the Apocalypse poured from the English presses. Joseph Mede's *Clavis Apocalyptica* (1627) was perhaps the most influential, but there were many others such as Thomas Brightman's *Apocalypsis Apocalypseos* (c. 1600)[11] and John Tillinghast's *Knowledge of the Times* (1654). Shortly before the start of the eighteenth century Samuel Petto, a Suffolk clergyman,[12] published his own study of Revelation (and other biblical apocalyptic passages).[13] Petto's work was typical of the age in which it was written: the end is coming and the prophetic 'signs of the times' are clearly discernible in the Church and in the world at large. Careful study of the prophecies, especially those contained in the books of Daniel and Revelation, will give a clear insight into how long this world has yet to last and what must happen before it comes to an end.[14]

Many of the above-mentioned works sought to locate the earth's present position on the map of world time, a sensible enough task given the preconception of the book of Revelation as a panoramic overview of the course of human and divine history. Such an approach to the book of Revelation (and much of what is said in this context is applicable also to the book of Daniel and some other parts of the scriptures such as 2 Thess. 2) has become known as 'world and/or Church historicism',[15] for

[11] Thomas Brightman, *A Revelation of the Apocalyps* (1611). The date of the writing of this work is somewhat unclear. Froom notes that Latin editions appeared in 1609 (Frankfurt) and 1612 (Heidelberg), and gives 1615 as the earliest date for an English edition (see Le Roy Edwin Froom, *The Prophetic Faith of Our Fathers* (4 vols., Washington, DC: Review and Herald Publishing Association, 1946–54), vol. II, p. 512 n. 18). However, there is in the John Rylands University Library of Manchester an English edition published in Amsterdam dated 1611 (ref. R127410).

[12] Froom, *Prophetic Faith*, vol. III, p. 131.

[13] Samuel Petto, *The Revelation Unvailed: Or, an Essay Towards the Discovering I. When Many Scripture Prophecies had Their Accomplishment and Turneth into History II. What Are Now Fulfilling III. What Rest Still to be Fulfilled, with a Guess at the Time of Them. With an Appendix, Proving, that Pagan Rome Was not Babylon, Rev 17, and that the Jews Shall be Converted* (1693). See also J. Bachmair *The Revelation of St. John Historically Explained* (1778); B. Blayney, *A Dissertation by Way of an Inquiry into the True Import and Application of the Vision Related in Dan IX verse 20 to the End, usually Called Daniel's Prophecy of the 70 Weeks* (1775).

[14] Little is to be gained here from a mere listing of further sources. However, the extent of the literature devoted to the book of Revelation in post-Reformation England should not be underestimated. Some indication of the richness of the sources can be gained from the bibliographical sections in David Brady, *The Contribution of British Writers between 1560 and 1830 to the Interpretation of Revelation 13:16–18 (The Number of the Beast): A Study in the History of Exegesis* (Tübingen: J. C. B. Mohr (Paul Siebeck), 1983); Richard Bauckham, *Tudor Apocalypse* (Abingdon: The Sutton Courtenay Press, 1978) and the second volume of Froom, *Prophetic Faith*.

[15] On the use of this term see further Arthur W. Wainwright, *Mysterious Apocalypse* (Nashville: Abingdon Press, 1993), pp. 49–66.

it sees the course of history from the time of John the Seer or Daniel the prophet to the apocalyptic return of Christ (and even a little beyond) as being punctuated by prophetic fulfilment. According to the historicist interpreter, time moves on to its predetermined goal and the book of Revelation (together with Daniel etc.) previews that course. The images and symbols contained therein are thus milestones which are able to give the traveller some reasonably clear indication of how far has been travelled and how much further there is yet to go. For example, some argued that the four horsemen of Rev. 6.1–8 previewed the early history of the Church from its period of purity and conquest during the age of Christ and the apostles (the rider on the white horse) to more troubled experiences and persecutions at the hands of the Roman state (the rider 'death' on the pale horse).[16] Similarly, according to some interpreters the vision of the fifth angel, the falling star, the bottomless pit and the swarming locusts (Rev. 9.1ff.) was a vision of the birth of Islam.[17] Taken together, so the historicists argued, these and the other symbols of Revelation give an overview of world and/or Church history.

This historicist approach to biblical-prophetic interpretation, which continues to enjoy some support today,[18] has enjoyed a long and distinguished history in the Christian tradition generally. Quite when or with whom it began is unclear. Central to its adoption, however, and to its gaining a firm foothold on biblical scholarship, was Joachim of Fiore (c. 1135–1202). According to Joachim, the history of the human race is to be divided into three ages, the age of the Father (the age of Law), the age of the Son (the age of Gospel) and the age of the Spirit (the age of Freedom). The book of Revelation, he argued, gives a detailed account of the course of these three ages (or 'states' as he referred to them). As such the book refers not only to that which was (from John's perspective) future, but also to that which was past. Joachim held that the third of these ages had dawned with the coming of St Benedict (c. 480–550). Thus the Church and people are currently living in the third and final stage in the course of history.

Joachim's views on the three ages and the extent to which the book of Revelation referred in part at least to events prior to the birth of the Christian Church did not gain widespread support. His suggestion that

---

[16] See, for example, *The Christian's Complete Family Bible, Containing the Sacred Text of the Old and New Testament at Large. And the Apocrypha. Illustrated with Notes and Comments whereby the Difficult Passages are Explained; the Mistranslations Corrected; and the Seeming Contradictions, found in the Oracles of Truth, Reconciled* (1739).

[17] Ibid.   [18] See chapters 8 and 9.

the book of Revelation gives a detailed account of the course of history, however, was to prove highly influential in later Protestant literature, and it is with some justification that Joachim is looked upon as the key figure in the establishment of historicism as a method in the western interpretative tradition.[19]

This basic approach to the biblical text, though not the detail, enjoyed some modest support over the course of the next 300 years. However, it was with the birth of Protestantism that historicism really began to exert an influence. On the continent of Europe the method was well represented. Luther's own views can be seen clearly enough from his comments found throughout his *Table Talk*,[20] and historicism is seen also in the work of the Swiss reformers Theodore Bibliander (1504–64)[21] and Johann Heinrich Bullinger (1505–75).[22]

Such continental developments are, however, outside the scope of the present enquiry, which is focused primarily on sources written in English and/or published on English soil. Among such literature, at least amongst the Protestant part of it, historicism was almost (though not quite completely) ubiquitous during the period from the Reformation to c. 1850. Further, as this book makes clear, historicism as a method continues to exercise a significant influence in non-critical approaches to the book of Revelation, including that adopted by the Jehovah's Witnesses, and especially in the Seventh-day Adventist tradition and its Davidian/Branch Davidian trajectory.[23]

While historicist interpreters of the book of Revelation (and with it Daniel, 2 Thess. 2 and several other portions of the scriptures) disagreed on almost every point of interpretation, and while the basic paradigm was continually updated to take account of more recent historical developments (the French Revolution, for example, saw a radical rethinking on several key issues), there are at least two major points of interpretation upon which almost all historicist interpreters

---

[19] On Joachim's biblical interpretation see Wainwright, *Mysterious Apocalypse*, pp. 49–53. More detailed is Bernard McGinn, *The Calabrian Abbot: Joachim of Fiore in the History of Western Thought* (New York: Macmillan, 1985), pp. 145–60. A full and detailed study of Joachim and his legacy is to be found in Marjorie Reeves, *The Influence of Prophecy in the Later Middle Ages: A Study in Joachimism* (Oxford: Clarendon Press, 1969).

[20] See further Froom, *Prophetic Faith*, vol. II, pp. 273ff.   [21] Ibid., vol. II, pp. 338–9.

[22] J. H. Bullinger, *A Hundred Sermons on the Apocalips of Jesus Christ*. This was first published in Latin in 1557, French in 1558 and English in 1561. For a summary see Froom, *Prophetic Faith*, vol. II, pp. 339–45, and E. B. Elliott, *Horae Apocalypticae; or, A Commentary on the Apocalypse, Critical and Historical*, 4th edn (4 vols., London: Seeley, 1851), vol. IV, pp. 430–7.

[23] In this context one should compare Kai Arasola, *The End of Historicism: Millerite Hermeneutic of Time Prophecies in the Old Testament* (University of Uppsala, 1990), whose central thesis, that Millerism was the swan-song of historicism, seems inaccurate.

have traditionally agreed. These are the 'year-day' principle and the identity of Antichrist. Both these aspects of the historicist paradigm are of central and direct importance in all of the studies presented in this book.

According to the exponents of the 'year-day' principle, one day in prophetic time periods is equal to a literal year. It was with this basic understanding in mind that historicist interpreters approached passages such as Rev. 11.3, which reads, 'And I will give power unto my two witnesses, and they shall prophesy a thousand two hundred and three-score days, clothed in sackcloth.' The 'thousand two hundred and threescore days' here mentioned, so the historicists argued, are to be understood as the same number of literal years. The 1,260 prophetic days of Rev. 12.6 were counted in the same way, as were the 42 months of Rev. 13.5 (one month is taken as thirty days, $42 \times 30 = 1,260$) and the 'time, and times and half a time' taken as three-and-a-half years of 360 days each, $3\frac{1}{2} \times 360 = 1,260$ of Rev. 12.14. This principle is of fundamental importance, for it enabled historicist commentators to chart and predict the fulfilment of particular prophecies with assumed accuracy. Further, since such a prophetic time period is mentioned in connection with the rise and career of the first beast of Rev. 13.5 and the persecution of the faithful witnesses in Rev. 11.3 (cf. Rev. 12.6, 14), it gave a key, so it was thought, to both the identity of the beast and the period of his dominance. Thus, for example, the Baptist commentator Benjamin Keach (1640–1704), whose views are examined in greater detail in chapter 2, argued that the year 1688 was a year of particular prophetic importance, being the conclusion of the 1,260 year-days of Antichrist plus the three-and-a-half year-days of the witnesses' death (Rev. 11.11). Similarly, it was on the basis of the year-day principle as applied to Dan. 8.14 that William Miller (the subject of chapter 7) came to the conclusion that Jesus was to return visibly to this earth in 1844.

The twentieth-century critical mind is perhaps liable to leap quickly to attack such an apparently ludicrous and arbitrary equation; why should 'a day' actually mean 'a year'? However, this 'year-day' view can claim some very impressive support. It is of course always possible that otherwise eminently sensible individuals may let logic and common sense slip when it comes to religious matters, but the fact that Sir Isaac Newton (among others)[24] took the view that 'in *Daniel's* Prophecies days

---

[24] The eminent scientist Joseph Priestley (1733–1804), famous for his work on electricity and oxygen, also took this view. See *The Theological and Miscellaneous Works of Joseph Priestley* (25 vols., 1817–31), vol. XII, p. 329.

are put for years'[25] suggests that the hypothesis, when seen in its proper historical context, is not completely devoid of some rational basis. The biblical text itself is of course central, in which context it is important to note Ezek. 4.6, where Ezekiel is told to lie upon his side for forty days, for, says the Lord, 'I have appointed thee each day for a year' (see also Num. 14.34). This year-day principle reigned supreme in Protestant literature to c. 1850. In Jewish exegetical methodology it may have an even longer history than it has in the Christian tradition, but this is beyond our present concern.[26]

The second major point among Protestant historicist interpreters concerned the identity of Antichrist, and upon this point almost all Protestant commentators agreed: Rome, which now meant the Roman Catholic Church, is Antichrist, and it is therefore that institution which comes under such sustained attack in the book of Revelation. This belief was not new with the Protestants; indeed, even Joachim had suggested, or at least hinted, that Antichrist would come in the form of a Pope.[27] However, among the Protestants the view quickly became firmly established and highly developed. The Roman Catholic Church is at least one, perhaps both, of the beasts portrayed in Revelation 13; Roman Catholicism is the great harlot of Revelation 17 and is also presented as Babylon in Revelation 18, etc. So widespread was this view concerning the identity of Antichrist that Keach once wrote confidently:

'tis evident to all who are men of any Reading, that most of our Eminent Protestant Writers, both Ancient and Modern, do affirm without the least doubt, that the Church of *Rome* is the great Whore spoken of [in] *Rev.* 17.[28]

Combined with the year-day principle, this view that Rome was Antichrist provided the basis for some very precise calculations. The known history of Antichrist could be compared with the information revealed in the scripture about the time periods relating thereunto. This provided, for the historicist, an outline of the history of God's people as they struggled to defeat that spokesperson of Satan and an indication of what the future held and how long it would be.

[25] Sir Isaac Newton, *Observations upon the Prophecies of Daniel and the Apocalypse of St John* (1733), p. 123.
[26] The possible application of the use of 'day' to mean a 'year' in early Jewish prophetical literature is found, for example, in 4 Ezra 7.43 (c. AD 100), where we meet the phrase 'a week of years', meaning seven years. Two useful essays on this and related aspects of the history of the year-day principle are found in William H. Shea, *Selected Studies on Prophetic Interpretation* ([Washington, DC:] General Conference of Seventh-day Adventists, 1982), pp. 56–93.
[27] Bernard McGinn, *Antichrist: Two Thousand Years of the Human Fascination with Evil* (San Francisco: HarperCollins, 1994), p. 142.
[28] Benjamin Keach, *Antichrist Stormed* (1689), p. 1.

Such notions, then, characterised the historicist method and supported the argument that at least the year, if not the day or hour (cf.
Matt. 24.36) of 'the end' (however conceived) could be known. If God
had revealed the future course of history to the Seer John and before
that to the prophet Daniel, so it was argued, then anyone could by the
application of sheer reason (not faith)[29] discern from these scriptures the
points at which prophecy and what was now past history coincided. As
might perhaps be expected, such works most often resulted in the
adoption of the view that the writer's own period was the one perched
on the brink of the apocalyptic conclusion of the present age. There
were of course exceptions, of whom John Wesley was one,[30] but many
who did attempt to set a date for the dawn of the eschatological kingdom
put the event at no great distance from their own present.

Historicist interpretations of Daniel and Revelation were, then, widespread. Neither were they limited to those on the religious margins or of
questionable intellectual ability. Indeed, even such intellectual giants as
the noted Oxford academic Thomas Goodwin (1600–80)[31] and, as was
mentioned above, the eminent scientists Sir Isaac Newton and Joseph
Priestley,[32] turned their hands to the task of this kind of prophetic
interpretation. This list of historicist biblical-prophetic interpreters
could easily be extended, though to do so here would serve little purpose.
Throughout this book the general context of the specific work of Bale,
Mede, Newton, Priestley and others is sketched in, and much more
detailed studies are undertaken of the work of some other interpreters. It
will be noted throughout that historicism, still very much alive in groups
such as the Seventh-day Adventists, has a long and prestigious pedigree.

Before we leave historicism, one further point of clarification is
needed. Historicist interpreters of the prophecies view the books of
Daniel and Revelation as a panorama of human history. A significant
event in the course of that history is yet to occur, namely the second
coming of Christ himself. Belief in the eventual second coming is
standard in the literature and is a belief in the literal and visible return of
Jesus in bodily form.

[29] This is a point adequately made by Christopher Burdon, *The Apocalypse in England: Revelation Unravelling, 1700–1834* (London: Macmillan, 1997).
[30] See further chapter 5.
[31] Thomas Goodwin was head of Magdalen College, Oxford from 1650 to 1660. He wrote many works dealing with the general topic of prophetic interpretation including a series of sermons preached in Holland in 1639. These were published posthumously in 1683 under the title *Exposition upon the Book of the Revelation*. See further Brady, *Number of the Beast*, pp. 181–2.
[32] See, for example, Joseph Priestley, *The Present State of Europe Compared with Ancient Prophecies* (1794) and his *Notes on the Books of Daniel and Revelation* in *Works*, vol. XII, pp. 309–43; vol. XIV, pp. 442–515.

However, while the nature of the event was a matter upon which almost all historicist commentators agreed, the timing of it was a matter of significant dispute. In general two positions emerged: premillennialism and postmillennialism.[33] The basic distinction between these two positions relates to the timing of the events of Revelation 20, the first four verses of which may be quoted here for the sake of clarity. They read:

And I saw an angel come down from heaven, having the key of the bottomless pit and a great chain in his hand. And he laid hold on the dragon, that old serpent, which is the Devil, and Satan, and bound him a thousand years, And cast him into the bottomless pit, and shut him up, and set a seal upon him, that he should deceive the nations no more, till the thousand years should be fulfilled: and after that he must be loosed a little season. And I saw thrones, and they sat upon them, and judgment was given unto them: and I saw the souls of them that were beheaded for the witness of Jesus, and for the word of God, and which had not worshipped the beast, neither his image, neither had received his mark upon their foreheads, or in their hands; and they lived and reigned with Christ a thousand years.

This prediction of a period of 1,000 years, that is, a millennium, of perfect bliss when the saints will reign with Christ while Satan lies bound in chains was taken with absolute seriousness by those who believed the Bible to be literally true and the book of Revelation to be an accurate prediction of what was to happen in the future. Premillennialists and postmillennialists differed, however, on the question of the chronological sequence of such events, and in particular the question of whether Christ would come before or after the events described in the verses quoted above. According to the premillennialists Christ would come *before* the onset of these events. Postmillennialists, on the other hand, argued that Christ would come only *after* the events. Indeed, according to the latter group the millennium itself was a period of preparation for Christ's final return.

The theological differences hidden within this apparently simple distinction are significant. There are of course exceptions, of which the Seventh-day Adventist Church is one,[34] but in general premillennialists held (and hold) to a very negative view of humankind. They generally consider that humanity and/or human society is rotten to the core, and

---

[33] On the distinction between pre- and postmillennialism see further D.W. Bebbington, *Evangelicalism in Modern Britain: A History from the 1730's to the 1980's* (London: Unwin Hyman, 1989), pp. 60–3, 81–6.

[34] See chapter 8.

that this state of things can be overcome only by the direct, cataclysmic intervention of God. Things are bad and will get worse. Individuals and society at large will slip further and further into the moral chaos until this world is so totally wicked that God will himself act (as he did in Noah's day) to put things right. In the letter discussed in chapter 6, Charles Wesley is seen to hold precisely to this view, and a further dramatic example of it is seen also in the work of William Miller discussed in chapter 7. In Miller's system the world was moving, whether humankind liked it or not, steadily towards its predetermined goal. Jesus would come back on 22 October 1844 and the golden age would begin. Humankind, in Miller's estimation, had little part to play in the process other than to sound the alarm and prepare for that grand event – hence the title of one of the Millerite publications, *The Midnight Cry* (cf. Matt. 25.6). Miller cannot be accused of sitting back and waiting for the purposes of God to be worked out in their own time, for he was a tireless preacher who did what he thought right to prepare for the inevitable. However, to Miller, as to a number of the other commentators discussed in this book, the human race is not in real control of its own destiny. Humans act and develop only under the irresistible influence of external forces which drive them on to an inescapable and predetermined future.

Those who hold the opposing view, on the other hand, suggest that Christ will appear only after the 1,000-year period, and that it is during this period that the ground is prepared for the Lord's return by means of a radical and hitherto unprecedented spreading of the gospel and consequent social reform. This precursory millennium (not always understood to be literally 1,000 years) might also see the destruction of the hitherto dominant Antichrist (= the Roman Catholic Church), who must be destroyed as a part of the effort to 'make the pathways of the Lord straight' (cf. Mark 1.3). This view is clearly seen in several of the commentators noted below, perhaps most obviously in the work of Benjamin Keach, who saw 1689 as the point at which the millennium had broken in and Antichrist had suffered the first of the many and ultimately fatal blows that were to be struck against him. The arrival on British soil early in that year of the Protestant King William and the subsequent driving out (or 'storming', as Keach has it in the title of his book) of Antichrist in the form of the Catholic King James II were, for Keach, a clear sign that the binding of Satan (cf. Rev. 20.2) had begun. The process would continue: things would get better as God worked through human agents to prepare for Christ's final return.

Postmillennialists, then, looked with general confidence to the future as they waited and expected to see the purposes of God being worked out through the medium of human agents. Keach's fellow Baptist James Bicheno was to argue a similar case relative to the events of the French Revolution.[35] The distinction between these views is profound, for they have altogether different answers to the fundamental question of how, to use the New Testament terminology, the kingdom of God will come upon earth.

Such a question was posed long ago by Harris Franklin Rall, in an article in which he sought to compare and contrast Methodism and premillennialism, which, according to Rall, stand at opposite ends of the theological spectrum.[36] As is shown in chapters 5 and 6, Rall's knowledge of eighteenth-century Methodist eschatological expectation is wanting, and his description of premillennialism deficient. However, his work is nevertheless of value, in that he clearly sees the potential conflict between a basically premillennial view of the human condition and that of the majority of Methodists. Indeed, according to Rall, while premillennialists are content to wait patiently for the coming of the Lord, John Wesley himself, in bringing the gospel 'to the brutish and besotted peasantry of his England', bore witness to his faith that it was 'the power of the Spirit of God through which God purposed to make a new world'.[37] That is to say, God is at work in the world through the medium of various institutions and individuals, and human beings and societies are at least in part responsible for their own development and improvement. Where premillennialists looked for the cataclysmic intervention of God at the end of the age to put things right, John Wesley (according to Rall) looked to the progressive and continual intervention of God within human history, institutions and Christian individuals as the means by which his kingdom would come. Such thinking may appear abstract, but it found concrete expression in works dealing with prophetic interpretation. Neither are such apparently theoretical views always without real, sometimes catastrophic, results. As we shall see, Waco is an extreme case in point.

While the historicist paradigm, together with its pre- or postmillennialism, the year-day principle and the view of the papal Antichrist, was dominant in English Protestant scholarship during much of the period

---

[35] See chapter 2.
[36] Harris Franklin Rall, 'Methodism and Premillennialism', *Methodist Review*, fifth series, 36 (1920): 209–19.
[37] Ibid., pp. 211–12.

from the Reformation to the middle of the nineteenth century, and continues to find expression in some groups today, it is not the only one that has been on offer in the broader pre- or non-critical marketplace. One other fairly major view on the interpretation of the book of Revelation is that which has become known as idealism. According to the exponents of this approach, the book of Revelation is not to be understood literally at all. Rather in its strange symbols and bizarre images one finds a general commentary on the struggle between good and evil. This view was found fairly widely in the early Church tradition, at least from the time of Augustine, Bishop of Hippo (AD 345–430), who was himself building upon the work of Tyconius in the late fourth century.[38] However, among Protestants idealism is rarely encountered, and even among Catholics it is relatively infrequently employed after c. 1550. Just one example, that of the English Catholic interpreter Robert Witham, is noted in chapter 4, and even he did not put forward a fully idealist reading of the Apocalypse.

During the period with which this book is concerned, then, idealism was not a major force. Most Protestants adopted the historicist view of the prophetic parts of the Bible, and in post-Reformation Catholic circles in particular, two other methods gained a measure of acceptance. These were preterism and futurism. As would be expected, each served its principal exponents well as they sought to use the biblical text to make sense of the world in which they lived.

Preterism and futurism are considered extensively in chapter 4 as a major part of the analysis of the Roman Catholic response to the Protestant historicist paradigm; some Protestant cases are also there noted. Just a few introductory remarks are offered here. According to the preterists, most of Revelation was fulfilled within a relatively brief period following the composition of the book. What little was yet to be fulfilled would not occur until the very last stages of the world's history. Thus, according to the preterists, the bulk of the prophecies of Revelation, while accurate predictions of future events when seen in the context in which they were written, now belonged to the past. The present was devoid of prophetic fulfilment. Most preterists, for example, argued that the sequence of seven seals in Revelation 6–8 was, from John's perspective, an accurate prediction of the conquest by Christianity of Judaism and paganism, a process largely complete by the middle of the fourth century. Similarly the beasts of Revelation 13 related not,

---

[38] See further *Tyconius: The Book of Rules*, translated with an introduction and notes by William S. Babcock (Atlanta, GA: Scholars Press, 1989).

as the historicists argued, to the Roman Catholic Church throughout the long course of its history, but rather to matters relating primarily to John's own day, perhaps to the emperor Nero himself. Such a view should not be confused with the modern critical contemporary-historical method of interpretation,[39] though clearly it is a forerunner of it. According to contemporary-historical analysis, all of Revelation relates to John's own time (he is of course allowed to make some guesses as to the future). Preterists argued rather that John was given an accurate vision of the course of events over the next several centuries. By the time of the preterist interpreters themselves, however, in the sixteenth century and beyond, these predictions had long since found their fulfilment. Some few events were yet awaited, but most had passed.

The second group, the futurists, differed. According to them some relatively small part of the biblical prophecies had been fulfilled in the past: those in Revelation 1–3 were generally taken as 'the things which are' (Rev. 1.19b) and hence were seen as related to John's own time. However, the vast majority, 'the things which shall be hereafter' (Rev. 1.19c), were not to be fulfilled until the last stages of the world's history. Like the preterists, then, though the case is argued in an entirely different way, the futurists took the view that the present was not the time for the working out of the prophetic plan. Like preterism, futurism was a mode of interpretation that flourished particularly among Catholics in the post-Reformation period. As Paul Boyer has shown, however, among modern non-critical interpretations of Daniel and the book of Revelation, futurism has gained a remarkable following.[40] It is futurism, for example, that informs the work of Hal Lindsey, whose book *This Late, Great Planet Earth* was the non-fiction best seller of the seventies, with claimed sales of over 25 million copies.

While much of what has been said above relates primarily to the period prior to c. 1850, the attraction of such speculation upon the biblical text clearly did not terminate at that time. Neither was it found only on English soil. Some few continental commentators have been mentioned above. It has further been said that futurism continues to be a significant force in North American biblical interpretation today, although that futurist phenomenon is not explored any further in this work. Chapters 7–9 of this book do, on the other hand, demonstrate just

---

39 Such confusion does exist in the literature on Revelation. See Mounce, *Revelation*, p. 27 for an example.
40 Paul Boyer, *When Time Shall Be No More: Prophecy Belief in Modern American Culture* (Cambridge, MA.: The Belknap Press of Harvard University Press, 1992).

how central historicism has been, and continues to be, to the Millerite–Seventh-day Adventist–Davidian/Branch Davidian tradition. The latter line of enquiry is particularly fruitful, and, it is suggested below, important, for it is clear from the evidence that while historicism and mainstream scholarly biblical studies were destined to go their separate ways during the course of the nineteenth century, historicism itself continues to live on, indeed to thrive, in this narrower, largely non-critical context.

It was suggested above that investigation into this kind of interpretative activity is not only 'fruitful' but also 'important'. The latter claim stems from the fact that while prophetic-interpretative speculation of the kind discussed in this book may have the appearance of a chaos of abstractions, it sometimes has very real consequences. This is seen particularly in the case of the Branch Davidians. However, the apparent negative aspect of the 'afterlife' of the book of Revelation seen so dramatically at Waco is not an isolated case, for the book has been a significant and important factor in many other outbreaks of apocalyptic zeal which have similarly led to death and destruction. Taking one further example almost at random from the many available, one might think of the Taborites, a group of extreme Hussites dating from the fifteenth century. The group, resident in Bohemia, had a clear conception of who the 'beast' of Revelation was (the Pope) and of their own duty to oppose him. The world was, so the Taborites argued, entering the period of Antichrist and the messianic woes. The opposition to Antichrist took the form not only of rejection of papal doctrine, but of the view, and action upon it, that it was the duty of the faithful to slay sinners in preparation for the second coming of Christ. Real lives were lost and real blood spilt as the Taborites put theory into practice and sought to prepare the way of the Lord.

No pity, they declared, must be shown towards sinners, for all sinners were enemies of Christ. 'Accursed be the man who withholds the sword from shedding the blood of the enemies of Christ. Every believer must wash his hands in that blood.' The preachers themselves joined eagerly in the killing, for 'every priest may lawfully pursue, wound and kill sinners'.[41]

The Taborites, like many of those individuals and groups examined in this book, wove much biblical material into their scheme. The book of

[41] Norman Cohn, *The Pursuit of the Millennium: Revolutionary Millenarians and Mystical Anarchists of the Middle Ages* (London: Paladin, 1970), p. 212. Numerous further examples of such thinking and action are found throughout Cohn's study.

Revelation was, however, absolutely central to their views concerning Antichrist. Again, then, its negative afterlife may be noted. Like the pale horse of Rev. 6.8, the text too sometimes finds death and hell following in its wake.

In chapter 3 further attention is drawn to a different aspect of Revelation's negative legacy, namely the use of it to support and/or reflect anti-Catholic sentiments in eighteenth-century England. In that chapter the use of the text by the strong Protestant majority to demonise the weak Roman Catholic minority is dealt with in some detail, with specific attention being paid to the means by which Protestant commentators managed to read into the text of Revelation their assumptions regarding the identity of Antichrist. Hence chapter 3 has particular significance in providing a contrast to the often-repeated remark that the Apocalypse is the voice of the underdog and that expositions thereof are often the vehicles by which the voice of the repressed and socially disadvantaged can be heard. Elisabeth Schüssler Fiorenza, for example, whose comments are not untypical, argues that

In contrast to mainline churches and theology, 'Bible-believing' Christians, who often belong to socially disadvantaged and alienated minority groups, give Revelation pride of place in preaching and life. They read Revelation as allegory and often utilize it as prophetic oracle predicting the schedule and plan for the end-time events which can be deciphered. Other oppressed and disadvantaged Christians read Revelation contextually as a political-religious typology that speaks to their own situation. Latin American or South African liberation theologies cherish Revelation's political world of vision for its prophetic indictment of exploitation and oppression as well as its sustaining vision of justice.[42]

Schüssler Fiorenza may well be right: the book of Revelation can be and often is 'utilized' by the kind of readers to whom she refers, and for the entirely positive and laudable ends she identifies. However, there is surely a need to balance her remark, for, as the history of its interpretation and influence clearly indicates, Revelation (and with it Daniel and 2 Thessalonians etc.) can be used no less effectively in the hands of oppressors, to demonise others and justify, or at the very least reflect, religious intolerance. The book appeals to those within the established Churches no less than to those on the margins.[43] It appeals to the

---

[42] Elisabeth Schüssler Fiorenza, *Revelation: Vision of a Just World* (Edinburgh: T. & T. Clark, 1991), p. 7.

[43] This is a point upon which Schüssler Fiorenza may be challenged, for her remark that in general 'mainline Christianity insisted upon its [Revelation's] canonical marginality' (p. 6) does not appear entirely accurate, at least when considered in the context of eighteenth-century England.

powerful no less than to the powerless; to the strong no less than to the weak.

It is apparent, then, that this study also raises once again the question of the relative contributions of text and interpreter in the process of interpretation. Is it the reader or the text that has control of the process? In all probability the answer comes somewhere between these two poles. Readers do bring to texts their own presuppositions, prejudices, interests and desires, and those subjective elements have a major impact on the way that the text is understood. However, the text imposes at least some element of order on the reader's thoughts and gives the interpretation a basic structure. The text may be pliable, but it cannot be dispensed with altogether.

This whole area of subjectivity and the relative roles of readers and texts has been of major concern to biblical scholars in recent years, and in literary theory more generally it has enjoyed even more sustained and longer-term attention. It is not the intention in this volume to enter into that discussion on the level of theory. Such approaches exist already.[44] However, it is intended that the discussion be entered into in another way. Through the presentation of individual case studies, some of the dangers inherent in reader-centred approaches to the scriptures will, it is hoped, be illustrated clearly. In particular two closely connected issues are raised.

First, it is noted throughout the studies presented here that it is indeed possible for readers to take near absolute control in the interpretative exercise. This is not to negate what was said above regarding the extent to which texts do exercise some influence in the overall interpretative exercise, but simply to accept that often the level of that control is very slight. The text yields to the interests of the reader, with the result that it is made to bear the weight of the reader's own prejudices and concerns. Often those prejudices and concerns are not the reader's alone, but are those of a wider community to which he (and all the interpreters dealt with in this book are male) belongs and under whose expectations he is labouring. This is of course not a new observation.[45]

The second point is a simple one. It is this: the end product of reader-dominated interpretations of texts is not always positive. This

---

[44] The question is at the heart of the work of a number of literary theorists, including the highly influential Stanley Fish and Wolfgang Iser. For a summary see The Bible and Culture Collective, *The Postmodern Bible* (New Haven, CT: Yale University Press, 1995), pp. 20–69.

[45] See *The Postmodern Bible*, pp. 20–69, and note especially the work of Stanley Fish, *Is There a Text in this Class? The Authority of Interpretive Communities* (Cambridge, MA: Harvard University Press, 1980).

observation is particularly important in the context of religious texts, since by virtue of their claimed association with the text itself (and the presumed author thereof, namely God), such interpretations share in the authority invested in the scriptures by the community to which those scriptures and their interpretations belong. This can be dangerous and have extremely negative results. Koresh is one among many examples, and while it may be possible to argue in the abstract that all readings of texts are of equal value, the claim looks less than satisfactory when seen alongside the charred bodies at Waco or even, less dramatically, the tear-stained faces of the disappointed Millerites as they turned to face the uncertain future on the morning of 23 October 1844.[46] Persecuted Catholics in eighteenth-century England might also have had good reason to complain that not all readings of biblical texts are equally good.

In this book, then, such issues are raised. Several chapters are particularly important in the context of these broader issues, and all address them to some degree. A further burden of these chapters is to illustrate a closely connected point, namely that in the process of determined interpretation to suit the reader's ends (and here negative ones are particularly in view), ingenuity knows almost no bounds. Interpreters determined to find papists in every nook and cranny of Revelation, Daniel and 2 Thessalonians 2 exercised quite phenomenal creativity, frequently of a highly sophisticated kind. The text was approached by such interpreters in much the same way as one might approach a mathematical problem. It was not in the least a matter of making a series of random and increasingly bizarre statements unconnected to each other or lacking any systematic structure. Rather, working with the key principles in mind (the basic historicist approach, the year-day equation and the papal Antichrist paradigm), most of the interpreters considered here constructed highly complex schemes designed to appeal not to the heart so much as to the head. It was Miller who described the Bible as a 'feast of reason', but, as is apparent in all the chapters below, that basic sentiment is not absent elsewhere. The application of that 'reason' was, however, done imaginatively, and the whole edifice rested upon the basic historicist principles. It is at this point, it is suggested, that the highest level of subjectivity enters in. Indeed, it is quite noticeable in the literature just how absent is any argumentation for the historicist approach, the year-day principle or the papal Antichrist paradigm. These

---

[46] See chapter 7.

three foundations, upon which the internally self-consistent and more often than not 'reasonable' interpretations of Revelation, Daniel etc. are built, are generally simply accepted as givens. They are seen as neither open to question nor in need of support. With these in place the Protestant edifice can begin to rise.

What has been said immediately above can, however, be divorced from the entirely separate question of the value of the study of *eis*egesis as a legitimate, indeed valuable, area for further research. Biblical texts are likely to give rise to a very personal and hence highly informative outpouring of the human soul. This is a point well illustrated in the studies here presented. Thus the history of *eis*egesis seems a fruitful area for academic enquiry. The fundamental concern of this discipline is to see the vital link that exists between the beliefs and concerns of the reader (which are of course dependent upon his or her cultural and historical context) and the kind of interpretation which that reader then gives to the text. George Tyrrell's famous remark that those seeking to reconstruct a life of Jesus are all too often in the position of looking into a deep well only to see there a faint reflection of themselves may well be valid.[47] However, those distorted images at the bottom of Tyrrell's well surely have some value, if not to the biblical scholar of the historical-critical school, at least to the historian of ideas, and perhaps to the literary theorist as well. Tyrrell was right to suggest that in the area of research into the historical Jesus subjectivity is a powerful force. However, the power of subjectivity is no less clearly seen in the area of prophetic interpretation and, as Waco among other examples illustrates, this is not just a matter of idle curiosity.

A final point of introduction: the studies presented here are limited in scope but range across a wide chronological, geographical and denominational field. Despite the range and diversity of approaches here presented, an underlying continuity between the chapters will nevertheless be noted. First the basic outline of the Protestant interpretative paradigm is brought into focus through an examination of the works of two seventeenth-century Baptist commentators, Hanserd Knollys and Benjamin Keach. In the works of both men the process of eisegesis can be seen as they seek to make sense of the events of the world in which they live. Such events, including, in Keach's case, the Glorious Revolution of 1688, are seen by both interpreters in the light of the events predicted in the book of Revelation. In chapter 3 this study is extended

---

[47] George Tyrrell, *Christianity at the Cross-Roads* (London: Longman's, Green & Co., 1910), p. 44.

further as one aspect of the Protestant paradigm, the view that the Pope
was Antichrist (a view clearly seen in the work of Knollys and Keach), is
examined in detail in its eighteenth-century context. Here the ingenuity
with which interpreters were able to find the Pope and/or Roman
Catholics in general mirrored in the symbols of Revelation is brought to
the surface in an attempt to illustrate the power of the eisegetical mind.
In chapter 4 the Catholic reaction to the Protestant paradigm is examined, with a specific focus upon English Catholic readings of the Apocalypse. As we shall see, Roman Catholics were no less ingenious than
were Protestants in inventing readings of the Apocalypse that suited
their own ends. Chapter 5 stays with the eighteenth century and ex-
plores the way in which the book of Revelation (and some other parts of
the scriptures) was interpreted in the early Methodist tradition, where,
somewhat surprisingly, and running counter to received Methodist
historical wisdom, a fairly traditional historicist, anti-Catholic, premillennial reading of the Apocalypse is clearly in evidence. Chapter 6
builds upon this general outline by providing a detailed account of
Charles Wesley's reading of the book of Revelation and his conclusion
that the world was to end in 1794. With chapter 7 the focus is shifted on
several fronts. In order to make the case that the kind of eisegetical
process seen so clearly in post-Reformation Britain was by no means
limited to that context, attention is shifted to nineteenth-century America. This chapter deals in particular with William Miller, who lived in
America during the first part of the nineteenth century but built upon
the classic British interpretations of the earlier period. In chapter 7 the
textual focus is also shifted to the book of Daniel, again with the
intention of demonstrating the adaptability of the basic historicist
model. It was on the basis of this model that Miller concluded from Dan.
8.14 that the world would end on 22 October 1844. One of Miller's most
successful denominational offspring, the Seventh-day Adventist
Church, is examined in chapter 8 with a particular emphasis upon the
view that that group took regarding the role of America in prophecy.
This theme is then taken up in the last chapter as the influence of such
thinking is followed into one of Seventh-day Adventism's splinter
groups, the Branch Davidians.

This geographical, chronological and denominational spread is fully
intended. Eisegesis is not the preserve of any particular nation, century
or religious affiliation. It is an activity engaged in by seventeenth-
century English Baptists no less than by late twentieth-century American Branch Davidians, and Roman Catholics no less than Methodists

have been schooled in the art. Indeed, while the claim could not be substantiated on the basis of the evidence presented in this book alone, the many hours that have been spent in libraries and archives, on the World Wide Web and in conversation during the preparation of the present book have given the cumulative impression that eisegesis is more or less endemic, at least in pre- or contemporary non-critical biblical studies. Perhaps in such circles, concerned as the members of them generally are to 'live by the Bible', the words of John the Seer himself should be more carefully considered. The words are characteristically threatening, but the basic advice seems useful.

For I testify unto every man that heareth the words of the prophecy of this book, If any man shall add unto these things, God shall add unto him the plagues that are written in this book: And if any man shall take away from the words of the book of this prophecy, God shall take away his part out of the book of life, and out of the holy city, and from the things which are written in this book. (Rev. 22.18–19)

CHAPTER 2

Hanserd Knollys, Benjamin Keach and the book of Revelation: a study in Baptist eisegesis

We saw in chapter 1 that interest in the books of Daniel and especially Revelation was widespread among English Protestant interpreters during the period c. 1550–1800.[1] Such an interest is reflected in the wealth of surviving materials devoted to these portions of the scriptures, materials which include not only published books and tracts, but also MS letters, sermons and notebooks.[2] The interest is spread across denominational ties: as will be seen in chapters 5 and 6, a significant interest in the proper interpretation of Daniel and Revelation is clearly noticeable in early Methodist sources; the Unitarian Joseph Priestley also paid much attention to such matters, as did the leading English Presbyterian Thomas Brightman (1562–1607) and a number of Established Church scholars such as Goodwin and Mede. It was not just among such notable groups as the sixteenth-century 'Fifth Monarchy Men' (so called since they believed that it was their task to establish the 'Fifth Monarchy', i.e. the one following the other four symbolised by the statue of Daniel 2)[3] that the interpretation of Daniel and Revelation was judged to be of primary importance. It was, rather, a concern expressed very widely indeed.

It is not surprising, then, to find that Baptist writers shared this general, cross-denominational and widespread interest in the prophecies. John A. Oddy has already given some indication of this interest in eighteenth-century Baptist sources, and highlights in particular the

---

[1] A earlier version of a part of this chapter was published under the title 'Benjamin Keach, William of Orange and the Book of Revelation: A Study in English Prophetical Interpretation', in *Baptist Quarterly* 36 (1995): 43–51. I am grateful to the editor of that journal for permission to reuse some of that material here.

[2] Such MS sources include the several sermons and notebooks to which reference is made in chapter 5 and the letter of Charles Wesley reproduced in full as an appendix to chapter 6.

[3] See further Bernard Capp, *The Fifth Monarchy Men: A Study in Seventeenth-Century English Millenarianism* (London: Faber, 1972); Philip George Rogers, *The Fifth Monarchy Men* (London: Oxford University Press, 1966).

work of James Bicheno (1752–1831), a Baptist minister from Newbury, Berkshire, whose interest in the prophecies was considerable.[4] It was Bicheno's view that the events of the French Revolution had particular prophetic significance. Indeed, the year 1789, according to him, marked the turning point of history, for it was in that year that the great Antichrist (the Roman Catholic Church) received a crushing blow.[5] Another Baptist commentator noted by Oddy, Joseph Tyso (1774–1852), is also of interest here. He, unusually (at least in Protestant circles), took the view that the main prophecies of Revelation were as yet unfulfilled. As we have seen in the previous chapter, and shall see further in chapter 4, this 'futurist' position was prominent among Catholic expositors of the period; however, to find it in the works of a Baptist is, as Oddy observes, quite extraordinary. Similarly the Baptist commentator John Gill, whose wider views on the identity of Antichrist are discussed further in chapter 3, also had a keen interest in the prophecies, arguing, among other things, that 'the conjecture is not improbable' that the end of Antichrist's (Rome's) reign will come in the year 1866.[6]

This very short list of Baptist commentators who expressed interest in the prophecies of Daniel and Revelation could easily be extended,[7] though to do so is not the intention here. Rather it is the purpose of this chapter to examine in some finer detail the work of two earlier Baptist commentators, Hanserd Knollys and Benjamin Keach, both of whom produced works in the midst of the excitement of the events in England around 1688. This date is of course highly significant, and the context in which both Knollys and Keach were working forms the backdrop to their eisegesis of the text. This was a period during which English Protestants in general, including Baptists, felt under some significant threat. Ever since the restoration of the English monarchy in 1660 there had been concern among Protestants regarding the possibility of the re-establishment of the Catholic faith in Britain. This fear was not groundless. Charles II, who reigned from 1660 to 1685, was widely

---

[4] John A. Oddy, 'Bicheno and Tyso on the Prophecies: A Baptist Generation Gap', *Baptist Quarterly* 35 (1993): 81–9.

[5] Ibid., pp. 84–5. Bicheno's interpretative scheme is dealt with more extensively by Oddy in his 'Eschatological Prophecy in the English Theological Tradition, c. 1700–c. 1840', Ph.D. thesis, University of London (1982), pp. 61–4, and in Froom, *Prophetic Faith*, vol. II, pp. 746–8.

[6] John Gill, *Exposition of the Bible* (NT, 3 vols., 1748; OT, 6 vols., 1766); 1809 edition, vol. III, p. 792. All references to it here are to the 1809 edition.

[7] Thus, for example, note might have been made of Sayer Rudd (d. 1757), whose work *An Essay Towards a New Explication of the Doctrines of the Resurrection, Millennium, and Judgment* (1734) was published two years before he left the Baptist community and conformed to the Established Church.

suspected of having Catholic sympathies, though if he did, he kept them largely out of the public eye. His brother, who was to succeed as James II, was, however, less inhibited, and his adherence to Catholicism was a matter of general knowledge. James was willing to practise his religion publicly, and his desire to see the removal of obstacles to the practice of the Catholic faith quickly found expression following his accession in 1685. Such deeds could hardly fail to give concern to those who considered Rome to be none other than Antichrist. Even the various moves made during this period towards some degree of religious tolerance were seen by dissenters as very much a mixed blessing, for while on the one hand such moves granted them a certain degree of freedom, they did the same also for the despised religion of the papists.[8]

That James should be on the throne at all was bad enough, but the unexpected arrival of an heir in the form of his son, born on 10 June 1688, was a matter of even more concern. The child would presumably follow in his father's Catholic footsteps and thus the possibility of an endless line of Roman Catholic English monarchs was raised. It must therefore have seemed to those living during this period as though the Roman Catholic religion was on the verge of establishing itself on English soil once again. The threat of domination by Antichrist was again very real. In addition to this issue of the possible restoration of Catholicism in England, which was of general Protestant concern, Baptists had the further problem that the period after 1660 brought some level of intermittent persecution.[9] From a Baptist perspective, then, the situation leading up to 1688 was not bright.

However, there was a sudden and dramatic turn of events. Barely had six months passed since the birth of James' son than James himself was on a ship sailing away from England, and with him went any expectation of a renewal of the Catholic faith in England. In the Catholic King James' place were now King William and Queen Mary, Protestants of unquestionable firmness in the faith. Antichrist had been ousted and the threat overcome.

It was in this context that both Knollys and Keach wrote. Knollys, the earlier writer, whose work was completed before the departure of James, was particularly concerned to strengthen and support his community

---

[8] See generally J. Miller, *Popery and Politics in England 1660–88* (Cambridge: Cambridge University Press, 1973). More specific is B. R. White, *The English Baptists of the Seventeenth Century* (London: Baptist Historical Society, 1983), pp. 109–10 and S. H. Mayor, 'James II and the Dissenters', *Baptist Quarterly* 34 (1991): 180–90.

[9] For a full study see T. E. Dowley, 'The History of the English Baptists During the Great Persecution, 1660–1688', Ph.D. thesis, University of Manchester (1976).

during hard times and to give hope for things to come. Keach, on the other hand, writing after the actual arrival of the Protestant King William, was keen to reflect upon the significance of this turn of events in the wider purposes of God. As we shall see, both drew extensively on the text of Revelation and both saw in it a picture of their own individual worlds.

HANSERD KNOLLYS (1598–1691)

Hanserd Knollys was a keen interpreter of the prophecies.[10] His major work, and the one considered here, is *An Exposition of the Whole Book of the Revelation* (1689),[11] though it was not the only volume he penned on the topic.[12]

The work on Revelation is typical of its seventeenth-century English context, and manifests a clear belief in the literal, visible second coming of Jesus.[13] This belief is postmillennialist, that is, Knollys believes that the second coming will take place only after the period of the millennium (Rev. 20.1–6), which he understands as a literal 1,000-year period during which the kingdom of God will advance upon earth.[14] It is during this millennium that the kingdom of God is established through the preaching of the gospel, the outpouring of the spirit and the destruction of the 'kingdoms of this world' (cf. Rev. 11.15).[15] At the end of the

---

[10] For a sketch of Knollys' life see the *Dictionary of National Biography* (hereafter *DNB*), vol. XIII, pp. 279–81. Knollys' life is also described (somewhat hagiographically) in Joseph Ivimey, *A History of the English Baptists* (4 vols; 1811–30), vol. II, pp. 347–59 and by B. R. White in *Hanserd Knollys and Radical Dissent in the Seventeenth Century* (London: Dr Williams's Trust, 1977).

[11] H[anserd] K[nollys], *An Exposition of the whole Book of the Revelation. Wherein the Visions and Prophecies of Christ are opened and Expounded: Shewing the Great Conquests of our Lord Jesus Christ for his Church over all His and Her Adversaries, Pagan, Arian and Papal; and the Glorious State of the Church of God in the New Heavens and New Earth, in these Latter Days* (1689). The *DNB* gives the date for this work as 1668, but this seems to be in error and is probably derived from Ivimey, *English Baptists*, vol. II, p. 357; there are several obvious direct literary overlaps between Ivimey's account of Knollys' life and work and that found in the *DNB*. The date given on the title page is 1689, though it was licensed on 12 September 1688. The work was thus completed before the arrival of William of Orange, an event which, as we shall see, was thought by the later writer Keach to have particular prophetic significance.

[12] Hanserd Knollys, *Apocalyptical Mysteries* (1669); *Treatise on Mystical Babylon Unveiled* (1679); *An Exposition of the Eleventh Chapter of Revelation* (1679); *The World that now is and the World that is to come; or the First and Second Coming of Jesus Christ* (1681); and several other similar works. He is also reputed to have been the author of a pamphlet entitled *Key of Prophecy; whereby the Mystery of all the Prophecies are Unclosed but especially Showing how the Little Horn of the Beast of the Bottomless Pit means the Parliaments of England which Killed the Two Witnesses and a Threefold King* (n.d.). This work is attributed to Knollys by J. W. Brooks in his work *A Dictionary of Writers on the Prophecies* (London: 1835), though this seems in error (see Brady, *Number of the Beast*, p. 152 n. 16).

[13] Knollys, *Exposition*, p. 5.   [14] Ibid., pp. 222–5.   [15] Ibid., p. 153.

thousand years will come the great day of judgement. It is at this time that Jesus returns visibly as Lord with power and great glory. Heaven and earth are dissolved to give way to a new heaven and a new earth.[16] Thus far Knollys fits in fairly comfortably with the general postmillennialist views of many of his contemporaries and predecessors.

Where Knollys does begin to diverge from this widely accepted interpretative scheme, however, is in his suggestion that the year 1688 will see the dawn of the millennial kingdom. This is to be expected, since those who do set dates for the culmination of this world's history generally conclude that the age in which they themselves are living is the one which is on the edge of the eschatological climax. For example, in a work published in 1706, the scholar William Whiston (1667–1752), who himself had some Baptist leanings, argued that the turning point of history was due to come in the year 1716. (Whiston's work will be considered more fully in chapter 3.) Later writers suggested later dates. Priestley argued that the conclusion of the 2,300-day prophecy of Dan. 8.14, and with it many of the prophecies of Revelation, was due to come 'in our own time'.[17] Similarly, as we shall see in chapter 6, Charles Wesley set the date of the end at 1794, arguing this on the basis of his interpretation of Rev. 13.18. Knollys is in good company, then, in that like other commentators he has interpreted the text of Revelation in such a way as to make it speak in very dramatic terms to his own time.

The dawn of the eschatological kingdom of God is not, according to Knollys, at any great distance. Indeed, although there is some slight room for error, the light will break somewhere very close to 1688.[18] This will be the time when Antichrist (the Roman Catholic Church) falls, Satan is bound (in accordance with Rev. 20.2) and the kingdom of God begins to advance upon earth. One thousand years after this date, it may be presumed, Knollys expects the literal, visible second coming of Jesus and the final great day of judgement. We can only conjecture what Knollys made of the apparent fulfilment of the first of these predictions. The last few months of 1688 must have found him in a pitch of some considerable excitement.

The precise details of Knollys' calculation of the 1688 date are not of primary concern here, but may be outlined briefly since they indicate the ingenuity of his approach and his determination to make the text fit his own concerns. In calculating the 1688 date he has paid particular attention to Rev. 13.5, which states that a certain beast, which he

[16] Ibid., p. 225.   [17] Priestley, *Works*, vol. XII, p. 329.   [18] Knollys, *Exposition*, p. 169.

understands as a prophetic symbol of the Roman Catholic Church, was given power to continue '42 months'. It is this period which he sees as the key to the whole prophetic timetable. The beast will last 42 (prophetic) months, and this he calculates as equal to 1,260 literal years. The method by which he achieves this figure is standard within the broader context of eighteenth-century English prophetical eisegesis. One (prophetic) month is equal to 30 days, so 42 months equal 1,260 days. Further, in prophecy one day is equal to a literal year,[19] so the 1,260 prophetic days (cf. Rev. 11.3; 12.6) are equal to 1,260 literal years. All Knollys has to do now is fix the time for the start of this period and he will arrive at the date for Antichrist's downfall.

Knollys puts the birth of the beast of Rev. 13.5 (Rome/Antichrist) in AD 428, when, he says, papal Rome arose from the ashes of pagan Rome. The beast will thus come to an end in 1688. He gives no clear explanation of the reasons for his adoption of the 428 date. It may have been that he was focusing on the reign of Celestine I, who was known for his attempts to expand the power of the Roman Bishop into both North Africa and the East, and to promote the view of the Bishop of Rome's universal headship. Celestine reigned from 422 to 432, and the midpoint of his reign would have been near the 428 date. Hence while the date given by Knollys for the birth of the beast looks fairly arbitrary, it is perhaps not quite as arbitrary as one might at first think.[20] That said, it remains a perhaps uncharitable suspicion that the real reason for the choice of the date is that it is 1,260 years prior to the year in which Knollys is writing. He may well be working backwards.

What is plain is that Knollys has appropriated the text for his own purposes and by his ingenious eisegesis (tempered perhaps by some concern for historical credibility) is able to make it speak directly to his own age. This process is quite understandable, for by it he has made the text relevant to his own Baptist community. The message that the dawn of the kingdom of God is nigh is one which is likely to be extremely attractive to a community such as Knollys', which, as we have noted above, was under significant stress during the period from 1660 to 1688.

By locating the fulfilment of prophecy just around the next corner, Knollys has been able to make the text of Revelation particularly significant for his own times. However, like the 'scribe trained for the kingdom' in Matt. 13.52, he is able to bring out from the scriptural

[19] Ibid., p. 162.
[20] I am grateful to an anonymous reader for Cambridge University Press for pointing out this possibility to me.

storeroom not just one, but a multiplicity of treasures. He finds in Revelation the confirmation of his hopes and spiritual dreams. In the same text he finds also justification for his altogether less uplifting prejudices. Thus to Knollys Revelation provides not just the glory of eschatological hope, but divine justification for his hatred of Catholics. This broader issue is discussed in detail with respect to other commentators in the next chapter, and only the briefest of summaries of Knollys' views is presented here.

For Knollys, the Roman Catholic Church is the great harlot of Rev. 17.5. Similarly, it is Roman Catholic error that is depicted in the vision of the swarming locusts that come up out of the bottomless pit in Rev. 9.3. Knollys' anti-Catholicism is thus characteristic of much of his entire exposition. In his comments on Revelation 13, however, this anti-Catholicism is perhaps at its clearest. It is therefore his remarks on this chapter of Revelation which come into focus here.

Both the first and the second beasts of Revelation 13, according to Knollys, refer to the papists and most especially to the Pope himself. They are dual descriptions of one and the same entity. The reference to the first beast's rising 'out of the sea' (Rev. 13.1) Knollys takes to indicate that it (papal Rome) arose out of 'some very great confluence of People, and Nations', arguing that papal Rome arose as a result of the destruction of pagan Rome by the hands of the various Gothic tribes and barbarians.[21] Pagan Rome fell, but out of its ashes, according to Knollys, was to arise the great Antichrist himself. Knollys is not confident concerning the exact date by which this process was complete, but, as has been seen, he suggests that it was no later than the year 428. This date marks the beginning of papal tyranny and the start of the 1,260-year period. By Knollys' own time, then, the reign of this beast is almost at its end.

Knollys' determination to identify the Roman Catholic Church as a positively satanic power is seen again in the way in which he argues that the beast of Revelation 13 is to be equated with the seventh and eighth heads of the beast of Revelation 17. In the composite beast described in that chapter Knollys finds a symbol of Rome in both its pagan and papal forms. Knollys notes that in Rev. 17.8 the beast is described as the one who 'was, is not, and yet is' and deciphers this enigmatic description for us. Rome 'was' formerly ordained by God to be the fourth monarchy of Dan. 7.23–5; Rome 'is not', in its papal form, ordained by God but by

²¹ Knollys, *Exposition*, p. 169.

Satan; and papal Rome 'yet is' the seventh head of the beast.[22] This is imaginative interpretation to say the least, and it seems fairly obvious that it is Knollys as reader rather than the text that is in control of this interpretative process. By such eisegesis Knollys is able to place the authority of papal Rome on a purely satanic foundation. The Roman Empire was ordained by God to rule the world; the Roman Church was ordained by Satan to corrupt true religion. Thus by his manipulation of the text Knollys has again made it serve his own purposes in a very dramatic way. Rome is demonised and set in stark contrast to truth and the way of God.

Knollys, then, lives in a very clear-cut religious world. On the one side is truth and on the other is error. It is not surprising that to a seventeenth-century English Particular Baptist there was no greater error than that of Rome. In fact, according to Knollys, the Roman Catholic religion is not just misguided: it is positively demonic. Romanism is the antithesis of true Christianity and is nothing short of a satanic conspiracy to pervert God's plan. Knollys has used Revelation to make this point graphically, and in his hands Revelation has become a highly charged weapon of religious propaganda. By it he is able to demonstrate that Catholics worship Satan. Even if one is not prepared to challenge Knollys on historical-critical grounds (and of course it would not be fair to do so), his work might at least be questioned on the basis of ethical considerations.

The beast (the Roman Catholic Church) will exercise its satanic and blasphemous authority for a period of 1,260 years. Turning to Rev. 11.2–3, Knollys notes that it is at this time that the 'holy city' (which he understands as 'the true Church') will be trodden underfoot by the Gentiles (whom he understands as the papists).[23] This, 1,260-year period is thus a dark time when truth is trodden down by error. However, though the true Church may be in the spiritual wilderness, its voice is not completely silenced, for God has set aside witnesses to keep the flame of truth alive. These, according to Knollys, are described in Rev. 11.3–12 and are identified by him as 'Ministers and Saints of God'. It is their business to oppose the beast during the period of his tyranny. Not surprisingly we find that Knollys sees reflected in this picture of the pure and faithful witnesses an image of his own group. Just as the satanic beasts refer to the papists, so the faithful witnesses refer to those God-fearing individuals who oppose the papists. According to Knollys, the

[22] Ibid., p. 205.   [23] Ibid., p. 125.

opposition which the witnesses (true Christians – in fact they turn out to be English Protestants) offer to the beast (the papists) is three-fold. These three elements reflect once again the religious tensions and conflicts of Knollys' own *Sitz im Leben*. First, the witnesses oppose the false teachings regarding free will, merit and condignity, holding up instead the doctrine of free grace and justification by faith in Christ. Second, the witnesses testify to 'the true and pure Worship of God in the Administration of his holy Ordinances' in contrast to the 'Idolatrous Worship of God' found practised by the 'Church of Rome, her Priests and Jesuits'. Nowhere is this clearer than in the witnesses' opposition to the 'superstitious and blasphemous Inventions of Transubstantiation of the Bread and Wine into the very True and Real Body and Blood of Christ'.[24] Third, the witnesses proclaim Christ as the king whose kingdom will have no end.[25] As has been seen, Knollys has demonised the Roman Catholic Church, and it is not surprising that the key elements of his criticisms come in precisely the areas that were of such great importance in Protestant–Catholic polemics: the sacraments, especially transubstantiation, and (as is clear from further reading of Knolly's work not here summarised) images.

Elsewhere in the *Exposition* Knollys focuses his attention particularly on several other key areas of dispute. The star which falls from heaven in Rev. 8.10 is, according to him, the fourth-century theologian (and condemned heretic) Nestorius. It was he who first corrupted the gospel in matters pertaining to the doctrines of original sin, justification and election, theological errors which were subsequently rife in Catholicism. As a Particular Baptist Knollys would naturally disagree with Rome on all these points. It was at this time too, Knollys adds, that penances were introduced along with praying to saints and various fasts and feast days and, in particular, the sacrament of extreme unction. These doctrines so corrupted the waters of pure doctrine that those who partook of them became poisoned and died (cf. Rev. 8.10–11).[26] There is much more in this vein; commenting on Rev. 9.20, for example, he notes the '*Popish* Doctrine of Devils', which includes the celibacy of priests, abstinence from meats and the use of images.[27]

Knollys' interpretation of Rev. 11.7–9 is particularly illuminating, for it once again illustrates very dramatically the extent to which his exposition is a product of his own *Sitz im Leben* and reflects his own religious prejudices. The passage reads:

---

[24] Ibid., p. 136.   [25] Ibid., p. 153.   [26] Ibid., pp. 102–3.   [27] Ibid., p. 115.

And when they shall have finished their testimony, the beast that ascendeth out of the bottomless pit shall make war against them, and shall overcome them, and kill them. And their dead bodies shall lie in the street of the great city, which spiritually is called Sodom and Egypt, where also our Lord was crucified. And they of the people and kindreds and tongues and nations shall see their dead bodies three days and an half, and shall not suffer their dead bodies to be put in graves.

Knollys takes the killing of the two witnesses by the beast as a reference to a significant decline in the spirituality of the true Church. The beast is of course Apollyon, the destroyer, that is, the Pope. The Pope succeeds in squeezing the spiritual life out of the true Church and hence silences its testimony.[28] This 'death' of the two witnesses lasts for three-and-a-half days (Rev. 11.9), during which time the bodies of the deceased lie unburied in 'the street of the great city'. Again Knollys is here quite ingenious: 'the street of the great city' is London and the fact that the bodies are unburied relates to the fact that the people of London never allow the truth to slip from their memories.[29] It is in England generally and in London in particular, according to Knollys, that the witnesses have given their testimony most evidently. Even at this time of great darkness, when the witnesses are 'dead', the memory of them still lingers on in London. It is no great surprise to learn that Knollys himself was a London man.[30]

The second beast in Revelation is identical with the first. It is simply another description from a different perspective. Little therefore need be said regarding Knollys' interpretation of this second beast, except to note that the virulent anti-Catholicism continues unabated throughout. One particular feature of the second beast does, however, call for some attention, and that is the number he is given in Rev. 13.18, namely 666. It was perhaps inevitable that this number should attract a great deal of eisegetical attention and, as will be shown in chapter 3 in more detail, solutions to the riddle of the number were numerous. Very popular was the view that the solution was to be found by adding up the numerical value of the beast's name. Another view was that the number referred not to the name of the beast, but either to the time at which he was to

[28] Ibid., pp. 138–9.   [29] Ibid., p. 140.

[30] Knollys was born in Lincolnshire and first went to London in 1636, but went afterwards to New England, returning again to London in 1641. His relationship with officialdom was somewhat stormy, resulting in several relatively brief periods in prison and abroad. However, though he did spend some time during the 1660s away from London, it was that city which was his base and it was there that the bulk of his teaching, preaching and writing was carried out (*DNB*, vol. XI, pp. 279–81).

arise or come to his end (1666 was a favourite) or else to the period
during which he was to exercise power.

Knollys, however, adopts a relatively uncommon interpretation of the
number 666. He does not, as did so many previous and later scholars, link
it to the numerical value of a particular title or description; nor does he
seek to use the number to calculate the time of the beast's end. Once
again note may be made of his ingenuity, and his determination that the
text fit his preconceived scheme. Rather than giving one of the standard
interpretations, he says that the number was foretold by John 'to be the
Beginning time of the Beast's *Universal* headship'.[31] (This is not to be
confused with the time when the beast was first to appear, that is, 428.)
This time was, according to Knollys, 'when the Emperor Phocas, by his
Edict, declared the Bishop of *Rome* to be the *Universal* Head of the Church'
(i.e. in 606). This year, Knollys states without producing any evidence in
support of the claim, is the 666th year after the beginning of the Roman
kingdom.[32] (There is a slight problem in the *Exposition* on this point, for on
p. 175 Knollys dates the decree of Phocas to 426. This is plainly wrong.
The best explanation is probably simply that it is a misprint, for elsewhere
(p. 179) Knollys correctly notes that it was Boniface III who was recognised by Phocas as the head of all Churches. Knollys surely knew the date
of Phocas' decree, or at the very least that Boniface III did not live in the
first part of the fifth century. To charge Knollys with such an historical
inaccuracy would be to underestimate the meticulous care with which he
has evidently constructed his arguments. Neither does the 426 date fit
with what Knollys says elsewhere about the rise of the beast in 428.)

Knollys is, then, clearly reading the book of Revelation from within
his own Protestant, indeed Baptist, context, and it is not surprising that
he consequently finds there the confirmation of all his worst fears and
prejudices. His remarks appear to most modern readers as at best
bizarre. Partly, of course, this is the result of the simple fact that the
modern reader is not likely to be sufficiently in tune with Knollys' basic
approach to Revelation to enable him or her to enter into a discussion
with Knollys on the meaning of the various symbols and figures contained in that book. Most modern readers do not read the book of
Revelation as a timetable of world events stretching from the time of
John to the end of the world. Neither do they share Knollys' extreme
anti-Catholicism. However, the modern reader might also find Knollys'

[31] Knollys, *Exposition*, p. 179.
[32] Ibid., p. 179. See further Brady, *Number of the Beast*, pp. 27–31, who gives some background to
Knollys' understanding of the number 666.

work strange in that he is apparently prepared to make the text say exactly what he wants it to. One might indeed marvel at the eisegetical trickery that has resulted in his arguing that the 'ships' which are destroyed in Rev. 8.9 are the '*Churches of mystical Babylon*'[33] (Rome). Equally strange, it might be argued, is the way in which he sees the 'street of the great city' in Rev. 11.8 as London.

It is plain that Knollys makes no attempt to rid himself of his seventeenth-century Protestant baggage. Perhaps it would be unreasonable to expect him to do so given his own historical context. However, it does seem, at least to the twentieth-century mind, that his work illustrates the fact that biases and prejudices do very seriously affect one's reading of biblical text, and further that such biases do not always bring positive results. Knollys has used Revelation to support what is in fact an unadulterated onslaught against an alternative form of religion to his own. The text has become a mirror of his own prejudices and biases. This may be understandable. Whether it is proper is another question altogether.

All this is not in any way to say, however, that his work is valueless. At the very least Knollys' *Exposition* tells us a great deal concerning the kind of intellectual world in which he lived. This world was clear-cut, supernatural and in the grip of a satanic conspiracy. It is also on the very threshold of eschatological regeneration and renewal. Satan, through his principal agent the Roman Catholic Church, is even now preparing for the final onslaught against truth which will result in the spiritual death of God's last witnesses. At this time only in England, most especially in London, will the truth linger on and refuse to disappear altogether. Consequently it is in England too that the remarkable regeneration begins and the dawn of the new age breaks. This may seem a strange world indeed to the modern mind, but there can be little doubt that it was the world inhabited not only by Knollys, but by many other seventeenth- and eighteenth-century English Protestants. Similar worlds are inhabited by numerous individuals and groups today, some of which will be examined in the last two chapters of this book.

BENJAMIN KEACH (1640–1704)

When seen in the broader context set out above, the work of Benjamin Keach is by no means extravagant in its claims to have detected in the

---

[33] Knollys, *Exposition*, p. 102; italic in the original.

events of 1688 the point at which history and prophecy coincide.[34] Keach is working with the benefit of hindsight and is aware of the arrival of William and Mary and the flight of James. He is hence able to weave these events into his reading of Revelation. This he does above all in the work which forms the chief focus of this section, *Antichrist Stormed* (1689), the title page and facing illustration of which are reproduced as figure 2. In many ways the work is typical of its age, in stressing the nearness of the end and interpreting contemporary events as signs of the impending eschaton. However, the precise slant of *Antichrist Stormed* is unique. In this work Keach puts forward the view that the arrival of William of Orange marked the drawing to a close of a prophetic period of $1,263\frac{1}{2}$ year-days. This is made up of the 1,260 days of Antichrist's rule as prophesied in Rev. 11.3 plus the $3\frac{1}{2}$ days during which the bodies of the witnesses would lie unburied in the streets (Rev. 11.9). The excitement and intensity with which this view is expressed make this work a highly illuminating source. Through careful analysis of the work some understanding of the eisegetical methodology employed by Keach (which was by and large the standard anti-Catholic historicism of his age) may be gained. Perhaps even more interestingly, however, *Antichrist Stormed* also provides an opportunity to catch a glimpse of the exciting world in which Keach, for a while at least, felt himself to be living. (A substantial extract from *Antichrist Stormed* is given as an appendix to this chapter, and could beneficially be referred to at this point.)

As has been seen already in considering Knollys' work, the view that the Roman Catholic Church was the incarnation of Antichrist was by no means unusual in eighteenth-century England. But the sources mentioned to this point are not the only ones relevant in this context. For example, Thomas Brightman (1562–1607) identified the whore of Babylon (Rev. 17.5) and the beasts of Revelation 13 with the Pope of Rome,[35] as did James Durham (1622–58).[36] The one-time Bishop of Galloway, William Cowper (1568–1619), is no less clear on the point, stating that the beast of Rev. 12.7 is none other than the 'Antichrist, the Apostate Bishop of Rome',[37] and Henry More (1614–87) concluded that

---

[34] For a sketch of Keach's life see *DNB*, vol. x, pp. 1142–3.

[35] Brightman, *Apocalyps*, pp. 349–50.

[36] James Durham, *A Commentarie Upon the Book of the Revelation* (1658). Traditional anti-Catholicism runs throughout Durham's work. Note, for example, the following remark, which is typical of many: 'It remaineth therefore, as was formerly concluded, that the Pope is the very Antichrist, and the papacy the very antichristian kingdom here described.' Durham, *Commentarie*, p. 573.

[37] See *The Workes of Mr William Cowper Late Bishop of Galloway. Now Newly Collected into one Volume. Whereunto is added a Commentary on the Revelation Never before Published* (1623), p. 1004.

Antichrist Stormed

Antichrist
STORMED:
OR,

Mystery Babylon the great Whore, and the great City, proved to be the present Church of Rome.
Wherein all Objections are fully answered.

To which is added, **The Time of the End,** or a clear Explanation of Scripture Prophecies, with the Judgment of divers Learned men concerning the final Ruine of the *Romish Church,* that it will be in this present Age.

Together with an Account of the Two Witnesses, who they are, with their Killing, Resurrection & Ascention

Also an Examination and Confutation of what Mr. *Jurin* hath lately written concerning the Effusion of the Vials, proving none of them are yet poured out. With Mr. *Cann's* Reasons to confirm the same.

Likewise a brief Review of D. *Tho. Goodwins* Exposition of the 11th chapter of the *Revelation,* concerning the Witnesses, and of that Street in which they should lie slain, proving it to be meant of *Great Britain.* And a brief Collection of divers strange Prophecies, some very Antient.

By *Benj. Keach,* Author of 𝔖𝔦𝔬𝔫 𝔦𝔫 𝔇𝔦𝔰𝔱𝔯𝔢𝔰𝔰.

To which is annext, A short Treatise in two parts. 1. The Calculation of Scripture numbers by Scripture only, without the help of Humane History. 2. Upon the Witnesses; giving light to the whole Book.

LONDON, Printed for *Nath. Crouch* at the *Bell* in the *Poultrey* near *Cheapside.* 1689.

Figure 2   Title page of Keach's *Antichrist Stormed* (1689)

since both the Pope and the great whore of Babylon described in
Revelation 17 wear a crown which bears an inscription beginning with
the word *mysterium*, the two are one and the same entity. Thus, according to More, the name 'Whore of Babylon' belongs to 'the Pope with his
clergy', for 'they are this *Great Whore that has made drunk the Inhabitants of the
Earth with the Cup of her Fornication*'.[38]

Given this widespread identification of Antichrist with the Roman
Catholic Church and the concurrent belief that the book of Revelation
charts the rise and fall of this satanic power, it is hardly surprising to find
Keach reflecting upon the prophetic importance of the events of 1688.
The raw facts, as Keach saw them, were that during the reign of Charles
II and James II the Roman Catholic Church had had an opportunity to
gain a firm foothold on English soil once more. However, by divine
providence (as Keach saw it) this had not happened. As Keach reflected
on this unexpected turn of events, he came to the conclusion that it had
been (as all was) part of God's plan. Antichrist, Rome, had been
'stormed' by the forces of good. Armed with this interpretation of
events, Keach sought in the scriptures confirmation of his view.

Beyond this detail Keach's basic historicist, anti-Catholic approach to
Revelation is standard within its seventeenth-century English context.
The book is understood by him as an overview of history (particularly as
it touches the Church) stretching from the time of John to the second
coming of Christ. He is standard also in his interpretation of many of the
other details of the book. For example, the opening of the six seals
described in Revelation 6 is taken by Keach as referring to the beginning of six consecutive periods, the last of which came to an end in c. AD
320.[39] The breaking of the seventh seal, which is accompanied in Rev.
8.1 by a short period of 'silence in heaven', he takes as a reference to the
start of 'A short time of rest for the Church and Saints of God, which
began in Constantines dayes and lasted as some conceive till the troubles
rose by the Arians'.[40] Such details are standard in the Protestant literature from the period.

The next major sequence in Revelation is the blowing of seven
trumpets, and again Keach is here fairly typical in the general thrust
(though not in all details) of his interpretation. The first six trumpets refer

---

[38] *The Theological Works of the most Pious and Learned Henry More, D. D.* (1708), p. 598. Italic in the
original.
[39] Keach, *Antichrist Stormed*, p. ii (Roman numerals are used here to refer to the unnumbered pages
of Keach's preface to this work).
[40] Ibid., p. ii.

to six consecutive historical periods which stretch from c. AD 379 to 1688. The blowing of the seventh trumpet (Rev. 11.15) marks a very significant turning point, for it is accompanied by the pouring out of the seven vials of God's wrath (Revelation 16). It is the beginning of this event that Keach dates to 1688, for he sees in the arrival of William the first stage in God's visitation upon Antichrist. The judgements of God have not yet begun to fall in all their terrible fullness, but they are due within a very short space of time. According to Keach, then, the blowing of the seventh trumpet marks the turning point of history. Up to this point Antichrist (Rome) has reigned supreme, but his days have now come to an end. With the arrival of William of Orange, the first blow has been struck and the fullness of the wrath of God is about to erupt upon his enemies.

Like Knollys, but with a different interpretative key, Keach sees the destruction of Antichrist as accompanied and in part accomplished by a parallel event, the raising up of the two faithful witnesses described in Rev. 11.1–14. These two witnesses testify during the dark period of Antichrist's rule, but towards the end of this period are slain by the 'beast that ascendeth out of the bottomless pit' (Rev. 11.7). However, after a short period God raises the witnesses from the dead and they ascend into heaven.

Keach's interpretation of this section of Revelation gives a glimpse of the exciting world in which he believed himself to be living. To Keach, the two witnesses symbolise the faithful servants of God down through the ages (he has particular regard for the Waldenses and Albigensians in this respect). It is they who bear testimony to the truth during the reign of the Roman Antichrist. The slaying of the witnesses is a reference to the exceptionally hard times which the faithful had to endure during the period from 1660 to 1688 in England. According to Keach, it was during this period (especially the latter part of it) that Antichrist made one final attempt to overthrow totally the faithful witnesses to God's truth. The attempt was substantially successful and the witnesses (English Protestants) died. In part this was a literal death, as the execution of 'that godly Woman and Martyr Mrs Gaunt' shows.[41] More generally, however, the death was a spiritual one accomplished by the 'emissaries of Rome' through their policy of

turning out of places of trust, many good Protestants, and the taking away of *Charters of Cities* and Corporations, silencing worthy Ministers, &c. nay, striking at the root and whole constitution of the English Government, nothing being

[41] Ibid., p. 145.

designed but the utter subversion of the Protestant Religion, things growing every day worse and worse, nothing appearing but the blackness of darkness, and that which was worst of all, many of Gods witnesses seemed to be strangely dispirited, whilest others truckl'd to the Enemies yoak, suffering Chapels to be erected for Popery and Cursed Mass Priests, and Jesuits.[42]

However, in 1688 freedom came in the person of King William. It is his arrival that marks the turning point. Now is the hour of deliverance and the dawn of the time when 'the knowledge of the glory of the Lord shall cover the Earth as waters cover the seas'.[43] King William thus plays a central role in the eschatological drama. Keach writes

I am persuaded that his present majesty is raised up to do great things for Christ; and tho' some may strive to obstruct the work of God, and uphold an interest for the Beast, yet they shall be blasted in their designs, and come to shame and ruin in the end; for God is risen up, and his Enemies shall be scattered.[44]

In a second publication Keach reflects further on this point and is in fact more confident that the time of the resurrection of the witnesses has already begun. Indeed he seems now to have no doubts that it is in the present time that 'the slain Witnesses are a-getting out of their graves'. King William is again praised as the one whom God has chosen to be a 'glorious Instrument' in his hands.[45]

For Keach, then, England is the focal point of this eschatological drama. The arrival of William of Orange and the expulsion of papal power from the shores of England marks the first in a series of deadly blows that will lead to Antichrist's final defeat. It is in England too that the resurrected witnesses are beginning to flex their missionary muscles. For Keach these are exciting times, the more so since Antichrist's ruin is accompanied by Christ's gain. The witnesses are soon to give their testimony and, states Keach, 'from that very time I conclude the Kingdom of Christ will begin'.[46]

Keach, like the vast majority of his contemporaries, is postmillennial in his eschatological expectation, that is, he believes that the literal return of Jesus to the earth will begin only after the period of 1,000 years during which the spiritual kingdom of Christ will advance. The literal return of Christ will thus presumably take place somewhere close to the

---

[42] Ibid., p. 146.   [43] Ibid., p. 188. The reference is to Isa. 11.9.
[44] Keach, *Antichrist Stormed*, p. 188.
[45] Benjamin Keach, *Distressed Sion Relieved* (1689). The remarks are found in the two-page 'Address to the Reader', which is not numbered.
[46] Keach, *Antichrist Stormed*, p. iii.

year 2688. Keach believes himself to be living at the time of the inauguration of the pre-advent millennial kingdom. In his own words,

tho' we cannot perfectly foresee what God is about to do, as yet, we being but in the morning of the approaching glory – yet are we full of expectation, that the work of God in respect of these great and longed-for blessings, will not go back again.[47]

According to Keach, then, the first blow against Antichrist has been struck. Antichrist has been stormed and is now heading for final destruction. However, the reference in Rev. 11.13 to the falling of a 'tenth part of the city' relates to the preliminary and partial destruction of Antichrist (Rome) in one part of his empire, and Keach sees this as relating to the fact that in 1688 the Protestant forces drove Antichrist from Britain, the first in a series of blows which would come to a conclusion with Antichrist's final overthrow in 1697.

Popery shall fall and go down, but all conclude that the tenth part of this great City falls first, and I doubt not but the providence of God hath brought us forth in the time of the accomplishment of that part of the Prophecy, for that great *Brittain* is that part of the great City, I see no cause to doubt.[48]

It is of course hardly surprising that Keach thinks of his own country as the one in which the eschatological drama is played out. It has already been noted that expositors who sought to give a date for the end of the world most often located that event fairly close to their own chronological setting; we saw in the work of Knollys that the same was true of geographical considerations.

Enough has now been said to indicate the general outline of Keach's thinking on the events of 1688 and the way in which he sought to relate those events to the book of Revelation. For Keach, William's arrival on the shores of Britain and the ousting of the Catholic King James II marks the dawn of the eschatological kingdom. Rome is Antichrist and Rome has been dealt a substantial blow by William of Orange. Antichrist has been stormed and driven out. This process will continue until the final overthrow of Antichrist in 1697. England is the epicentre of these eschatological events, and it is outward from England that the kingdom of Christ upon earth will advance.

Seen within a seventeenth-century English Protestant context, Keach's work *Antichrist Stormed* (and with it *Distressed Sion Relieved*) is typical in its claim to have detected in the events of history evidence of the working out of God's plan. It is typical also in its attempt to relate

---

[47] 'To the Reader', in Keach, *Distressed Sion Relieved.*   [48] Keach, *Antichrist Stormed*, pp. 137–8.

contemporary events to the book of Revelation, which was seen during Keach's time as giving an overview of history from the time of the prophet John to the end of the world. Keach employs fairly standard interpretative principles in seeking to work out his exposition and reflects by and large the kind of prophetic eisegetical school existent in England at the end of the seventeenth century. His work, however, like that of Knollys, is exceptionally interesting in that it gives a glimpse of what must have been a very exciting world. Keach believes that 1688 saw the first rays of the eschatological dawn. It is his view that William of Orange is none other than God's chosen instrument. By him God has dealt the first precursory blow to his great enemy the Antichrist of Rome. Even now are the slain witnesses to God's truth getting out of their graves and preparing for a period of evangelism the like of which the world has never before seen. In just eight more years Antichrist will come to final ruin and the pre-advent millennial kingdom of Christ will begin.

Keach's work raises a number of issues and illustrates several points. Throughout it has been noted that Keach fits fairly well into a school of interpretation that was dominant in his day. The seriousness with which he approached the text is obvious, and the seriousness with which he sought to explain contemporary events in the light of what he found in Revelation no less so. There were many before Keach who had sought to do the same thing, and there were many others who came after him. But Keach is an individual whose circumstances were peculiar to him. Consequently, his understanding of Revelation, like all others, reflects those individual circumstances and is highly personal. In the area of prophetic eisegesis, then, it is clear that text and interpreter interact. To explore those dynamics is not only to understand a little of the power of the text, its *Wirkungsgeschichte*, but also to enter, albeit briefly, into the thought world of the interpreter.

Neither is Hanserd Knollys' work at all unusual in its general tone; rather it was part of a general school of prophetic interpretation dominant in England during the period with which this study has been primarily concerned. Knollys' work on Revelation, like that of Keach, is illuminating, however, for it clearly illustrates the extent to which, in seventeenth-century Protestant England at least, the book of Revelation could be interpreted in such a way as to confirm the suspicions, fears and religious prejudices of the reader. The text has clearly been hijacked and put at the mercy of its interpreter. In the case of both Knollys' and Keach's work, of course, it is relatively easy for the modern readers to spot this process, since they are unlikely to share the extreme religious views of a seventeenth-century Particular Baptist. It is perhaps much more difficult for those same readers to see past their own biases and prejudices.

It is of paramount importance to note that Knollys' work was far from atypical. It is true, as has been said, that Knollys was particularly outspoken and sharp when it come to what he perceived to be devil-inspired Roman error, but the general view that Rome was Antichrist pervades the literature on Revelation from this period. Thus Knollys belonged to what Stanley Fish would call an 'interpretative school'[49] and his work simply reflects the kind of interpretative principles which were in force in the world of a seventeenth-century Particular Baptist. Indeed, Fish might well draw from Knollys' interpretation of Revelation (or any of the many hundreds of others like it) adequate evidence to support his view that the text contributes nothing in the overall interpretative exercise. The actual text of Revelation seems almost incidental to Knollys' purposes. In Fish's terms, the text has pretty well 'disappeared'.

It remains of course to be asked whether this is an altogether happy state of affairs. After all, few today would be prepared to defend what Knollys has done with the text, and in an ecumenical age some might even judge Knollys's attempt to find satanic papists in every nook and cranny of the text of Revelation to be morally reprehensible. Such judgements would of course be anachronistic. However, there is surely some lesson to be drawn from Knollys' work, and perhaps it is this: subjectivity in biblical interpretation may well be inescapable, but to let it reign unchecked seems unwise. In fact, the one who reads Knollys' work might be forgiven, even in the context of the present ebbing of the historical-critical tide, for complaining that not all readings are equal and that such things as authorial intention do matter. Knollys has forced upon the book of Revelation the role of sacred supporter of his own prejudices, frustrations and fears. Perhaps it was inevitable that he should have done so; whether the inevitability is also legitimate is, however, another question.

APPENDIX[50]

An Essay towards the understanding the Time set in the Scriptures respecting the Witnesses, left in the Word for the Use and Benefit of the Church.

[49] Fish, *Is There a Text in this Class?*
[50] From Keach, *Antichrist Stormed*, pp. 224–31; spelling, punctuation and italic are reproduced without alteration.

And First, why two Witnesses? First, either because the Scriptures tell us, That in the Mouth of two or three Witnesses everything shall be established. Two are sufficient, and less cannot; holding forth this truth to us; That let God's faithful Servants be never so much reduced as to their number, yet he hath not left himself without sufficient Witness in this World. Or, Secondly, To signifie unto us the greatness of that Apostacy that should be from the truth, of which the false Church should be composed, the whole Earth wondring after the Beast, and that but few comparatively should be found faithful in the time of the Holy Cities being trodden underfoot by the Gentiles. Or, Thirdly, Signifying to us, That as the Church at the time of Christ's coming was but one National Church, therefore represented by one Candlestick, *Zech.* 4.2 Now under the Gospel the true Church of God, the Mystical Body of Christ her Head, consists of several visible Churches, and therefore is represented by two Candlesticks, *Rev.* 11.4

Secondly, Who those Witnesses are? *Ans.* Leaving them to their own thoughts, who take them to be either the two Testaments, or Magistracy and Ministry, or two particular Persons, I conceive them to be the faithful people of God, that have obtained Grace to hold the truth of Christ in all Ages in a faithful adherence to him, under all the Apostacies that have been made from them and Oppositions that have been made by them that have Apostatized from them that have not loved their Lives unto the death, for the Love they have had to Christ and his Gospel.

Thirdly, The time of their Prophesie is set down, Rev. 11.3. and is 1260 days, that is, so many years, which time is contemporary with the Gentiles treading under foot the Holy City for forty two months. Now although in forty two full Months there are more days by about eighteen than 1260, yet the Text seems to give us to understand that these times shall begin and end together, though thus differently reckoned, the one by the Sun, the other by the Moon, as may more fully appear in the next consideration of their work.

Fourthly, Their work is implied in the name given them; they are called Witnesses. To make a person a true Witness, he must have a full knowledge of what he says or testifies, 1 *John* 1. 1, 2, 3. Therefore they are Gods Children here intended, that have experienced the things they testified unto; for the matter of their Testimony is that *Act.* 1.8. to testifie to Christ his Person and Offices, the alone Mediator, as revealed, opened and held forth in the Gospel, which is that upon which the true Church is built, *Eph.* 2. 19, 20, &c. And which is the Temple not given to the Gentiles whilst the Court and Holy City is given to them to tread underfoot forty two Months, all which time the Witnesses here intended are to Prophesie and Testifie to those truths, that others under a name and profession of Christ Apostatized from, and intruded their false Doctrines and Corruptions instead of the truths and true Worship of God, *Acts.* 20. 28, 29, 30. 2 *Thes.* 2. 1, 2, 3, 12. &c. 1 *Tim.* 4. 1, 2, 3. &c. 2 *Tim.* 3. 1, 2, 3, 4, 5. 1 *Pet.* 3. the whole chapter, 2 *Pet* 2 the whole chapter, the Epistle of *Jude,* all are prophetical of great Apostacies that would be from the Truths and purity of the Gospel. Now, I say, the work of the Witnesses is, to stand up for the defence of the

Gospel, and they shall do so for 1260 years together, and then they are slain and lye dead for three days and a half, that is three years and a half, then the Spirit of life from God shall come upon them.

Fifthly, Their finishing their Testimony, this must either respect their Testimony it self or the time allotted to them, that is, the 1260 years; I conceive the first is intended, for after or when they are upon the finishing it, there is a fresh War made upon them, in which, they that make the War upon them prevail, so as to overcome them, and kill them, and then they lye dead for three years and $\frac{1}{2}$ now how long time this shall take up, is not said. And if the holy Spirit who had been so exact, in setting down the time of 1260 years of their Prophesy, and the three days and $\frac{1}{2}$ of their lying dead, had omitted a time between both, the Church of God had been in as great uncertainty, as if no time had been set almost. Therefore if we take the finishing their testimony to respect their work, then it is our concernment to consider wherein this finishing part doth lye; And that I conceive to be in a witness to the Kingly Office of Christ. His Prophetical and Priestly Offices were first Witnessed to; And this hath been lastly contested for, even to blood, in the last wars in *England*, as the other had been upon which this last War had been commenced. The Testimony being further confirmed in the Martyrdom of many of those concerned in the finishing of this Testimony. The sufferings of the Church in these late years has been carried on against her otherwise than in former ages, in other Methods, and under other names and pretences, all bespeaking that the time of finishing the Testimony is come, and the War commenced, and it may be an overcoming, if not killing also.

Sixthly, Where shall this be? *Ans.* It will be there where this finishing part of the witness to Christ is born, for there the last War is (which is the last effort which Antichrist shall make against the Church of God) and overcoming, and killing will be: And where they shall lye dead, and where they shall rise? when the Spirit of life from God comes upon them; Now where shall all these things be? The Holy Spirit tells us, it shall be in the Street of the great City, *Rev.* 11. 8. ot in all the Ten, but in one Street, and upon their resurrection the tenth part of the City falleth, not the whole City at once, *v.* 13. So that in the Street, or Kingdom where the Testimony hath been finished, there all the rest follow, and there the deliverance of the Church shall begin, to an utter overthrow of all her Persecutors and Mortal Enemies.

Seventhly, When shall this be? *Ans.* To know the beginning, and end of these times and things, there are two ways of calculating. The one is beginning at the Head of a number, so reckoning forward to its end; The other is back-wards, as *Daniel* did, *Chap.* 9. beginning our reckoning at the end of the number, and so reckoning to the beginning; Now by one of these two ways, in Gods time we shall infallibly know. But to the Question, I suppose both ways may be a help to us now, and Scripture numbers have a dependance one upon the other, and there lies the harmony of them, when that is understood. The great number, which includes all the rest, throughout the sufferings of the Church of God, under the three last of *Daniels* four monarchies, is that of 2300 years, which I have indeavoured to carry on by Scriptures to the end of it, within forty five or forty four years, from this year of Our Lord 1686. There are two other great numbers in *Daniel, chap.* 12,. one of 1290. the other 1335. which is forty five more than the other; so that altho' they both begin together they do not end together, by 45 years. That they begin together is evident, for the 45th is the addition of so many to the 1290. therefore blessed is he that lives to the forty five longer than the 1290. for altho' the Churches deliverance shall begin at the 1290. it shall not be compleated till forty five more; Therefore blessed is he that lives till that time: so that when ever these 1335. years begin, they end with the 2300 years also. Again, the 1290 is thirty more than 1260. in *Rev.* 11 therefore tho' they end together yet they cannot begin together. And because of this, expositors have generally judged, that the 1290. in *Daniel* relate to the *Jews*, and the 1260. to the *Gentile* Church, but by what reason I cannot be satisfied. Hence they head this 1290. at *Julian's* attempting to rebuild the Temple; The reason of which was this, he had apostatized from Christianity, and restored the *Gentile* Worship and sacrifices, and as an affront to Christians, put the *Jews* upon Sacrificing also, who told him that it was not lawful for them, but in the Temple at *Jerusalem*, therefore he orders them to build it, which they attempted to do, but could but attempt, for God by his immediate power prevented them. This *Julian* began his reign in 365. and Reigned but three years, so that this opinion time hath confuted; For add 1290 to 368, it makes but 1658. at which time they reckon'd the *Jews* would be called; but no such thing hath been: Therefore they expounded all these places, which we read Sacrifices, with a supplement, in *Dan.* 8. 12. *chap.* 11.31. *chap.* 12.11. to intend the Jewish worship, which *Julian* intended to set up in confront to Christianity, to be the abomination that makes desolate, for all or any of which I see no reason. It is properly translated Sacrifice in one place, as *chap.* 9. 26, 27. And this doth relate to the taking away of the Sacrifices then in being, of Gods own appointment, which accordingly were taken away, as Christ himself also admonished. *Mat.* 24.15. by *Titus* –&c.

But the abomination which makes desolate, I conceive is some corruption in the Gospel worship, the true worship of God; and therefore seeing we, as before, find the Apostle concerned so much in forewarning the Church by a Spirit of Prophesie, of what had also been expressly foretold by the Spirit of God; If it was expressly foretold, it must be written some where or other: and take the Apostles own exposition, 1 *Tim.* 4. 1, 2, 3. Why may we not rather reckon this to be the abomination, to astonishment foretold by *Daniel*, and this came in the 383. year, when *Syricius* was Bishop of *Rome* and continued 15 years; in his time Marriage was forbidden to the Priests, and in the 425. year *Celestinus* was Bishop of *Rome* and continued eight years; He assumed the temporal power, as 2 *Tim.* 3. 1, 2, 4, 5. and why we may not head these numbers here, I would be glad to understand. In the last of which I conceive Antichrist did make his first visible appearance in the World: so that add the 1260 to 425 it makes 1685, and you bring it to the end of 2300 days within forty five years, or a year or two, which time I conceive is alloted to pour out the Vials, and to accomplish the great revolutions in, that shall come upon the Earth, in order to the possessing of the Kingdom, that shall be given to the Saints of the most high,

Dan. 7. 26, 27, 28. There is time expressed by time, times and dividing of time, three times in Scriptures, as *Dan.* 7. 25. 12. 7. *Rev.* 12. 14. I find time thus expressed but in one place more, and that is *Dan.* 4. 23. where it's certainly taken for years and by what rule we will construe it otherwise in other places I see not. And that in *Dan.* 12. 11 seems plainly to relate to a special time of the Enemies accomplishing to scatter the power of the Holy People, then all shall be finished, (*i. e.*) the sufferings of the Church, or deliverance shall thence begin, and bear date from the end of these three years and $\frac{1}{2}$. In Dan 7.25. He tells who shall act this last part, compared with *Rev.* 11 and in *Rev.* 12. 14. how God even in that time will provide for his Church, when the Devil pours out his last wrath upon her, knowing his time is short, and what time this should be, except the last three years and $\frac{1}{2}$ of the Witnesses lying dead; I cannot see the time when *Babylon* shall say in her Heart, she sits a Queen, shall see no sorrow, Widowhood, or loss of Children any more, having accomplished what she had been 1260. days labouring at, the slaughter and death of the Witnesses, whom she hath now dead at her feet; Therefore they make merry, send gifts to one another, not knowing how near utter destruction is at her door, she being like *Pharaoh* of old, but a noise, and past her time. For I conceive the Witnesses cannot be said to Prophesy when dead, therefore this time follows immediately upon the end of the 1260 days of their Prophecies; which ending in 1685 according to the preceding computation; at which time Popery came to be inthron'd in this Nation, accomplished the slaughter and death of the Witnesses; the time of whose lying dead, which was to be three years and an half, being added to 1685, amounts to 1688 and an half which was the very time of Gods lifting up his hand by his present Providence to save these distressed Nations.

CHAPTER 3

Revelation 13 and the papal Antichrist in eighteenth-century England

In the previous chapter we saw that the Baptist writers Knollys and Keach read Revelation in such a way as to make the text particularly relevant to their own circumstances. Much of what they read into it was relatively benign; however, their use of it was by no means uniformly positive. This is seen particularly in the way in which they read into Revelation the prevailing anti-Catholicism of their day, including their insistence that the Pope was Antichrist. In this chapter[1] the theme of anti-Catholic readings of Revelation is explored further and an investigation is conducted into the way in which the book of Revelation, especially chapter 13, was used to support the view that the Pope and/or the Roman Catholic Church in general was the Antichrist.[2] Naturally it has been necessary to limit the discussion somewhat, and this has been done primarily by restricting the investigation to works on Revelation produced in the eighteenth century.

In this chapter, then, an attempt is made to outline the way in which the book of Revelation was used in a way complementary to the general anti-Catholic views of eighteenth-century English Protestants. This use of Revelation must be seen in the context of the underprivileged status of Catholics during that period, whose lines did not fall in pleasant places. The reasons for this situation are complex indeed, and go back at least as far as the social, religious and political tensions spilling over from the Henrician reformation of the sixteenth century. The very real 'Gunpowder Plot' of 1605 had not been forgotten, and neither had the

---

[1] An earlier version of part of this chapter was published in the *Bulletin of the John Rylands University Library of Manchester* (hereafter *BJRULM*) 79 (1997):143–60. I am grateful to the editor of that Journal for permission to reuse some of the material here.

[2] Wainwright, *Mysterious Apocalypse*, pp. 21–103 gives a useful overview of pre-critical scholarship on Revelation; pages 49–66 of that study are particularly relevant. The second volume of Froom, *Prophetic Faith* covers the period in considerable detail, though the anti-Catholic, premillennial views of the author somewhat colour his evaluation of the commentators he surveys. Brady, *Number of the Beast* is also useful, though it deals with only three verses.

fabricated 'Popish Plot' of 1678. Both were seen as evidence of Rome's continued desire to rule once again over the religious consciences of the English. Similarly, the three Jacobite rebellions of the first part of the eighteenth century (1708, 1715, 1745) were seen as obvious examples of Rome's desire to restore a Catholic monarch to the throne of England.[3] Such fears led to persecution and social exclusion. In dealing with Protestant anti-Catholic readings of Revelation, then, it must be remembered that this is an instance of the use of a text by the strong to demonise the weak. Thus the claim made in the introduction seems a reasonable one: Revelation is a text that can be used no less effectively by the powerful than by the powerless.

The focus of this chapter is the use made of Revelation 13, and the discussion concentrates upon just two commentators, William Whiston and John Gill. There follow in addition some further general remarks on more popular sources (hymns, sermons, tracts, annotated bibles). This is designed to show two things: first, that anti-Catholic readings of the book of Revelation were detailed and ingenious, and second, that they were not limited to academic monographs. Despite the limited nature of the study, however, some general conclusions can be drawn, for the work here surveyed is fairly typical and is indicative of the broader conspectus.

Chapter 13 of the book of Revelation is one which could not but attract the attention of anyone determined to find in scripture a picture of 'the enemy' (whoever that is thought to be). In its own context it almost certainly relates to the persecution of Christianity under the Roman Empire, and perhaps under Nero in particular. Historicist readers of Revelation, however, saw in this chapter a picture of their own day. It describes the rise and blasphemous career of two 'beasts'; the first comes up 'out of the sea' and the second 'out of the earth'. The description of these beasts which follows clearly indicates that they are powers opposed to God. The first blasphemes terribly and the second ensures that any who do not worship the first beast are killed. The two therefore work together to deceive the inhabitants of the earth. Throughout the course of the seventeenth and eighteenth centuries this

---

[3] The situation of Catholics in Britain during this period is discussed generally in Colin Haydon, *Anti-Catholicism in Eighteenth-Century England c. 1740–80: A Political and Social Study* (Manchester: Manchester University Press, 1993). See also Raymond D. Tumbleson, *Catholicism in the English Protestant Imagination* (Cambridge: Cambridge University Press, 1998). A briefer account is found in David Butler, *Methodists and Papists: John Wesley and the Catholic Church in the Eighteenth Century* (London: Darton, Longman and Todd, 1995), pp. 1–19. Butler also prints an illuminating list of penal laws in force against eighteenth-century English Catholics (pp. 205–10).

particular passage of scripture was the subject of intense debate, and, as chapters 7–9 of this book indicate, it has remained central in non-critical approaches to the biblical text to this day. Opinion on its correct interpretation was naturally divided; however, most Protestant interpreters were agreed at least that the arch villain of the passage was none other than the Pope and/or the Church of Rome in general. It was the career of this blasphemous institution which most English Protestant interpreters from this period held to be charted in the chapter.

The identification of the Church of Rome as the great Antichrist was standard in post-Reformation England (and Luther's views on the matter are of course well known).[4] An early expression of it is found in the work of John Bale (1495–1563), and the general thrust of his work was repeated in numerous commentaries throughout the latter part of the sixteenth and into the seventeenth centuries.[5] Keach's comment, written in the seventeenth century, that 'most of our Eminent Protestant Writers, both Ancient and Modern, do affirm without the least doubt, that the Church of *Rome* is the great Whore spoken of [in] *Rev.* 17'[6] has been noted already and seems well founded, and the tradition continued in the eighteenth century.

William Whiston (1667–1752)[7] was Sir Isaac Newton's successor as Professor of Mathematics in the University of Cambridge, although he is better known to biblical scholars as the translator of Josephus.[8] Whiston's views on Revelation were put forward in his work *An Essay on the Revelation of Saint John*, first published in 1706 and revised several times thereafter.[9] His interpretation of Revelation is ingenious and often

4 See, for example, Jaroslav Pelikan and Helmut T. Lehman (eds.), *Luther's Works* (55 vols., Philadelphia: Fortress Press, 1958–86), vol. XXXIII, pp. 392–5.
5 The most important work in this line of tradition is arguably that of Joseph Mede (1586–1638), whose *Clavis Apocalyptica* (1627) was to prove highly influential over the course of the next two centuries.
6 Keach, *Antichrist Stormed*, p. 1.
7 For a brief life of Whiston and a complete list of his publications see *DNB*, vol. XXI, pp. 10–14. The main source for the life is the *Memoirs of the Life and Writings of Mr William Whiston, Containing Several of His Friends Also, and Written by Himself* (1749; 2nd edn 1753). A general treatment of his apocalypticism may be found in James E. Force, *William Whiston, Honest Newtonian* (Cambridge: Cambridge University Press, 1985).
8 Whiston's translation, which is still in print, was originally published in 1737 under the title *The Genuine Works of Flavius Josephus, the Jewish Historian, in English* (1737).
9 *An Essay on the Revelation of St. John so far as it Concerns the Past and Present Times to Which Are Added Two Dissertations ... with a Collection of Scripture Prophecies relating to the Times after the Coming of Messiah* (1706). Whiston's other works on prophecy include *The Accomplishment of Scripture Prophecies* (1708), *The Literal Accomplishment of Scripture Prophecies* (1724) and *An Essay on the Revelation of Saint John so far as Concerns Past and Present Times, Second Edition, Greatly Improv'd and Corrected* (1744). Whiston also deals with some prophetic matters in his *A Short View of the Chronology of the Old Testament, and of the Harmony of the Four Evangelists* (1702).

strays from the well-beaten exegetical path of his predecessors; both these elements may be seen in the extract from the *Essay* which is given as an appendix to this chapter, and which might be usefully read at this point.

An outline of Whiston's overall scheme can be seen in the diagram reproduced as figure 3. He divides the history of the world into three epochs: the period of 'emptiness' (he appears to have טוהו in error for what presumably should be תוהו),[10] the period of law and the period of the Messiah. Each of these periods is '2000 [years]' long. There follows the Sabbath-millennium of Revelation 20. Whiston constructs his interpretation around this basic framework, seeking to integrate the various sequences of seals, trumpets, vials and woes into it (understood of course along standard historicist lines, including the all important year-day principle).

Whiston is not working here without an interpretative context. The view that the world would end after 6,000 years has a long history in Christian thought. As Wainwright notes,[11] it is found clearly already in the *Epistle of Barnabas* (late first or early second century AD), where, after reminding his readers of the commandment to keep the Sabbath holy, the writer continues:

Consider, my children, what that signifies, he finished them in six days. The meaning of it is this; that in six thousand years the Lord God will bring all things to an end. For with him one day is a thousand years; as himself testifieth, saying, Behold this day shall be as a thousand years. Therefore, children, in six days, that is, in six thousand years shall all things be accomplished.[12]

Thus for Whiston as for Barnabas the final end will come after 6,000 years, which for Whiston, since he dates creation at 4000 BC, is in the year AD 2000. However, for Whiston the year 1716 is also particularly significant, for it is in this year, he argues, that the millennial dawn will begin to break and the pre-millennial period of preparation will begin. This year will mark the beginning of the end of Antichrist, and here he draws extensively on Revelation 13.

The view that the year 1716 held particular prophetic significance was peculiar to Whiston, and the means by which he arrived at it somewhat unusual; these are examined in greater detail below. On Revelation 13 in general, however, Whiston is fairly typical of the general trend of his

[10] The word *tohu*, that is, 'emptiness', should be spelt with an initial (reading right to left) ת (*taw*) rather that a ט (*teth*).
[11] Wainwright, *Mysterious Apocalypse*, p. 231 n. 1   [12] *Epistle of Barnabas* 15.3–5.

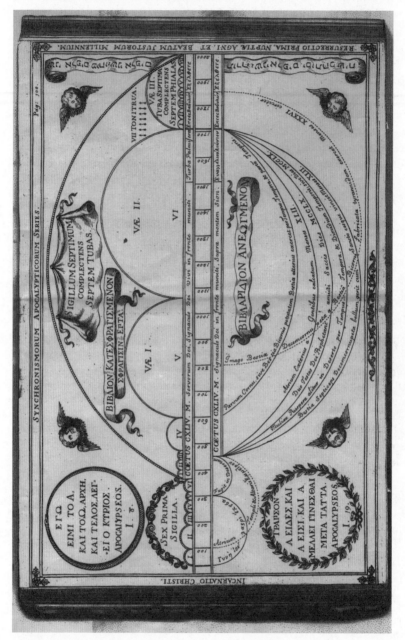

Figure 3   Whiston's diagram of the prophecies (1706)

contemporary eighteenth-century Protestant interpreters. He saw the
Catholic hierarchy clearly portrayed in Revelation 13, most especially in
verses 11–18. In the vision of the rising of the beast, according to
Whiston, 'we have a plain account of the Rise of *Antichrist himself*, strictly
so called; or of the *Pope of Rome*'.[13] This Antichrist has the outward
appearance of a lamb (he calls himself the vicar of Christ), but speaks
like a dragon:

exalting himself above all that is called God; Excommunicating and Destroying
Princes; Absolving Subjects from their allegiance; Introducing new, false, and
pernicious doctrines and practices; Commanding Idolatry in the worship of
Angels, Saints, Images and Reliques; Tyrannizing over the Consciences of
Men; and Anathematizing all who will not submit to his ungodly doings.[14]

Whiston is of course reflecting the common assumptions of his day.
The Pope is Antichrist, therefore it must be the Pope who is depicted in
Revelation 13. The text suits Whiston's purpose well, for its rich imagery
is pliable in the extreme, and so is able to regurgitate to Whiston's
satisfaction all the religious prejudices and preconceptions he feeds into
it. Indeed, as one reads Whiston on the matter of the identity of the
beast, one is struck by the obvious sense in which he assumes what he
wishes to prove, namely that the Pope is the beast of Rev. 13.11ff. To be
sure, he cites other writers who have said the same thing and appeals to
the common consensus for support, but there is little if any attempt
actually to argue the case. The best argument he offers is that in
fulfilment of Rev. 11.13–14 the papal beast works (actually he adds
'seems to' before the verb 'work' at this point in the biblical text)

a multitude of strange Miracles; and pretends to abundance of lying Wonders;
by which he strangely prevails with, and amuzes, and enslaves the World; and
so deceives them into an implicit obedience to his Dictates.[15]

Whiston then goes on to note that

[a]ll which characters are so peculiar to, and notorious in the Pope and his
Subordinate Ecclesiastical Hierarchy, that I need spend no more words about
them.[16]

In his attempt to ascertain the time of the beast's rising and the length
of his blasphemous career, Whiston becomes even more ingenious.
Drawing on Daniel as well as Revelation, he argues that the beast will
last for a 'time and times and the dividing of time' (Dan. 7.25). Whiston

---

[13] Whiston, *Essay*, p. 243.   [14] Ibid., p. 243.   [15] Ibid., p. 244.   [16] Ibid., p. 244.

argues here, as did most of his contemporaries, that a 'time' is a year and that 'times' is therefore two years. On the meaning of the phrase a 'dividing of time', however, he is unusual. The most natural understanding of this phrase, states Whiston, is a month, for the month is the principal division of the year;[17] the phrase 'time and times and the dividing of time' therefore indicates a period of three years and one month. This is taken as 37 months at 30 days per month or 1110 literal years. Armed with this information, Whiston approaches the question of when this period is to end. The little horn of Dan. 7.8, equated to the Lamb-like Beast by Whiston, arose in AD 606 when the Pope took to himself the title of 'universal bishop' and began the reign of 'Ecclesiastical Tyranny'.[18] The period will thus end in 1716.

Whiston has carried off a master-stroke: not only does his interpretation of the text now support his view of the religious opposition, thereby enabling him to stake out his existential claim in terms of his religious allegiance and standing, but it assures him that the beginning of the end is not far away, and hence gives him a definite locus on a clearly mapped-out chronological scale. For Whiston the final coming of Christ is still some 300 years away. However, he expects the dawn of the premillennial kingdom in 1716. It is in this year, he argues, that Antichrist, the Roman Catholic Church, will fall.

Whiston is of course reading the book of Revelation through Protestant-tinted spectacles, and it is not surprising that he consequently finds there the confirmation of all his worst fears and prejudices, as well as the affirmation of his hopes and millennial dreams. The powerful symbolism of the text and the determined interests of the reader have formed together an explosive mixture. It would of course be unfair to criticise Whiston for not conforming to the norms of modern historical-critical biblical scholarship, and that is not the intention here. However, what should be noted is that in bringing to the text his own prejudices and beliefs, Whiston has made his interpretation more or less pure eisegesis. He is reading into it what he wishes to find there, and the text has served the needs and desires of the interpreter well. In fact, in Whiston's interpretation the actual text appears almost incidental and is certainly not the controlling factor. Had 'Old Mother Hubbard' been in the canon in place of Revelation 13, it may be conjectured that Whiston might well have concluded that the cupboard represents the Roman Catholic Church barren of any spiritual sustenance, the bone for which

---

[17] Ibid., p. 4.   [18] Ibid., p. 245.

the dog longed is a symbol of righteousness and communion with God, and the dog itself a symbol of the hungry Christian soul which is starved as a result of papal error. Thus while the text has certainly been used by Whiston, it can scarcely be said to have had an influence upon him. As has been said in a more general context,

The interests of the readers and interpreters affect how texts are used and understood. In many cases, especially legal codes and religious scriptures, these interests are those of a community, not simply of individual readers. But it is still the aims or interests of the readers, rather than the intentions of the authors, which are decisive.[19]

However, although subjectivity in biblical interpretation may be inescapable, it should surely not be allowed to reign unchallenged. To many modern readers Whiston's work may seem illegitimate, being, as it is, the product of an unholy alliance of an almost infinitely malleable text and the powerful emotions of the interpreter, all put to negative ends. Whiston's work is at some considerable distance, both culturally and chronologically, from the present day, and this, perhaps, makes it possible to see relatively clearly the extent to which he has used the text for his own purposes. Further, these purposes are negative, for one result is that it has confirmed Whiston's views that the Pope and his hierarchy, and by extension Catholics in general, are servants of Satan whose desire it is to pervert truth and thwart the plans of God for the salvation of humankind. In the context of eighteenth-century England this is the voice of the persecutor, not the persecuted, and the eisegesis is used to support the strong, not the weak. Not all eisegesis is good eisegesis. Texts can be used to negative no less than to positive ends. In Whiston's interpretation of Revelation this is seen, for what we have here is the spectacle of a Cambridge academic (albeit one who was later to be expelled from the University for deviant views on the Trinity) using a text to support and prop up the demonising view of the small and largely underprivileged Catholic minority.

Whiston's basic points (though not the details) are reflected also in the work of the eminent Baptist minister John Gill. Although he had little formal education, he became skilled in Hebrew, Latin and Greek and in 1748 was awarded the degree of DD from the University of Aberdeen. He was the author of numerous works, including a multi-volume biblical commentary. Much of his work on Revelation was standard within a

[19] Robert Morgan with John Barton, *Biblical Interpretation* (Oxford: Oxford University Press, 1988), pp. 270–1.

broader eighteenth-century context, and hence is indicative of the broader stream. It comes as no surprise, then, to discover that Gill had no doubts regarding the identity of the beasts of Revelation 13. The whole chapter, he states, describes the rise of the great Roman Antichrist who at the instigation of Satan seeks to deceive and destroy God's people on earth. Commenting on Rev. 13.11, Gill writes that the second beast which is there described is

The same with the first beast, only in another form; the same for being and person, but under a different consideration; the same Antichrist, but appearing in another light and view: the first beast is the pope of Rome ... this other beast is the same pope of Rome, with his clergy, cardinals, archbishops, bishops, priests &c.[20]

Gill then goes on to describe the actions of this papal Antichrist, who has come up from the 'bottomless pit of hell' (cf. Rev. 9.1ff.):

Pretending great humility and holiness, shewing signs and lying wonders, obliging to idolatry, and exercising tyranny and cruelty on all that will not confess his religion.[21]

This onslaught continues unabated. As with Whiston, Gill offers little argument in favour of his position. Rather he simply states and restates the common assumptions of his day. Again like Whiston, he offers an imaginative reading of Revelation 13. Particularly imaginative are his thoughts on the number 666. Rev. 13.18 reads

Here is wisdom. Let him that hath understanding count the number of the beast: for it is the number of a man; and his number is Six hundred threescore and six.

This is an enticing text, and needless to say it attracted a great deal of attention before and during the eighteenth century. Brady has noted some of that tradition in great detail.[22] It must be remembered that the commentators dealt with here understood Revelation as a time-map of history which lays out either in chronological order or in several cycles the events that will come upon the world, from the time of John the Seer to the coming of the New Jerusalem and the eradication of all wickedness. Given these basic assumptions there was clearly scope for some imaginative interpretations of the number 666, for in each successive age the number was thought to be of particular and contemporary significance.

[20] Gill, *Exposition*, p. 794.   [21] Ibid., p. 794.

[22] Brady, *Number of the Beast*; David Brady, '1666: The Year of the Beast', *BJRULM* 61 (1979): 314–36.

Two main positions emerged on the correct way to decode this number. According to one group of scholars, the number should be seen as being in some way related to a particular date and/or time period. Thus there were those who felt that the number was to be understood as the number of years during which Antichrist would rule. (In 1693, for example, Samuel Petto[23] argued that the period of Antichrist was from c. 1050 to 1716.[24]) Some other interpreters, however, thought that the number provided a clue to the time of the rise of the Antichrist. Samuel Petto refers to the view of 'Mr Stephens', who put forward the theory that the number of the beast refers to a period of 666 years from 60 BC to AD 606, which latter year marked the beginning of Antichrist's rule when the Pope of Rome took to himself the title 'universal bishop'.[25] The view that the Antichrist was to arise exactly 666 years after the birth of Christ is as old as Bale,[26] but seems to have found little general support. Much more prevalent was the view that Antichrist's rise would be exactly 666 years after some other significant event in the history of the Church, for example the writing of the Apocalypse itself. As will be seen, Gill himself puts forward a form of this argument.

The third date-related interpretation saw the number as in some way reflecting not Antichrist's rise, but his downfall. In the latter context it was perhaps not surprising that the year 1666 gave rise to intense eschatological speculation.[27] Indeed, Gill himself refers to this earlier view that Antichrist would fall in 1666 or, more colloquially, in '666', 'the number of the thousand being dropped, as it is in our common way of speaking'.[28] Samuel Petto, writing in 1693 and hence within living memory of the events of 1666, himself gives testimony to the view that 'some' having referred the number of the beast

to the time of his Fall had raised expectations on the year 1666. Supposing that *John* left out the Millenary number, but time hath confuted this, that year being

---

[23] Samuel Petto, *The Revelation Unvailed* (1693), p. 36.

[24] Such an explanation of the number 666 is also a central component of the interpretation proposed by the German expositor Johann Albrecht Bengel (*Apparatus criticus* (1734), *Erklärte Offenbarung Johannis* (1740), *Gnomon Novi Testamenti* (1742)). Bengel's work is highly complex and need not be entered into fully here. However, we may note that the period 1143–1810 (Bengel argued that the actual period indicated by 666 in Rev. 13.18 was 666 and six-ninths) was central to Bengel's scheme. Bengel's work on Revelation was highly influential. It left its mark, for example, on John Wesley (see John Wesley, *Explanatory Notes upon the New Testament* (1754), p. 932) and upon his brother Charles – see chapter 6. On the view that 666 refers to the number of years in Antichrist's reign see further Brady, *Number of the Beast*, pp. 177, 215, 216, 221.

[25] Petto, *The Revelation Unvailed*, p. 34.   [26] Brady, *Number of the Beast*, pp. 26–7.

[27] See further Brady, 'Year of the Beast'.   [28] Gill, *Exposition*, vol. III, p. 796.

past and he not fallen; unless you will begin either at the Passion of Jesus Christ, or the time of writing the Revelation.[29]

The other, perhaps larger, group of interpreters, however, saw the number as being the numerical value of the letters of the beast's name. The word 'Lateinos' (λατεινος) was a particular favourite, but there were other suggestions, for example 'Romanus' (Ῥομανυς) and 'Vicarius Filii Dei'. Historical-critical scholars will of course be aware of the various attempts to get the numerical value of the letters in the name of Nero to add up to 666. It is not easy, but it can be done.[30] Those who were not wedded to an historical-critical framework for their interpretation, however, had a much freer hand, and expositions abounded.

Gill sets to work on the problem with characteristic ingenuity and argues that in fact the number signifies both the name of the beast and the date of his rising and falling. The name of the beast is straightforward enough. The key is the word 'Lateinos' which, when written in Greek, adds up to the required number.[31] Similarly, he observes, the Hebrew רומיית (Romiith) adds up to the same figure.[32] But Gill goes ingeniously on: France is particularly Catholic and a common name of French kings is 'Louis', which may be latinised to 'Ludovicus', and the numerical value of the letters in 'Ludovicus' is, says Gill, 666. Hence we have a further key. Antichrist, Rome, will fall when a king by the name of Louis is on the throne of France.[33] (The linking of Ludovicus with the number 666 was not altogether uncommon, especially, naturally enough, after the outbreak of the French Revolution. Gill may have been influenced in this interpretation by the work of his fellow Baptist, Sayer Rudd (d. 1757), who published *An Essay Towards a New Explication of the Doctrines of the Resurrection, Millennium, And Judgement* in 1734.[34])

The time of the rise of Antichrist can similarly be worked out from the number. The key, says Gill, is to be found by considering the square root of 666, which is, as close as can be discerned, 25.[35] Add 25 to the date of

[29] Petto, *The Revelation Unvailed*, pp. 34–5.
[30] See, for example, G. B. Caird, *The Revelation of St John the Divine* (London: A. & C. Black, 1984), pp. 174–77. As Caird notes, if the Latin Neronius Caesar is Hellenised to Neron Kaisar and then put into Hebrew as נרון קסר, the numerical result is 666.
[31] Gill, *Exposition*, vol. III, p. 797. According to Gill, who was typical of a very long line of tradition stretching back to Irenaeus, l = 30, a = 1, t = 300, e = 5, i = 10, n = 50, o = 70 and v = 200. Whiston opts for the same solution and prints his workings on p. 257 of his *Essay*.
[32] Gill, *Exposition*, vol. III, p. 797.   [33] Ibid., vol. III, p. 797.
[34] On Rudd see further Brady, *Number of the Beast*, pp. 40–5 (although he seems to misread Gill on this point) and Froom, *Prophetic Faith*, vol. II, p. 681–2.
[35] The view that the importance of the number 666 is to be found in its square root was put forward in the course of over 200 pages by Francis Potter (*An Interpretation of the Number '666' or 'The Number of the Beast'* (1642)). See further Brady, *Number of the Beast*, pp. 111–24.

the crucifixion (taken as AD 33) and the result is AD 58. This was the year of the birth of Antichrist (though Gill does not say what is significant about the year). Add 666 years to this date and one lands on AD 724, the date at which, according to Gill, Antichrist reached his 'manhood' and engaged in controversy over the worship of images. He is presumably thinking of the iconoclastic controversy of c. 725–c. 842.[36] Thus, it seems, Gill is able to link the number 666 to the Roman Catholic Church on several points. His case is therefore 'proved': the Roman Catholic Church is Antichrist, as the uncanny recurrence of the number 666 (or its square root) in the history and descriptive titles of that institution prove. Thus the Pope is the instrument of Satan and Catholics are his servants. The popular attitude to Catholics in Gill's eighteenth-century England is hence justified.

It may of course be argued that the work of both Whiston and Gill cannot really be taken as representative of anything other than the views of a relatively small scholarly (though pre-critical) elite. However, it has been noted that the work of these two scholars is typical of the broad trend and represents the views not of the few but of the many. In English Protestant scholarly circles anti-Catholic readings of Revelation were absolutely standard and a force to be reckoned with. Such readings represent the scholarly paradigm of the period, and are indicative of a broad interpretative school.

But evidence of such views is not limited to strictly scholarly sources alone or confined to academic monographs or biblical commentaries. In a hymn first published in 1762, Charles Wesley wrote (as a poetic comment on Rev. 12.10–12):

> Now is the saints' salvation come,
> The strength that slays that beast of *Rome*,
> The Kingdom of our God below,
> The power of Christ against our foe,
> Which forces Satan to submit,
> For ever bruised beneath our feet.[37]

In a hymn designed for public consumption and use, then, Charles Wesley is linking Rome to the great beast/dragon of Revelation 12–13. And his mind is drawn once again to Revelation when considering his son Samuel's defection in 1784 to 'the *Romish* sect'[38] (an institution

---

[36] Dates according to F. L. Cross and E. A. Livingstone (eds.), *The Oxford Dictionary of the Christian Church* (Oxford: Oxford University Press, revised edn, 1997), pp. 815–16.

[37] G. Osborn, (ed.), *The Poetical Works of John and Charles Wesley* (13 vols., London: Epworth Press, 1868–72), vol. XIII, p. 234.

[38] Ibid., vol. VIII, p. 424.

elsewhere described as 'the *Babylonish* beast').[39] In words clearly reminiscent of Rev. 13.13–14 he wrote

> Thy power be in his weakness seen,
> Nor let him the commands of men
>   Rashly mistake for Thine,
> Nor heed to lying wonders give,
> Or legendary tales receive
>   As oracles divine.[40]

Pamphlets, tracts and sermons which similarly use Revelation as a vehicle for anti-Catholic sentiments are copious and no significant attempt to enter into that literature can be made here. In passing, however, we may note the work of the Anglican divine Thomas Simmons, in a sermon preached on 5 November 1714. (The date of course is significant: Simmons is reflecting on God's mercy in delivering England by thwarting the Gunpowder Plot of 1605.) Simmons makes frequent allusion to the book of Revelation in arguing that God is on the side of the Protestants and against papists.[41] Indeed, despite the fact that he hardly ever quotes directly from the book of Revelation (the reference to the 'Souls under the Altar' (cf. Rev. 6.9) is one exception),[42] the text is clearly in his mind as he constructs his arguments. Thus, for example, he refers to the previous condition of the Church when it was 'in the Wilderness' and when 'Popery as a Deluge over-flowed almost all the Face of the Christian World'.[43] Such remarks clearly reflect Rev. 12.6, 13–15, and further allusions are found in references to those who hold to the 'testimony of Jesus'[44] (cf. Rev. 1.9; 6.9; 11.7; 12.11, 17; 19.10). Simmons then goes on to argue that with the coming of William and Mary, God delivered a part of the Church from popish, i.e. satanic, domination. (Simmons was not the first to make this suggestion, as chapter 2 has shown.) The rest of the work continues in this vein, and it is apparent that it is largely from Revelation, and the prevailing anti-Catholic readings of it, that much of Simmons' imagery and argumentation is drawn. This sermon, then, gives one example (and others could have been listed easily enough) of the use of Revelation to support fervent anti-Catholicism among the populace.

[39] Ibid., vol. viii, p. 398.
[40] ST Kimbrough and O. Beckerlegge (eds.), *The Unpublished Poetry of Charles Wesley* (3 vols., Nashville, TN: Kingswood Books, 1988–92), vol. i, p. 310; Butler, *Methodists and Papists*, p. 186.
[41] *The Sure Side: or, God and the Church. A Sermon Preached on the Fifth of November, 1714 in the Parish of St. John Wapping* (1714).
[42] Simmons, *The Sure Side*, p. 15.   [43] Ibid., p. 8.   [44] Ibid., p. 13.

Perhaps even more illuminating than sources such as hymns, tracts and sermons, however, are the marginal notes and brief exegetical remarks found in many editions of eighteenth-century bibles. Such notes, unlike, it might be argued, more extended scholarly treatises, were likely to be of significant influence among the rank and file. A survey of such material reveals the anticipated results: the kind of interpretation found in many eighteenth-century bibles is wholly consistent with the general thrust of the more extended and scholarly treatments discussed in detail above. One might note, for example, *The Family Bible* of 1771.[45] On the words 'The name of blasphemy' (i.e. the one written on the heads of the beast of Rev. 13.1) the editors quote with apparent approval the words of Philip Doddridge (1702–51)[46] that any who do not (with hindsight) see in this prophetic picture a reference to the papal hierarchy 'must have very little acquaintance with the arrogant titles which have been assumed or admitted by the Popes'.[47] The editors again quote Doddridge (who himself is quoting Newton) on the meaning of the number 666. The number refers, it is argued, to the name of the beast, namely 'Latium' (*sic*) in the original language. However, the number also refers to the time of the beast's arising, which, it is claimed, was 666 years after the writing of the Apocalypse in AD 96, i.e. in AD 756 (*sic*) 'or thereabouts', when the Pope became a temporal monarch.[48] Again the eisegetical process is clearly visible here, and again the eisegesis is used to foster and support a demonizing view of a religious minority. Exactly the same process can be seen in other editions of the Bible. To note more individually seems unnecessary, but the *Family Expositor Bible* (1763) is one further example to which reference may be made.[49]

In eighteenth-century England, then, the book of Revelation was widely used. The emotional and intellectual energy invested in it and the ingenuity with which it was made to suit the interpreter's ends are apparent. Such a process is of course not of necessity a bad thing.

---

[45] *The Family Bible; or, Christian's Best Treasure. Containing, the Sacred Text of the Old and New Testament, with Annotations from Grotius, Boyle, Prideaux, Pearson, Tillotson, Poole, Whitby, Henry, Burkitt, Doddridge, &c. &c.* (1771).

[46] Philip Doddridge was a nonconformist minister. His six-volume work *The Family Expositor; or a Paraphrase and Version of the New Testament; with Critical Notes* was published during the period 1739–56, the last volume being edited and published posthumously by his close associate Job Orton. Doddridge's work is now more readily available in the one-volume reprint edition of 1825 (*DNB*, vol. v, pp. 1063–9).

[47] *Family Bible*, p. 1434.   [48] Ibid., p. 1434.

[49] *Family Expositor; Containing the Sacred Text of the Old and New Testament; Illustrated with a Commentary and Notes, Historical, Geographical and Critical, Taken from the Most Eminent Commentators Ancient and Modern… Wherein the Text is Explained, Doubts Resolved, Scriptures Paralleled, and Various Readings Observed* (1763).

Religious texts can and often do bring support and hope to those badly
in need of it. In general terms the book of Revelation fits this pattern,
and commentators like Wainwright seem justified in pointing to the use
of Revelation in the works of black South Africans such as Alan Boesak
and Latin Americans like Dagoberto Ramírez Fernández to support the
view that

> [i]n every age and in most branches of the Christian church the Apocalypse has
> made its impact through worship, bringing comfort in times of sorrow, giving
> expression to dreams and hopes, and providing the language and images of
> adoration and praise.[50]

The book is able to give inspiration and hope to the socially disadvantaged, the persecuted, the poor and the weak.[51]

However, though the book can and often does appeal to the weak
and/or the persecuted, it has no less an attraction for the strong and/or
the persecutor. It may appeal to and inspire the higher religious emotions, but it may also be used to express wholly less noble sentiments. In
this chapter we have caught a glimpse of that, for in the hands of some,
indeed most, eighteenth-century Protestant interpreters, the book became a means of divinely sanctioning their contemporary society's
anti-Catholicism. Catholics were servants of Antichrist and Satan, and
hence their influence upon Christendom must be negated.

This negative aspect of the afterlife of the book of Revelation does not
stand alone. In chapter 7 the bitter disappointment of the Millerites will
come into focus while in chapter 9 the case of the Branch Davidians will
be considered in some detail. At Waco the result of a misreading of the
Apocalypse was very real. That misreading was the wanton use of the
text to encourage and support a group in its wholly negative and in the
end disastrous understanding of the world, satanic forces, and its own
place in the eschatological drama.

APPENDIX[52]

In this fifth Vision; (which includes the sixth also, of the Image of the Beast, of
which hereafter;) we have a plain account of the Rise of *Antichrist himself*,

---

50 Wainwright, *Mysterious Apocalypse*, p. 222. Wainwright then expands on these sentiments, arguing
   that the Apocalypse has strengthened the faith of those facing natural and man-made disasters,
   and appeals particularly to those who believe themselves to be in a situation of crisis. He does refer
   briefly to the possible negative use of the book (p. 229), but does not consider this at any length.
51 Ibid., pp. 177–87.
52 From Whiston, *Essay on the Revelation of Saint John*, pp. 243–8; spelling, punctuation and italic are
   reproduced without alteration.

strictly so called; or of the *Pope of Rome and his subordinate hierarchy*: having indeed the appearance of *a Lamb;* professing to be the Vicar of Christ, who is the *Lamb of God;* Servant of the Servants of God; Successor of the blessed Apostle St *Peter;* the great Pastor of the Church, to feed the flock of Christ: but *speaking like a Dragon;* exalting himself above all that is called God; Excommunicating and Destroying princes; Absolving Subjects from their allegiance; Introducing new, false, and pernicious doctrines and practices; Commanding Idolatry in the worship of Angels, Saints, Images and Reliques; Tyrannising over the Consciencies of men; and Anathematizing all who will not submit to his ungodly doings. *He exercises all the power of the first Beast before him;* maintains *Imperium in Imperio;* requires the like or greater submission to his decrees as the Supream Temporal Power expects; and gives out all his Laws in the fight, and by the permission of the several Kings by which the distinct Kingdoms of the *Roman* Empire are govern'd. *He causes all to worship the first Beast, whose deadly wound was heal'd,* i.e. He is the common Center and Cement which unites all those otherwise distinct Kingdoms; and by joining with them procures them a blind obedience from their Subjects; and so He is the occasion of the preservation of the Old *Roman* Empire in some kind of Unity, and Name, and Strength: which otherwise had been quite dissolv'd, by the Inundations and wars succeeding the settlement of the Barbarous Nations in that Empire. He also, does, or seems to do, a multitude of strange miracles; and pretends to an abundance of lying wonders; by which he strangely prevails with, and amuzes, and enslaves the World; and so deceives them into an implicit obedience to his Dictates. All which characters are so peculiar to, and notorious in the Pope and his Subordinate Ecclesiastical Hierarchy, that I need spend no more words about them. What is chiefly to be here considered is the *time of his rise,* and his duration; both of them to be taken from *Daniel,* where, as we have prov'd, he is described under the Name of *the Little Horn;* and therefore, according to what has been there already advanc'd, ought to begin *some time after* the Rise of the Ten Horns or Ten Kings of the *Roman* Empire; and to continue until their Destruction *in being,* but *in Power* no longer than they do so, *viz.* till the end of his 1110 and of their 1260 years. Now as to the Epocha of the Exaltation of the Papal Power, I take it to be plainly AD 606. 150 years after the Epocha when the Ten kings were first risen AD 456. And certainly this date agrees so well with History that nothing can do more so. Thus says one very truly, 'Concerning the Emersion of the two-horned beast out of the Earth, I find a great Consent in the Commentaries, Controversies, and Stories of the Church: that the two-horned Beast began in the Universal Headship under the Emperor *Phocas. Crakanthorp* in his Treatise against *Spalato* calleth it the Corner-Stone of the Building. And in very deed many Authors, if you put them upon it to state the original of the Beasts Kingdom, they do generally in a manner pitch upon the year 606.' And to be sure Pope *Boniface* the third in that year receiving first from the Tyrant *Phocas;* and the Popes, his Successors ever after claiming the Stile of *Head of the Church,* and *Universal Bishop* of the same, and accordingly ever after pretending to, and upon all occasions exer-

cising an usurped Power agreeable to so presumptuous a title; this Epocha of
the Pope's Ecclesiastical Tyranny is so Eminent and Remarkable in History,
and has occasion'd such mighty disputes between the *Romanists and Protestants*,
and has been so often pitched upon by this who have attempted this Prophecy,
tho' they could find so little direct Foundation in Scripture for it, that I need
not use many words to shew the exactness of its correspondence with *Daniel's*
Prophecy, and that from hence began that famous Period when *Times, and
Laws, should be given into the hands of* this *Little Horn for a Time, and Times, and a
Division of Time*, or for 1110 Prophetick Days. Dr *Heylin*, a Learned Man who
seems not much to have concern'd himself with the Apocalypse, from the
great difference there was in History between the *Bishops* of Rome *before*, and
the *Popes* of Rome *after* this Epocha, in his Catalogue intirely distinguishes the
one from the other: and having given us a list of the 65 first *Bishops* of *Rome* till
AD 605 and noted that *Sabinius I* was the last of the Roman *Bishops*, not having
that arrogant Title of *Universal Bishop*, or *Head of the Church*. He finishes that
Branch of the intire Catalogue: and then beginning the second with this Title,
The Popes of Rome challenging a Supremacy over all the Church, From, A. D. 606 and
Boniface III. He gives us the Catalogue of the Popes till his own time, being in
number 179. And it is very well worth our Observation that when just before
that time the Bishop of *Constantinople* had obtained the title of *Universal Bishop*,
the then Popes, *Pelagius* and St. *Gregory*, vehemently oppos'd it; and downright
affirm'd that whosoever took the Title of Universal Bishop upon him was a
Fore-runner of Antichrist; equal to Lucifer in pride, and had the name of
Blasphemy upon him. So that when immediately after, St *Gregory's* next successor but one, *Boniface* the third, accepted of that very Title; and what was
more, both himself and his successors exercis'd that Tyrannical Power therein
imply'd; it is plain by Pope *Pelagius* and St. *Gregory's* opinion that either
Antichrist himself, or at least his Forerunner, who was equal to Lucifer in
pride, and had the name of Blasphemy upon him, began to sit in the See of
Rome. This whole History I shall first give you in the words of that great Man,
A. B. *Laud* in his excellent Book against *Fisher* the Jesuit; and then in the
forenamed Popes own words. The A. B. then giving an account of the gradual
Rise of the Popes to their greatness under the Christian Emperors; and being
come towards the end of the sixth Century, He thus proceeds. 'About this time
brake out the ambition of *John Patriarch* of *Constantinople* affecting to be Universal Bishop. He was countenanced in this by *Mauritius* the Emperor; but sourly
opposed by *Pelagius* and Pope *Gregory*; in so much that St. *Gregory* plainly says
this pride of his shews that the times of Antichrist were near. So as yet; (and
this was near upon the point of six hundred years after Christ;) there was no
Universal Bishop, no one monarch over the whole Militant Church. But
Mauritius being depos'd and murdered by *Phocas*, Phocas conferred upon *Boniface* the third that very Honour that two of his Predecessors had declaim'd
against, as Monstrous and Blasphemous, if not Antichristian. Where, by the
way, either these two Popes *Pelagius* and St. *Gregory* err'd in this weighty
Business about an Universal Bishop over the whole Church; or if they did not

erre, *Boniface* and the rest which after him took it upon them, were in their very predecessors judgment Antichristian.'

(There follows a lengthy series of extracts – about 500 words – from Pelagius and St Gregory, in the original Latin.)

It is therefore evident, That As in the present Hypothesis, the Pope arose *among* the ten Kings in place; his Authority and theirs being in the very same Countries and Kingdoms; and *after* them in time, as Antichrist was to do; so that at this *Epocha* AD 606, his Power was advanc'd to a height abundantly sufficient to begin the Date of his overbearing Dominion and Tyranny over the Christian Church: which being so, and his Duration but 1110 years, as we have already observed, we have great reason to expect the period of his *Grandeur* and *Tyranny*, at the Period of those 1110 years i. e. at the same time with that of the ten Kings AD 1716. and his utter destruction, with that of the whole *Roman* Empire, at our Saviour's coming: according to the several Scripture Prophecies hereto relating.

CHAPTER 4

Catholic Apocalypse: the Book of Revelation in Roman Catholicism from c. 1600 to 1800

In the previous chapter we noted the standard view among Protestant interpreters of the book of Revelation regarding the identity of Antichrist: it was almost universally thought that the Pope and/or the Roman Catholic Church in general was the incarnation of that epitome of evil. This is seen clearly in Protestant interpretations of Revelation 13, but the eisegesis goes beyond this. While no attempt has been made here to document the case, it is true to say that this understanding of Antichrist is similarly reflected in the views put forward in Protestant interpretations of Daniel (especially such passages as Dan 7.24–5)[1] and 2 Thessalonians (especially 2 Thess. 2).[2] It was also noted in the previous chapter that numerous commentators showed great ingenuity in seeking to interpret the text to support this view. The interpretation of the number 666 in Rev. 13.18, for instance, attracted a great deal of attention and is a particularly good example of the eisegetical process at work. The way in which the various parts of the composite beasts in Revelation 13 were interpreted during this period also illustrates the same point. In chapter 2 the same eisegetical process was seen in action as Keach, Knollys and others sought to read into the text of Revelation a picture and understanding of the world in which they themselves lived.

The history of the interpretation of the Apocalypse has attracted some significant attention before, and those important and sometimes extensive studies are now well known. However, research in this area is almost exclusively focused upon the use and application of the book of Revelation in Protestant sources; there are a few exceptions, but the work that has been done on the interpretation of Revelation in the

---

[1] See, for example, *Family Expositor*.
[2] See, for example, 'The Fifth Lecture upon the Second Epistle of Paul to the Thessalonians', in *Lectures upon the First and Second Epistles of Paul to the Thessalonians: Preached by that Faithfull Servant of God M. Robert Rollock, Some-tyme Minister of the Evangell of Iesus Christ, and Rector of the College in Edinburgh* (1606).

Catholic tradition is principally that contained in more general studies.[3] Thus despite an ever-growing body of secondary literature devoted to Revelation's reception history, relatively little is known regarding the history of Catholic understandings of the book. This is a serious gap and one which this chapter seeks partially to fill. How, in the context of the anti-Catholic Protestant interpretative paradigm outlined in chapter 3, was the book of Revelation (and with it parts of Daniel and 2 Thessalonians) read by Catholic scholars in the two or three centuries following the Reformation? How were the Protestant charges rebutted? These are the questions addressed here.

The focus of this examination is chiefly on the interpretation of the Apocalypse in Catholic sources from the seventeenth and eighteenth centuries, though some sixteenth-century texts do receive a brief mention. There is a heavy, though not exclusive, concentration on materials published in English and/or in England.[4] In the section dealing with individual writers, only a small number can be examined in the detail they deserve. However, while the rather narrow focus of this chapter needs to be acknowledged clearly at this point, an attempt has naturally been made to select authors who seem typical of general trends in the wider Catholic tradition. Indeed, in the process of collecting the data for this chapter, every entry in Blom et al.[5] has been examined, and significant time spent at Catholic archives in the United Kingdom. The survey presented here, then, is limited but fair.

Enough has already been said in chapters 1–3 to indicate the main contours of English Protestant biblical-prophetic interpretation up to and during the eighteenth century. As we have seen, the basic approach adopted was that of anti-Catholic historicism, though of course there

---

3 The literature is not vast. However, there are some useful summaries. E. B. Elliott's still very impressive survey of the history of interpretation of the book of Revelation is found in *Horae Apocalypticae*, vol. IV, pp. 275–633, and remarks on Roman Catholic commentators occur sporadically throughout. On pages 464–506 of that work Elliott pays particular attention to interpreters such as Ribera, Alcazar (spelt 'Alcasar' by him) and Bossuet. Wainwright, *Mysterious Apocalypse* is extremely useful in giving a general overview of the interpretation of Revelation in the pre-critical period (pp. 21–103), but deals only briefly with Catholic expositors (pp. 61–5). Most recent is Jean-Robert Armogathe, 'Interpretations of the Revelation of John: 1500–1800', in John J. Collins, Bernard McGinn and Stephen J. Stein (eds.), *The Encyclopedia of Apocalypticism* (3 vols., New York: Continuum, 1998), vol. II, pp. 185–203, which, despite its wide-ranging title, is primarily concerned with continental Roman Catholic sources. On Walmesley in particular see especially Geoffrey Scott, '"The Times are Fast Approaching": Bishop Charles Walmesley OSB (1722–1797) as Prophet', *Journal of Ecclesiastical History* 36 (1985): 590–604.
4 Much of the material used in this chapter is located in the special collections at the John Rylands University Library of Manchester, UK and at Ushaw College, Durham, UK. The holdings of the Gradwell Library, Upholland, UK have also been examined.
5 F. Blom et al., *English Catholic Books, 1701–1801* (Aldershot, Hants: Scolar Press, 1996).

were numerous variations on this overarching theme. For example, a number of English expositors, including the highly influential Thomas Brightman, took the view that the book is to be read as a sequential unfolding in chronological sequence of events from the time of John down to the dawn of the millennial kingdom.[6] In this Brightman was followed by (among a mass of others) Joseph Mede[7] and John Tillinghast (1604–55).[8] Bale,[9] on the other hand, took a cyclical approach. According to him the seven seals of Revelation 6–8 are seven periods of the (true) Church. These are successively the period of Christ and the apostles; early heresy and persecution; later heresy (Arianism and Pelagianism in particular); the dawn of the papacy and Mahometanism; the great persecution at the hands of Antichrist (the Roman Catholic Church); Antichrist's convulsion at the hands of Wycliffe, Huss and the reformers; and the period of silence following Antichrist's fall when the Jews shall be converted and the gospel will spread to all. The seven trumpets of Rev. 8.7–11.15ff. go over the same ground from a different perspective. Moving into the later chapters of Revelation, Bale continues with this historicist line. Revelation 11, for example, speaks of witnesses to the truth in general and their slaughter during the period of the sixth age of the Church at the hands of the papal Antichrist. Revelation 13 describes the overall career of Antichrist. Luther also took this cyclical view. According to him, the seven seals give an overview of political history as it affects the Church; the seven trumpets, on the other hand, give an overview of spiritual events. These are, however, variations on the general historicist theme, whose framework is always that the book of Revelation gives an overview of history and the Pope is Antichrist.

It is hardly surprising, given this general context, that the relatively few English Catholic commentators who turned their hands to the interpretation of these same passages should be concerned to counter this widely held, if somewhat variously presented, Protestant view. The response came in three basic forms: preterism, futurism and 'counter historicism' – a term that has been created for the purposes of this discussion. As will be seen, the three categories are by no means mutually exclusive. There is also a fourth method of approach, that of

---

[6] Brightman, *Apocalyps*. [7] Mede, *Clavis Apocalyptica*.
[8] John Tillinghast, *Knowledge of the Times* (1654).
[9] On Bale see especially Bauckham, *Tudor Apocalypse*, pp. 21–36 and *passim*; Bale's work is summarised also in Elliott, *Horae Apocalypticae*, vol. IV, pp. 437–44 and in Froom, *Prophetic Faith*, vol. II, pp. 395–401.

the 'idealist' school, which suggests that the book is to be read as a symbolic account of the battle between good and evil. This is all but absent in Protestant sources, and seems to have had little impact on English Catholic interpreters during this period, though one meets it occasionally; an interesting example occurs in the work of Robert Witham, whose *Annotations on the New Testament* is discussed below. The title page of that work is reproduced as figure 4.

A basic outline of the preterist and futurist schools of prophetic interpretation has already been given in chapter 1. There it was noted that according to the futurists most of the prophecies of Revelation await their fulfilment in the future – generally in the three-and-a-half literal years of Antichrist preceding the end of the world. (This period of three-and-a-half literal years is of course that of the 1,260 days, the time, times and half a time and the 42 months mentioned in Dan. 12.7; Rev. 11.2, 3; 12.6, 14; 13.5; the futurists did not adopt the year-day principle.) The preterists, on the other hand, argued that the book of Revelation dealt mainly with events of the first few centuries of the Christian era only, though again space was often left for the events of the last three-and-a-half years of the world's current history. The counter-historicist school saw things differently. According to proponents of this view, the Protestants were right in seeing the books of Daniel and Revelation, and other portions of the Bible, as a 'time map'. Present events do shadow the prophecies. However, on the details of the correspondence between scripture and history, so Roman Catholic historicists argued, the Protestants erred. Thus, for example, some Catholic expositors saw Luther and Lutheranism as the 'beast from the bottomless pit' described in Revelation 9;[10] the destroying figure there described was not, as many Protestants had claimed,[11] to be equated with the Pope and his clergy.

These three approaches to prophetic interpretation allowed room for considerable overlap, especially between the futurist and counter-historicist school on the question of the identity of Antichrist and the length, location and nature of his rule. The extent of that overlap is seen

---

[10] Bellarmine took this view (Froom, *Prophetic Faith*, vol. II, p. 499). Wainwright (*Mysterious Apocalypse*, p. 61) points out that the view was also put forward by Bertold Purstinger, Bishop of Chiemsee, and that Serafino da Fermo saw in Luther not only the fulfilment of the prophecy of the falling star (Rev. 8.10), but also the fulfilment of that of the first beast of Revelation 13.

[11] Such a view was put forward by a number of commentators during the period with which we are here concerned. It is reported, for example, in the annotations accompanying the text of the *Family Expositor*, where it is associated with King James [I]. See also Durham, *Commentarie*, pp. 434ff., who is very clear on the matter.

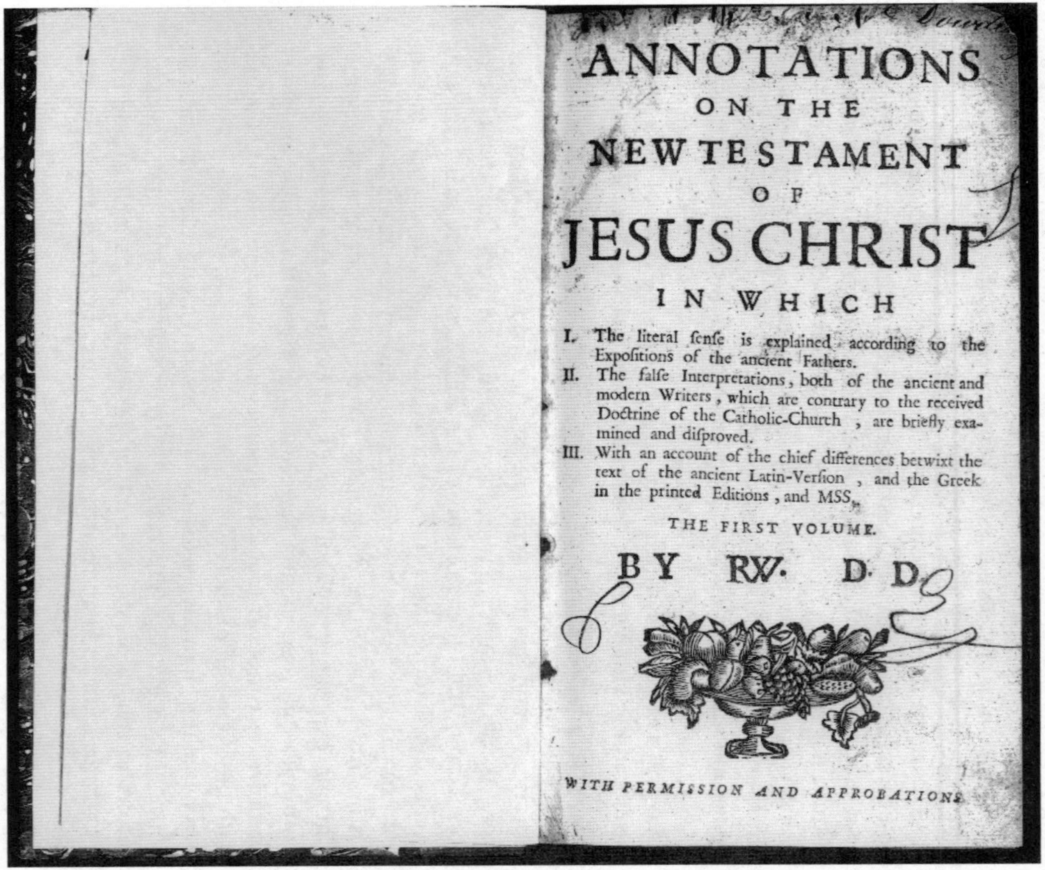
ANNOTATIONS
ON THE
NEW TESTAMENT
OF
JESUS CHRIST
IN WHICH

I. The literal ſenſe is explained according to the Expoſitions of the ancient Fathers.
II. The falſe Interpretations, both of the ancient and modern Writers, which are contrary to the received Doctrine of the Catholic-Church, are briefly examined and diſproved.
III. With an account of the chief differences betwixt the text of the ancient Latin-Verſion, and the Greek in the printed Editions, and MSS.

THE FIRST VOLUME.

BY R.W. D.D.

WITH PERMISSION AND APPROBATIONS.

Figure 4 Title page of Witham's *Annotations* (1730)

very clearly, for example, in the work of Charles Walmesley (1722–97),[12] which will be considered more fully below. His interpretative scheme has a distinctly counter-historicist framework, but his comments on Antichrist show an adoption of the futurist scheme on that particular issue.

It is clear why Catholic scholars were so concerned with the task of countering the Protestant prophetic-interpretative paradigm that had by the beginning of the eighteenth century become so firmly entrenched in biblical studies. At least from Luther on, and perhaps even before, the book of Revelation had provided a useful weapon in the arsenal of those who wished to launch an attack upon the papacy, and a means by which the demonisation of that institution could take on the appearance of having divine sanction. Nothing less was at stake than the question of the supernatural origins of the Church. Was it of God or of the Devil? Was it the Bride of Christ or the Whore of Satan? Little wonder, then, that Catholic expositors spent considerable time and energy in seeking to meet the challenge that had been posed. In the remainder of this chapter some specific examples of that counter-attack are surveyed, grouped as they relate to the three approaches of preterism, futurism and counter-historicism. Two points will be of note throughout: first, that the text has once again yielded to the interests of the reader (this time the beleaguered Catholic community as it sought to defend itself in the face of the Protestant onslaught) and second, that this was a process in which some were prepared to invest significant intellectual energy and verve.

Perhaps the most significant figure in the origin of this preterist method of interpretation was the Jesuit from Seville, Luis de Alcazar (1554–1613).[13] He is often credited with establishing the preterist scheme of interpretation in the post-Reformation Roman Catholic tradition. In his commentary on Revelation Alcazar put forward the view that the book spoke only of the period of the early Church, predicting its

---

[12] Walmesley was born in Wigan, Lancashire, and educated for the priesthood at Douai and Paris, where he obtained the degree of DD at the Sorbonne. He was prior of the Order of St Benedict, based in Rome, but returned to England to become Vicar Apostolic of the western district, which he administered for over thirty years. He was a noted mathematician and a Fellow of the Royal Societies of London and Berlin. Information from Joseph Gillow, *A Literary and Biographical History, or Bibliographical Dictionary of the English Catholics: From the Breach with Rome, in 1534, to the Present Time* (5 vols, n.d. [1885–1902]), vol. v, pp. 569–70.

[13] On Alcazar see Froom, *Prophetic Faith*, vol. II, pp. 506–9 and Elliott, *Horae Apocalypticae*, vol. IV, p. 484. According to Froom (*Prophetic Faith*, vol. II, p. 507), Alcazar's 900-page work on the Apocalypse, published posthumously, was the fruit of some forty years' labour.

conquest over Judaism and paganism.[14] Nero is the Antichrist and the New Jerusalem the Roman Catholic Church. The millennium of Revelation 20 is the period of the Church and hence the period currently enjoyed by Catholic Christians. The book of Revelation does not speak of the future or, except in its description of the millennium, the present. The Antichrist has been and gone and was not the Pope. Alcazar is unusual in the extent to which he was prepared to apply the preterist logic consistently; for him, the whole of the book of Revelation related to the past.

Other Catholic scholars, while adopting in broad outline the preterist scheme as proposed by Alcazar, were not so certain that the book of Revelation had no future application. In particular, most allowed for the coming of an individual Antichrist figure in the future, although, some argued, this final Antichrist had been prefigured in the past by individuals such as Antiochus and Nero. Thus, for example, the influential French biblical scholar and theologian Bishop Jacques Bénigne Bossuet (1627–1704)[15] adopted a basically preterist scheme throughout the course of his work *L'Apocalypse avec une Explication*,[16] suggesting that the bulk of the book describes the victory of Christianity over pagans and Jews in the first few centuries of the Church's existence. According to Bossuet, the first six seals deal with the Church's eventual victory over paganism, while the trumpets describe the victory over the Jews and Jewish-Christian heresies. The woman clothed with the sun of Revelation 12 is the Church and the male child to whom she gives birth is Constantine. Bossuet went on to argue that chapter 13 describes the events under Julian the Apostate, chapters 14–16 describe the fall of Rome at the hands of the Goths, and chapters 17–19 go over the same chronological ground, giving more detail on specific points. Only in the

---

[14] Luis de Alcazar, *Vestigatio Arcani Sensus in Apocalypsi*. Froom gives 1614 as the date for this work (Froom, *Prophetic Faith*, vol. II, p. 809). The date of the edition held at the Ushaw College Library, Durham, UK (ref. 1.c.3.2) is 1619. Some other publication details given by Froom are also different from those of the Ushaw and Rylands volumes. This suggests that the work had been reprinted by 1619, an indication, perhaps, of Alcazar's popularity.

[15] For an outline of Bishop Bossuet's life and literary career see John J. Delaney and James Edward Tobin (eds.), *Dictionary of Catholic Biography* (London: Robert Hale, 1961), p. 164. Brief notes on his method of interpretation are found in Froom, *Prophetic Faith*, vol. II, p. 636 n. 60. More extensive treatments are found in Elliott, *Horae Apocalypticae*, vol. IV, pp. 480–4 and Armogathe, 'Interpretations', pp. 195–7.

[16] Jacques Bénigne Bossuet, *L'Apocalypse avec une Explication* (1689). Froom, *Prophetic Faith*, vol. II, p. 813 gives 1690 as the date for this work (a date which he may have derived from Elliott, *Horae Apocalypticae*, vol. IV, p. 480 n. 4, upon which he was clearly dependent for most of his information on Bossuet). The copy in the Ushaw Library is clearly dated 1689, suggesting a reprint in 1690, an indication perhaps of its popularity.

final section of Revelation, specifically in Rev. 20.7–15, is the coming and career of the future Antichrist brought into focus. The millennium is the period of the Church (as Augustine had said), but just before the end of the world the great Antichrist will arise.

Another Catholic writer worth considering at this juncture is Augustin Calmet (1672–1757), a French Benedictine, who first published his *Commentaire Littéral* in 1707–16.[17] There were major elements of the preterist scheme in his work. On the question of Antichrist, however, he was less inclined to preterism. A summary of his thinking on this issue is to be found in his dictionary of the Bible. In the article on Antichrist, he puts forward the view that though Antichrist may have been prefigured in such persons as Antiochus and Nero, the 'true' and 'real' Antichrist, who is to come before the second advent of Jesus Christ,

will bring together in his person all the malicious characteristics which have been seen only separately in the different people who, because of their impiety, have deserved to be called figures or precursors of Antichrist.[18]

For Calmet, then, the real Antichrist is still in the future. He will come shortly before the end of the age to wage war upon the true followers of Christ and seek to extinguish truth. In common with other futurist interpreters, Calmet sees Antichrist in very literal and political terms. He will wage a real war and put down real kings. Jerusalem will be the seat of his empire. This is again a commonplace in Catholic literature from the period. In the last stages, the remaining persecuted faithful will cry out and Christ will descend from heaven with the angels to destroy Antichrist and his hordes.

An element of preterism was then reasonably well represented in Catholic sources of the period, though the linguistic medium and provenance of that view was not primarily English. The extent to which these studies influenced English Catholic views of the Antichrist is not easy to assess, as few relevant sources seem to have survived. However, a modified form of the preterist scheme is reflected in no less central an

---

[17] I have consulted the edition held at Ushaw College, Durham: Augustin Calmet, *Commentaire Litteral Sur Tous Les Livres de L'Ancien et Nouveau Testament* (8 vols., 1724–6).

[18] He wrote:

réünira dans sa personne tous les caractères de malice, que l'on n'a vû que séparément dans ces différents personnages, qui par leur impiété ont mérité le nom de figures ou de précurseurs de l'Antechrist.

Dictionnaire Historique, Critique, Chronologique, Geographique et Littéral de la Bible, rev. edn (4 vols., 1730), s.v. 'Antechrist' (*Dictionnaire*, vol. I, pp. 166–71), p. 166.

English Catholic text than the Doway Bible.[19] The notes appended to this important text for our understanding of English Catholicism were primarily the work of Richard Challoner (1691–1781).[20] In them he reflects more of the futurist than the preterist scheme, but on a few points his sympathy with preterism comes across. For example, when commenting upon the beasts of Revelation 13, he observes that while these beasts do point forward to agencies yet to come (futurist), they also have reference to those which have already had their day (preterist); they are both Antichrist future and Antichrist past.

We may note here also that when Charles Walmesley came to write his own interpretation of Revelation in the form of his *General History of the Christian Church*, he felt it necessary to deal in particular with what he considered to be the erroneous views put forward in the preterist interpretations of Bossuet and Calmet. This suggests that the influence of the earlier continental preterism both was felt in Walmesley's England and, in his view, was something which must be countered. It is worth noting in passing that there is some evidence also of the influence of preterism on Protestant sources.[21] Preterism was adopted by Hugo Grotius (1583–1645), the Dutch statesman, historian and theologian.[22] By far the best example of this approach in England is that of Henry Hammond (1605–60).[23]

[19] *The Holy Bible Translated from the Latin Vulgat: Diligently Compared with the Hebrew, Greek, and Other Editions in Diverse Languages.* The history of the Doway (Douay/Douai) Bible is complex. Editions appeared in 1582 (NT), 1600 (NT), 1609–10 (OT), 1621 (NT), 1633 (NT), 1635 (OT), 1738 (NT), 1788 (NT), 1809 (OT and NT), 1816–18 (OT and NT), 1834 (NT). All included notes, which in the later editions are quite extensive. The Doway is sometimes known as the Doway-Rheims (the English College at Douay relocated to Rheims in the period 1578–1593, and it was there that the first edition of the NT was published). In addition to the Doway there are three other Catholic bibles relevant to the present study. The first of these is that of Cornelius Nary, who produced a modernised NT in 1718. This text was based, it seems, upon the Doway, though some have held that it was 'independent' of that text (see William E. Addis, Thomas Arnold and T. B. Scannell (eds.), *A Catholic Dictionary*, 9th edn (London: Kegan Paul, Trench, Trubner & Co., 1917), p. 287). The second is that of Robert Witham (see further below), who in 1730 published a revision of the Doway NT. The third is that of Richard Challoner, who published a NT in 1749 and a complete Bible in 1750. Challoner's text was itself revised by McMahon in 1783 (NT) and 1791 (OT and NT). These texts are discussed further below. For a more complete account of these developments see Reginald Fuller, Leonard Johnston and Conleth Kearns (eds.) *A New Catholic Commentary on Holy Scripture* (London: Thomas Nelson & Sons, 1969), pp. 48–9.

[20] Challoner was born in Lewes, and converted to Catholicism from Presbyterianism in his youth. He was educated at the seminary in Douai, and spent twenty-five years there. He became coadjutor Bishop of London in 1741, and full bishop in 1758, spending in all forty years in pastoral and apologetic work. See further *The New Catholic Encyclopedia* (14 vols., Washington DC: McGraw-Hill, 1967), vol. III, pp. 437–8.

[21] Froom, *Prophetic Faith*, vol. II, pp. 509–10.   [22] See ibid., vol. II, pp. 521–4.

[23] Henry Hammond, *A Paraphrase and Annotations upon all the Books of the New Testament*, 4th edn (1675). Hammond, who has been called 'the father of English Biblical Criticism', was an eminent Anglican divine, and was one of the royal chaplains before the English Civil War. See further Froom, *Prophetic Faith*, vol. II, pp. 524–5.

At the other end of the prophetic biblical interpretative spectrum to the preterists were the futurists. According to this group the fulfilment of the bulk of the prophecies of Revelation, and with it much of the other biblical prophetic material, such as 2 Thess. 2 and Daniel 7–12, is to be located in the future. Not all of the prophecies of Revelation were, however, related to the end time. Some relatively small part had found their fulfilment already in the past. As would be expected, this division in the futurist literature was not made at random. Rather, the argument was that one should distinguish between those things which 'are' from the perspective of John and those things which 'are to be'. Such a division is based upon Rev. 1.19, which reads, 'Write these things which thou hast seen, and the things which are, and the things which shall be hereafter.' This was read in the context of Rev. 4.1, which then goes on 'After this I looked, and, behold, a door was opened in heaven: and the first voice which I heard was as it were of a trumpet talking with me; which said, Come up hither, and I will shew thee things which must be hereafter.' In accordance with this view the futurists argued that some parts of Revelation, in particular chapters 1–3 (the things which 'are'), had already been fulfilled, and indeed were largely a description of John's own times. Chapters 4–22, however (the things which 'must be hereafter'), await their fulfilment in the last stages of the world's current history. Thus the present age is largely devoid of prophetic fulfilment. This last point is an important one. It must be remembered that it was in the context of the onslaught upon the Pope and the Roman Catholic Church in general that the preterist and futurist counter readings were launched. Emptying the present of prophetic fulfilment had the altogether happy consequence, for the Roman Catholic commentators here surveyed, of disarming the Protestant claims regarding the nature and identity of Antichrist.

The rise of futurism is generally associated with the name of Francisco Ribera (1537–91),[24] a Spanish Jesuit scholar who published a lengthy commentary on the Apocalypse in c. 1590.[25] It was his view that only the first few chapters of the Apocalypse relate to the past. The remainder are to be fulfilled in the literal three-and-a-half years of

---

[24] Ribera was born at Villacastin, in Spain. He was educated and taught at the University of Salamanca, where he was recognised as a major scriptural scholar, and an expert in Latin, Greek and Hebrew. He was the confessor and biographer of St Teresa of Avila. See further Froom, *Prophetic Faith*, vol. II, pp. 489–93.

[25] Francisci Riberae, *In Sacram B. Ioannis Apostoli & Evangelistae Apocalypsin Commentarij* (1623). The date of the first printing of this work is unclear, but Froom notes an edition from 1593 (Froom, *Prophetic Faith*, vol. II, p. 836). A copy carrying this date is located in the Ushaw College Library, Durham.

Antichrist's reign, immediately preceding the return of Christ. Antichrist, suggested Ribera, and in this he was followed by many other Catholic commentators, was to be an individual figure who would reign in Jerusalem during his brief career immediately prior to the inauguration of the perfect age.[26] This 'perfect age' is not, according to Ribera, the millennium of Revelation 20; it is, however, symbolically portrayed in Revelation 21 as the city descending from God. On the millennium of Rev. 20.1–7 itself (the only place in Bible where the expression χίλια ἔτη occurs with the meaning of '[the] millennium'), Ribera agreed with Augustine in arguing that the period was not to be taken as a literal thousand years. Rather, he stated, it is the period between Christ's death and the coming of Antichrist. However, the millennial rule is enjoyed in heaven, not, as Augustine had suggested, on earth. It is the blessed state into which the souls of the faithful departed enter.

A similar futurist scheme was put forward by the Italian archbishop and cardinal (and later saint) Robert Bellarmine (1542–1621).[27] Like Ribera, Bellarmine argued that Antichrist was to be an individual Jew who would reign in Jerusalem for three-and-a-half years (this was the loosing of Satan spoken of in Rev. 20.7). This would precede his destruction and the dawn of the perfect age.[28]

The extent of the direct influence of such works as those by Ribera and Bellarmine upon English Catholic expositors is not easy to gauge. However, what is relatively clear is that futurism did gain a foothold in the English Roman Catholic scholarly community. A good illustration of this may be seen in the seventeenth century work of the English Jesuit James Mumford (or Montford; 1606–66).[29] He put forward the view, in

---

[26] A summary of Ribera's work is found in Elliott, *Horae Apocalypticae*, vol. IV, pp. 466–8.

[27] Bellarmine was born in Tuscany, the nephew of Pope Marcellus II. He entered the Society of Jesus at eighteen, and was perhaps the most able of all the Jesuit apologists of the Counter-Reformation. He became Archbishop of Capua, but resigned the position when appointed chief theological adviser to the Holy See. A summary of his life and literary career is to be found in Delaney and Tobin, *Catholic Biography*, pp. 118–19. His views on Revelation are discussed briefly in Wainwright, *Mysterious Apocalypse*, p. 62, and more fully in Froom, *Prophetic Faith*, vol. II, pp. 495–502.

[28] Note also Froom's comments on the Catholic futurists Blasius Viegas (1554–99), Cornelius Lapide (1567–1637) and Thomas Malvenda (1566–1628) in *Prophetic Faith*, vol. II, pp. 502–5. Wainwright, who seems dependent upon Froom at this point, gives the primary references (*Mysterious Apocalypse*, p. 238 n. 57).

[29] Mumford was born in Norfolk, and entered the Society of Jesus at Watten in 1626. Following his appointment as Rector of Liège he returned in 1652 to England, where he engaged in missionary endeavour. In 1657–8 he was arrested and imprisoned in Norwich. He was later released. In addition to his work *The Catholike Scripturist*, to which reference is made here, he wrote *A Remembrance for the Living to Pray for the Dead. Made by a Father of the Society of Jesus* (1660), *A Vindication or Defence of the Dialogues of St Gregory* (n.d.), *De Misericordia Fidelibus Defunctis Exhibenda* and *The Question of Questions, which rightly Resolved, Resolveth all our Questions in Religion* (1658). See further Gillow, *English Catholics*, vol. V, pp. 83–4.

a direct attack upon the Protestant position, that Antichrist was not yet come, nor would he come 'until we be close bordering upon the very last end of the world'.[30] The appendix to this chapter contains Mumford's attempt at countering the chief points of the Protestant paradigm; the reasoning is concise and self-contained, and gives a valuable insight into the thought processes operating on both sides of the argument. Reference should be made to it at this point.

Mumford's concerns in this work are limited to the question of the coming of Antichrist. However, from the relatively brief remarks he makes on this issue, it is plain that he is working within the broader futurist paradigm. In making his case, he runs through several lines of argument standard in Catholic counter-Protestant views of Antichrist, and typical of the futurist scheme overall. For example, he argues that scripture clearly teaches that Antichrist is an individual, not a system or a sequence of men (i.e. the Popes), and indeed will be a Jew from the tribe of Dan.[31] As Challoner was later to do, Mumford appealed to 2 Thess. 2.4 in support of this assertion. Similarly scripture (and it is clear that Revelation is in view) indicates that Antichrist will rule only for a short time ($3\frac{1}{2}$ years, 1,260 days, 42 months), but the Popes 'have reigned these many ages'. (Mumford, like the futurists in general, did not align himself with the 'year-day' principle.) This Antichrist will come shortly before the end of the world. Scripture also teaches that Antichrist will have his headquarters in Jerusalem; this is not true of the Pope. This is all very typically futurist and overlaps significantly with the work of Ribera and Bellarmine.

Whether Mumford was fully futurist in his general views on the correct interpretation of Revelation cannot be discerned from this one source. He is concerned only with the question of the identity of Antichrist, not with a full exposition of Revelation. However, from what he says it does appear that he is working with a basically futurist conception in mind. This is interesting given the date (1662), since it suggests that the influence of more extensive continental futurist expositions of the book of Revelation had gained headway in England well before the work of Challoner and Walmesley. Indeed, from the few other sources that have been traced to date, it seems that futurism was very much alive in seventeenth-century English Catholic readings of Revelation.

---

[30] Mumford, *The Catholike Scripturist, or, the Plea of the Roman Catholikes Shewing the Scriptures to Hold forth the Roman Faith in above Forty of the Chief Controversies now under Debate*, 2nd edn (1662), pp. 74–9.

[31] This understanding of the origin of Antichrist, based on various biblical and other texts, had been widely held in mediaeval times and later. See further McGinn, *Antichrist*, p. 296 n. 12, and Richard Kenneth Emmerson, *Antichrist in the Middle Ages: A Study of Medieval Apocalypticism, Art, and Literature* (Seattle: University of Washington Press, 1984), pp. 79–80.

The influence of futurism in English Catholic sources is clearly seen also in the Doway Bible. The notes accompanying this Bible, which were largely the work of Challoner, in places show evidence of preterist interpretation, but in general strongly suggest that Challoner was working within the futurist paradigm. For example, commenting upon the first beast of Revelation 13 (the beast from the sea), the note says

This first beast with seven heads, and ten horns, is probably the whole company of infidels, enemies and persecutors of the people of God, from the beginning to the end of the world. The seven heads are seven kings, that is, seven principal kingdoms or empires, which have exercised, or shall exercise tyrannical power over the people of God; of these, five were then fallen, viz. the Egyptian, Assyrian, Chaldean, Persian, and Grecian monarchies: one was present, viz. the empire of Rome; and the seventh and chiefest was to come, viz. the great Antichrist and his empire.[32]

When read in the context of other remarks, such as those made on Dan. 7.8, 7.25, 9.27 and 2 Thess. 2.3,[33] this statement clearly indicates that it was the editor's view that Antichrist, while perhaps prefigured in other epitomes of evil (as Calmet also had suggested), is himself yet to come. Indeed, his coming will be very close to the end of all things. The persecution inflicted by him will last three-and-a-half literal years, culminating in his own destruction. It is worth noting also that in the Doway Challoner shows an overt interest in directly countering the Protestant paradigm. Commenting upon Rev. 11.3 (the vision of the locusts), he notes:

These may be devils in Antichrist's time, having the appearance of locusts, but large and monstrous as here described. Or they may be real locusts, but of an extraordinary size and monstrous shape, such as were never before seen on earth, sent to torment those, *who have not the sign (or seal) of God in their foreheads.* Some commentators by these *locusts* understand heretics... Others have explained these *locusts,* and other animals, mentioned in different places throughout this sacred and mystical book, in a most absurd, fanciful and ridiculous manner: they make *Abaddon* the pope, and the *Locusts* to be friars mendicant, &c. Here it is thought proper, not to enter into controversy upon that subject, as the inventors of these fancies have been already answered, and fully refuted by many controvertists: besides, those who might be imposed on by such chimerical writers, are in those days much better informed.[34]

The 1809 edition of the Doway has more extensive notes (added after Challoner's own death in 1781), and makes the same points even more clearly. For example, the very full notes offered by the editors on 2

[32] *Doway Bible,* p. 264. [33] Ibid., respectively pp. 879, 880, 882, 213. [34] Ibid., p. 261.

Thess. 2 have grown from just a few lines in the earlier edition, although the same basic point is made: Antichrist is yet to come and will appear only 'near the world's end'. The Protestant leaders and other heretics may have been precursors of this man of sin, but they were not the great Antichrist himself.[35]

In the Doway, then, Challoner's (and the later editors') basic futurism is seen clearly enough. It appears sporadically also elsewhere. Indeed, as early as 1735 Challoner had written:

> Protestants will have it, that the Pope or Bishop of *Rome* is *Antichrist*. The contrary is evident from their bible 2 Thess. ii.4 where it is said of Antichrist the Man of Sin, that he *opposeth and exalteth himself above all that is called God, or that is worshipped; so that he as God sitteth in the temple of God, shewing himself that he is God.* No Pope ever did this, *Item*, 1 John ii.22. where it is said that Antichrist *denieth that Jesus is the Christ:* which the Pope confesseth and maintaineth; and therefore cannot be *Antichrist.*[36]

In opposition to the view that the Pope was Antichrist, Challoner was already putting forward here, as he was later to do in the Doway notes, the view that Antichrist was yet to come. Antichrist was a literal figure who would appear shortly before the end of the world to wreak havoc upon the faithful. The coming of the 'man of sin' (2 Thess. 2) and the 'little horn' (Dan. 7.8; 8.9) was hence yet awaited. Challoner's earlier interpretation of Revelation, and with it the other portions of the Christian prophetic scriptures, thus runs along similar futurist lines to that of the continental Catholic expositors noted above.

Enough has now been said to indicate that the futurist approach to the book of Revelation was a significant influence in English Catholic sources from the period c. 1600–1800. That influence is seen in the Doway, in Mumford and, perhaps most importantly, in the work of the highly significant figure of Richard Challoner, and there were others.[37] Indeed, the evidence suggests that it was primarily on the basis of the futurist

35 *The Holy Bible Translated from the Latin Vulgat: Diligently Compared with the Hebrew, Greek, and Other Editions in Diverse Languages* (2 vols., 1809), p. 317.
36 Richard Challoner, *The Touchstone of the New Religion: or Sixty Assertions of Protestants, Tried by their own Rule of Scripture alone, and Condemned by Clear and Express Texts of their own Bible*, 7th edn (1795), p. 20. *The Touchstone* was first published in 1735, with further editions appearing in 1735, 1741, 1748 and 1788.
37 In this context note in particular 'Whether the Pope be Antichrist?', in Anon, *A Plain and Rational Account of the Catholick Faith; with a Preface and Appendix in Vindication of Catholick Morals, from Old Calumnies Revived and Collected in a Scurrilous Libel, Entitled,* A Protestant's Resolution, &c., 3rd edn (1721), pp. 16–20; and 'Antichrist, the head of al Heritikes, is to come: nere the end of this World', in T. W., *An Anker of Christian Doctrine. Wherein the most Principal Points of Catholike Religion, are Proved by the Only Written Word of God* (1702), pp. 474–95.

paradigm that Catholic writers from the period approached the book of Revelation. In this way they sought to counter the almost unanimous voice of Protestant interpreters regarding the nature and identity of Antichrist. (Again, it is worth noting here in passing that one does meet the occasional Protestant in the literature. The futurist case is argued, for example, by the Baptist writer Joseph Tyso, whose work was considered from a different perspective in chapter 2,[38] and the coming of a future Antichrist is predicted by Robert Shelford[39] and by Thomas Stackhouse, vicar of Beenham in Berkshire.[40] Froom notes some other cases.[41])

Counter historicism, the third method of interpretation evident in Roman Catholic treatments of the Apocalypse, appears to have had relatively few adherents. This reluctance on the part of the Catholic commentators to propose a counter-historicist reading of the text is perhaps less than surprising, since it was a method that was very difficult for them to maintain. The difficulty arose from the fact that the author of Revelation appears to have written about Roman imperial power and it was a relatively easy step for Protestants to take to make this same text relate now to Roman Catholicism. Catholic commentators wishing to divorce the text altogether from its original 'Roman' context had much more of an uphill struggle. Nevertheless, some attempted it. The result-ant interpretation was perhaps the most rewarding in terms of religious propaganda, for it not only disarmed the Protestants in their unabated attack upon Rome, but actually turned the tables on them altogether. Where the futurists and the preterists were satisfied to argue that certain parts of Revelation, for example the swarming locusts of Revelation 9, were not symbols of Roman Catholics, but rather of some horrific creatures yet to come, counter historicists could argue the stronger case 'it's not us, it's you'. Without doubt the best example of this approach is that provided by Charles Walmesley.

Walmesley's *General History of the Christian Church*, written under the pseudonym of Signor Pastorini,[42] is a detailed exposition of Revelation,

---

[38] Joseph Tyso, *Elucidation of the Prophecies* (1838).

[39] 'A Treatise Shewing the Antichrist not to be yet Come', in Robert Shelford's *Five Pious and Learned Discourses* (1635), pp. 229–326.

[40] Thomas Stackhouse, *A New History of the Holy Bible, from the Beginning of the World to the Establishment of Christianity*, 2nd edn (2 vols., 1742–4), vol. II, pp. 1621–3.

[41] Froom, *Prophetic Faith*, vol. III, pp. 730–3.

[42] Signor Pastorini [Charles Walmesley], *The General History of the Christian Church, from her Birth to her Final Triumph and State in Heaven, Chiefly Deduced from the Apocalypse of St. John the Apostle* (1771). The *History* went through numerous editions. *The Catholic Encyclopedia* (16 vols., Washington, DC.: McGraw-Hill, 1913–14), vol. XV, p. 540) suggests ten, which, if it errs, is on the side of caution. Copies of editions from 1771, 1782, 1790, 1794, 1797, 1798 and 1800 are listed in Blom et al., *English*

probably the most detailed to come from the pen of an English Catholic during the course of the eighteenth century. In it he presents a basically counter-historicist interpretation. In the adoption of this methodology Walmesley differed not only from his Protestant contemporaries, but also from the majority of those in his own Catholic tradition. However, he is fully aware of being out of tune with the Catholic expositors who had gone before him. At the beginning of the book he expresses the hope that when the reader has completed an examination of his work, he will join with Walmesley himself

in thinking, that the celebrated Commentators, Bossuet and Calmet, have too much contracted this admirable Prophecy by confining it's contents to so short a period as the four first centuries of the Christian aera, and applying the whole, except the two last chapters, to the persecutions the church suffered from the pagan Roman Emperors, and to the destruction of the Roman Empire.[43]

The preterist view is then, for Walmesley, improperly employed in the understanding of Revelation. It is apparent that he also rejected a fully futurist exposition, though, as has been noted, on the question of the coming of Antichrist he was in accord with the basic futurism of many of his Catholic contemporaries and predecessors. In place of these interpretations he sets forth his counter-historicist reading.

Walmesley's system is complex, and he presents intricate arguments in support of it. It is built upon the fundamental assumption that the book of Revelation is to be seen as an outline of seven periods in the history of the Christian Church. The seven periods are (roughly – Walmesley does not commit himself to very specific dates) 33–320; 320–406; 406–620; 620–1520; 1520–1820; 1820–the day of judgement; and finally the period of 'eternity'. The history of the Church during these periods is, according to Walmesley, the subject of the book of Revelation; in making this basic claim he is of course sharing common ground with the majority of Protestants. It is with this basic programme in mind that he approaches the text.

In common with several Protestant commentators, examples of whom have been given at the beginning of this chapter, Walmesley does

Catholic Books, 1701–1800. Gillow, *English Catholics*, vol. v, p. 570 also lists editions and reprints dated 1770, 1806, 1812, 1815, 1816, 1820 and 1821 and refers to 'very frequent repr. in America'. According to Gillow, the *History* was translated into French in 1777 and 1790; Latin (n.d.); German in 1785 and Italian in 1798. Such a publication record suggests considerable interest in the subject matter. For this chapter the second English edition (1782) located at the Gradwell Library, Upholland, has been used. A copy of the first edition is located at Ushaw College, and of the third at the Franciscan Library, Kilkenny.

[43] Walmesley, *History*, p. iv.

not read the book of Revelation as a continuous narrative beginning in either 1.1 or 4.1 and lasting to the end of the book. Rather he views the book as a series of cycles, each dealing with the entire course of the history of the Church, but not all in the same detail or from the same perspective. Thus according to Walmesley the history of the Church from Pentecost to eternity is outlined in the sequence of the seven seals. The same history is outlined again in the sequence of the seven trumpets and the seven vials. The rest of the book adds further detail to this outline. The history of the Church in the first period (33–320) is, according to this interpretation, described under the first seal, the first trumpet and the first vial. Thus Walmesley wrote: 'The first Seal, Trumpet, and Vial, have exhibited a general description of the first preaching of the Christian Religion, the persecutions that attended it, and the Divine vengeance on the Authors of those persecutions.'[44] In several other places too the same period is described (Revelation 12, 19, 20). The second period (c. 320–406) is described under the second seal, the second trumpet and the second vial, as well as in several other places. This argument is extended to cover all seven seals, trumpets and vials. As the title of the book indicates, Walmesley takes the view that the periods stretch from the beginning of the Christian Church to the second coming of Christ and the onset of the perfect age.

For Walmesley much of what is described in Revelation has already occurred. Here he is on common ground with the Protestants, though naturally the details of his scheme are quite different. He is not in agreement on the question of the identity of Antichrist, who is yet to come. The fact that the events are future means that they cannot be known perfectly. Walmesley writes:

Hitherto the account we find in History of the different ages, has contributed to explain the Prophecies relating to them: but with respect to the age we are now entering upon, as it yet remains sealed up in the womb of futurity, we can have no light but what must be drawn from the Prophecies themselves.[45]

Despite this statement, however, on the question of the identity of Antichrist, his career and end, Walmesley is quite specific. Antichrist will not come from the tribe of Dan and indeed will not even, contrary to common expectation, be Jewish. Rather, states Walmesley, Antichrist will be born of Mahometan parents, and will be a great prince of the Mahometan Empire. This Antichrist is described in Revelation 13 (the second beast) and also in Daniel 7. His name, written in Greek, is

44 Ibid., p. 95.   45 Ibid., p. 98.

μαομετις, which has the numerical value 666 (μ = 40; α = 1; ο = 70; μ = 40; ε = 5; τ = 300; ι = 10; ς = 200).

There follows in Walmesley's work an extended and extremely detailed discussion of the sixth period (that of Antichrist), which need not be entered into here. The period he describes is characterised by great bloodshed and martyrdom. Antichrist is assisted by the false prophet, sets up a kingdom and raises an army. Literal battles are fought and literal blood spilt. The Jews are converted in Jerusalem, to which they have flocked, by one of the two witnesses of Revelation 11. These two witnesses are Enoch and Elijah; Enoch will convert the Gentiles, Elijah the Jews. The preaching lasts 1,260 days (cf. Rev. 11.3; 12.6). The eschatological battle finally follows between the forces of evil (which includes devils in human form) and those of good. Christ returns and slays Antichrist and his satanic hordes. The final judgement follows, and Christ establishes a kingdom which will last for ever.

Many of the events which Walmesley crowds into this period are found in passages other than Revelation. There is little to be gained from listing all the biblical material upon which he draws, or providing a fuller analysis. It is, however, worth noting just how complex the system is, and the extent to which he was evidently familiar with, and concerned to explain the meaning of, relatively obscure parts of the Old Testament text. In presenting this scheme, he has disarmed the Protestant claim that the Roman Catholic Church is Antichrist, a view to which he often refers. His views on the coming of Antichrist are fairly standard among Catholic commentators from the period (both futurist and preterist), though many of the mass of details appear to be new with him.

Finally, attention must now be directed to another Catholic commentator who does not fit neatly into the scheme so far adopted. Robert Witham[46] in 1733 issued his two-volume *Annotations on the New Testament*.[47] This is a substantial work which deals systematically with the biblical texts, including those which held pride of place in the Protestant

---

[46] Robert Witham appears twice in Gillow, *English Catholics* (vol. II, p. 239, vol. V, p. 370) and on both occasions is mentioned in the context of a dispute with Dr Charles Fell upon the latter's publication of *Lives of the Saints* (4 vols., 1729). Witham's criticisms of Fell were published in London in 1732. In the second entry the reader is referred to the entry on Witham. However, no such entry exists.

[47] R[obert] W[itham], *Annotations on the New Testament of Jesus Christ in Which I. The Literal Sense is Explained according to Expositions of the Ancient Fathers II. The False Interpretations, both of the Ancient and Modern Writers, which are Contrary to the Received Doctrine of the Catholick-Church, are briefly Examined and Disproved III. With an Account of the Chief Differences betwixt the Text of the Ancient Latin-Version, and the Greek in the Printed Editions, and MSS* (2 vols., 1733).

anti-Catholic arsenal. Witham's work is especially interesting in the present context since he integrates a definite element of idealism into his basically futurist interpretation of the Apocalypse. This is a method that is noticeable mainly by its absence in both Protestant and Roman Catholic works from the period.

In Witham's work we find a robust defence of Catholicism in the face of Protestant claims regarding the nature and person of Antichrist. That defence comes mainly in the form of attack, in the presentation of a counter reading of the disputed texts that, according to Witham, makes better sense of the text. On 2 Thess. 2, for example, he takes a determined stand. The 'man of sin' there described is not, as the Protestants have claimed, the Pope, but rather one individual man who is to come shortly before the end of the world. Witham appeals to the standard futurist logic regarding the 'man of sin'. Thus by the words of 2 Thess. 2.3–4, he states,

is described to us the great Antichrist, about the End of the World, according to the unexceptionable Authority, and Consent of the ancient Fathers. 'Tis as ridiculous as malicious, to pretend with divers late Reformers that the Pope, and all the Popes since the Destruction of the Roman Empire, are the *great Antichrist, the Man of Sin*, &c. Grotius, Dr. Hammond, and divers learn'd Protestants have confuted and ridicul'd this groundless Fable, (of which more on the Apocalypse.) It may suffice to observe here, that Antichrist, the *Man of Sin*, the *Son of Perdition*, the *wicked one*, according to all the Ancients, is to be one particular Man, not so many different Men. 2dly, That he is to come a little while before the Day of Judgement. 3dly, That he will make himself adored, and pretend to be God, what Pope did so? 4thly, That he'll pretend to be Christ, &c.[48]

This view is expanded in Witham's comments upon the book of Revelation, where he has a great deal to say. He begins by outlining the three possible ways in which the book may be read. Though the labels are not his, the methods to which he is referring are, without doubt, preterism (he refers the reader to Alcazar); futurism; and the 'mystical way' of interpretation, which seeks to unpack the metaphors and allegories of the book, that is, idealism.[49] The historicist reading is represented only disparagingly, with fairly frequent references to what is for Witham the 'fact' that it is so fanciful and absurd that it is not worth taking the trouble to refute it.[50]

Witham then launches into his own study of the text: a study which is self-consistent only to the extent that it is a thorough-going rejection of

---

[48] Witham, *Annotations*, vol. ii, p. 258.   [49] Ibid., vol. ii, p. 450.   [50] Ibid., vol. ii, p. 481.

historicism. In fact his own sympathies are not easily disentangled from the views of others that he presents, though a reading of his comments on chapters 4–16 suggests that he was inclined to the preterist interpretation, at least for this section. Despite this apparent sympathy with preterism, however, he often gives the futurist reading an airing and the reader is generally left to decide which one to take. Either of course serves equally well for Witham's main purpose, which is to refute the Protestant claim regarding Antichrist. Thus, for example, when discussing the possible interpretation of Revelation 9 (the locusts from the bottomless pit), he notes how according to some this represents the confusion of all things that is to take place during Antichrist's time (the futurist reading). Alternatively, he states, it may refer to the incursions of the Goths and 'those barbarous People, that made an Irruption into the Roman Empire, in the time of Decius, about an. 250' (the preterist reading). Another alternative, again along preterist lines, is that the locusts represent heretics, particularly 'those Hereticks, that spring from the Jews, and with them denied the Divinity of our Saviour Christ, as Theodotus, Praxeas, Noetus, Paul of Samosata, Sabellius, Arius, &c.'. These, according to Witham, are all possible interpretations. However, the views of writers such as 'Mr Willet, who, Brightman-like, makes *Abbadon* the Pope, and Locusts to be Friars mendicant', are so obviously the result of invention and fancy as to make their refutation nothing more than a waste of time. Occasionally, however, Witham does treat the reader to 'a taste of such licentious Expositions of the divine Oracles' as those put forward by Brightman.[51]

The futurist and preterist readings are presented side by side for much of the commentary on the first sixteen chapters of Revelation, though, as has been noted, it appears that Witham himself has more sympathies for the preterist approach. When one arrives at chapter 17, however, Witham suddenly appears to change course. He moves off in an interesting direction, and one which seems, from the point of view of the history of prophetical eisgesis, somewhat anachronistic. He writes:

I must repeat what I have already taken notice of, both in the Preface to the Apocalypse, and sometimes in the Annotations, that there are three ways of expounding all the Visions of this Revelation, from the end of the 3d Chapter to the end of the 10th Verse chap. 20. which all of them seem grounded on the Opinions of the ancient Fathers. According to the first all these Visions are only to be fulfill'd in Antichrist's time, a little before the End of the World. According to the 2d, the Visions may be apply'd to particular Events, which happen'd

[51] Ibid., vol. II, p. 463.

in the first 3 or 4 Ages under the persecuting Heathens, till by Constantine, and the succeeding Christian Emperors, Idolatry by degrees was extirpated, and the Faith of Christ triumph'd over all it's Enemies, whether Jews or Pagans. According to the 3d, by the great City of Babylon, is mystically and metaphorically signified all wicked great Cities in the World, all the multitude of the wicked dispers'd in all nations, their short and vain Happiness; their Persecutions and Oppressions of the good and faithful Servants of God, who live piously in this World, and who are call'd to be Citizens of the Coelestial Jerusalem in the Kingdom of God, where he reigneth for ever with his Angels and Saints, and where they all reign with him, happy in his Sight and Enjoyment. I am more and more inclined to this 3d Exposition, by reading this 17th Chapter, with the Contents of the 18th, 19th and 20th Chapter till the 11th Verse, and by reading what S. Hierom says in general Terms in his Ep. to Marcella, tom. 4. part. 1. pag. 166. Nov. Edit.[52]

The reader of Witham's exposition may well be surprised by this sudden change of tack, for the idealist reading of Revelation has not been much in evidence to this point. An idealist interpretation of Rev. 17.1–20.11 follows, though Witham continues with his earlier policy and outlines also the preterist and futurist positions.

Witham suggests a three-part division of Revelation. Chapters 1–3 contain prophecies to the seven churches, though what is said to them is important to others 'in the like Dispositions'.[53] The things that are here spoken of are to come to pass 'shortly', that is, before the end of the first century. The second part of Revelation is found in chapters 4–20. Here, according to Witham, we find outlined the history of Christ's Church as it triumphs over 'all its Enemies, the Devil, Jews, Heathens, Hereticks'.[54] It covers the period from Christ to the establishment of the Church under Constantine in 325. Witham takes the rider on the white horse linked with the opening of the first seal (chapter 6) to be Christ, armed with the piercing bow of gospel truth. The image of the rider and the horse is not, however, chronologically limited to the ministry of Jesus. Rather it represents Christ the conqueror, who conquers not only through his ministry, but also through the ministries of his 'Apostles, Preachers, Martyrs and other Saints'.[55] The preterist reading of this section appears to be Witham's favoured one, though he also makes reference throughout to those who would see this material as relating only to events surrounding the end of the world and the coming of Antichrist, and there is the significant disruption of the idealist twist for 17.1–20.11.

[52] Ibid., vol. ii, pp. 510–11.   [53] Ibid., vol. ii, p. 452.   [54] Ibid., vol. ii, p. 466.
[55] Ibid., vol. ii, p. 472.

The third part of Revelation is found in the remainder of the book. This section, states Witham, deals with the events that are to take place shortly before the end of the world; here, of course, preterists and futurists generally agree. This is the period of Antichrist. Commenting on chapter 21, Witham writes:

From the seventh[56] Verse of the foregoing Chapter, begins, as it were, the third Part of the Apocalypse, containing the coming of Antichrist, the great Day of Judgement, the Punishment of the wicked, and the eternal Happiness of God's elect in Heaven, or in the coelestial Jerusalem, which S. John describes in this Chapter, as it were like a large City beautified, and enrich'd with Gold, and all manner of precious Stones, &c.[57]

Witham's comments on 20.7–15 come largely in the form of his approving quotation of Augustine, who argued that the first resurrection spoken of in 20.5 is the resurrection of the soul from death. The '1,000 years' is not, as the millenarians have claimed, a literal thousand years during which time the faithful will reign with Christ upon earth, but rather the period of the Church; '1,000 years' means only 'a long time'. Satan is 'bound' during this period by virtue of the fact that his power is severely limited by the proclamation of Christ through the Church. However, Satan's time will come. He will have three-and-a-half years of unrivalled power immediately before the end of the world. This is the period of Antichrist.

In the work of Witham, then, there is to be found a fairly extended treatment of the book of Revelation. He employs three methodologies (futurism, preterism and idealism) to counter the Protestant paradigm and speaks approvingly of all three. Consequently, it must be said, his work is not self-consistent. This is perhaps not really the point, however, for his main interest clearly is not so much to launch a reading of Revelation that is right, but rather to prove that the reading adopted by the Protestants is wrong. Though he would presumably not have agreed with the remark, his policy seems to have been that any stick is good enough to beat a dog with.

It has now been shown that throughout the seventeenth and eighteenth centuries the book of Revelation came under careful scrutiny by a number of Catholic scholars. The preterist scheme of interpretation, which had been launched by Alcazar in the sixteenth century, continued to have an influence on later writers such as Bossuet and even, in

---

[56] There is a slight contradiction here since in other places Witham states that this third part of the book of Revelation does not begin until verse 12.

[57] Witham, *Annotations*, vol. II, p. 538.

a modified form, the notes accompanying the various editions of the Doway English Bible. Futurism, which had an able exponent in the person of Ribera, continued to influence later Catholic biblical scholars, both on the continent and in England. Indeed, it was futurism which provided the most significant counter-Protestant reading of Revelation (and with it Daniel and other passages such as 2 Thess. 2) during this period. However, the attempt by Walmesley to launch a counter-historicist reading of Revelation should not be underestimated. The energy he invested in this project and the detail with which it is worked out are obvious.

The overriding concern of Catholic commentators on Revelation during this period was to disarm the standard Protestant view that the Pope and/or the Roman Catholic Church was the Antichrist. This was done almost, though not quite, exclusively by relating those passages in Revelation, Daniel and 2 Thess. 2 to an expected individual who would come in the future – not too distant a future, but the future – to play his satanic role in the divine drama. Even Walmesley took this view, though, as has been noted, his interpretation bears significant overall similarity to the historicism of the Protestants.

Scrutinising this interpretative process is more than just an interesting exercise in hermeneutical history. The use of the book of Revelation, and in particular the Antichrist texts, to which attention has been drawn, indicates a hermeneutical fluidity which modern interpreters would perhaps do well to note. The anti-Catholic Gordon riots[58] of the latter part of the eighteenth century are but one example of the level of animosity that existed between the Protestant majority and the Catholic minority in England during this period. Revelation served its Protestant masters well in providing fuel for this religious-polemical fire. The responses to this demonising hermeneutical programme provided by English Catholic apologists such as Mumford, Challoner, Walmesley, the editors of the Doway Bible and others, though they look strange in a modern context, are entirely understandable in their own.

---

[58] These began in London in June 1780 as a protest and petition to Parliament against the 1778 Catholic Relief Act, which provided a small measure of relief against some of the restraints from which Catholics suffered. They turned into a week of riots, looting and arson in which nearly 300 people died. See Cross and Livingstone, *Dictionary of the Christian Church*, p. 691, or for a fuller account *New Catholic Encyclopedia*, vol. VI, p. 631.

APPENDIX[59]

1. Because there is never a pulpit in England in which the Pope hath not been preached, by all our Ministers to be not only Anti-Christ, but also *the Anti-Christ*, who is so much spoken of and detested in Scriptures, I thought fitt to make my deare country men see with theyr own eyes, how unconscionably these theyr Ministers so universally deale with them in this point, in which they can not but see (if indeed they reade and will understand) how flatly, and point blank this doctrine is against most manifest Scripture.

2. *First.* The Scripture teacheth clearly that Anti-Christ is one particulare determinate man, and not any ranke of severall distinct men successively living one after the other as the Popes do. Hence 2 Thess. 2.3. Anti-Christ is called *That man of sin the sonne of perdition. The adversary.* And Apoc. 13.14. An image shall be made of this particular person, where as no such image can represent those hundreds of Popes who have sitt in S. Peters chaire. Again there it followeth that this particular man shall have a speciall name, and such a peculiar number shall express this name: *For it is the number of a man.* A Man, I say and not many men succeeding one an other as Popes are. Whence it followeth. *The number of him is six hundred sixty six.* Of that *Him,* whom Christ allso insinuated to be one particular *man* when he sayed Io. 5.43. *If an other shall come in his Name him you will receave.* Whereas no one of the Popes was yet receaved by the Iewes. Wherefore of the Pope it is false to say the Iewes *have received him.* And this is the second reason why the Pope according to Scripture is not Antichrist.

3. *Thirdly,* this one particular man shall not come untill we be close bordering upon the very last end of the world. Mark 13.24. *But in those days after the tribulation* (of Anti-Christ) *the Sunne shall be darkened.* Popes have never beene ever since S. Peters days, and that which you call Popery hath beene (as you confess) above these thousand years and yet the Sunne shines upon the world as clearely as ever.

4. *Fourthly,* this one speciall man shall reigne but for a short time, where as these Popes (upholders of confessed Popery) have reigned these many ages. Anti-Christ shall reigne but three yeares and a half, *a time, and times, and half a time.* Dan. 7.25. And Apoc. 12.14. Hence Dan. 12.11. this time is further expounded to be *a thousand two hundred and nynety days.* And the Church a litle after this persecution began, shall fly into the wilderness *for a thousand two hundred and sixty days.* And for this time of 1260. *days the two witnesses shall prophecy.* Apoc. 11.3. For the persecution of Anti-Christ shall last but *two and fourty months* as it there expressly sayd. And Apoc. 13.5. *Power was given (to the beast) to continue two and fourty months.* The time therefore of Anti-Christs reigne shall be short, *For the elect the days shall be shortned* Matth. 24.22. So Apoc. 20.3. it is sayed that the divel shall be lett loose for the short time of Anti-Christs reigne. *After these things he must be loosened a little time.* That is after Christ hath bound up the divel, during the

---

59 From Mumford, *The Catholike Scripturist,* pp. 74–9; spelling, punctuation and italic are reproduced without alteration.

long time of the new Testament (described there by the complete and perfect number of a thousand yeares) he shall be lett loose for the short time of the reigne of Anti-Christ.

5. *Fiftly*, all the Ministers in England, or out of England, can never be able to shew that the Pope did ever kill two such witnesses as Anti-christ is clearly sayd to kill Apoc. 11.6. That is *two witnesses who shall prophesy one thousand two hundred and sixty days cloathed in sackcloath, who shall have power to shutt the heavens that it may not raine in the days of there prophesy; and power of the waters to turne them into bloud. And to strike the earth with all plagues as often as they will.* If your Ministers will prove the Pope to be Antichrist they must not only prove that he did kill two such witnesses, as they are (for the true Anti-christ must do this) but allso they must prove that the Pope did kill two such witnesses in *Ierusalem* leaving theyr bodyes lying in the streets thereof. For this allso the true Anti-christ must do, because it followeth v.7 *The beast shall kill them. And theyre bodyes shall lye in the streets where theyr Lord was crucified*, that is in Ierusalem.

6. *Sixtly*. Hence appeares that the chefe seate of Anti-christ shall be at Ierusalem where he shall most shew his power and glory whence it was allso sayd before that the Iewes should receave him, and the Holy Fathers commonly say he shall be born a Iew, of the Tribe of Dan, which is the cause why that Tribe was not numbered with the rest Apoc. 7. neither could the Iewes receave him if he were not borne a Iew. None of these things agree to the Pope and yet they all agree to Antichrist.

7. *Seaventhly*, the beast which shall sett up the power of Antichrist *shall make fyre come downe from heaven to earth in the sight of men.* Apoc. 13.13 Tell me what setter up of the Popes power did ever doe this?

8. *Eightly* there allso v. 17 it is sayed that he also shall effect *that no man shall buy or sell but he that hath the Character or name of the beast or number of his name.* In what Popes dayes was this verified?

9. *Ninthly* and lastly 2. Thess. 2.4. That one speciall man, (who is called *that man of sin*) *is extolled above all that is God or all that is worshipped.* Now whosoever is extolled above judges, and Kings, sometimes called Gods (as all just men are) but *to be extolled above all that is called God*, he must be extolled above *God himselfe*, who (in the very first place) *is called God.* So he that is extolled not only above Princes and Kings, but above saints and Angels, and God himselfe. No neither doth the Pope extoll himselfe or is extolled by any of his adherents above the Apostles or Angels, and much less above God himselfe *shewing himselfe that he is God*, as there sayed Antichrist shall do

CHAPTER 5

Methodists and the millennium: eschatological belief in early British Methodism

In the previous chapters some of the eisegetical tradition relating to Daniel and Revelation has been explored, and we saw that Revelation in particular is a text that seems open to a variety of interpretations, its assumed meaning being almost entirely dependent on the whim of the interpreter. In this and the following chapter the discussion is broadened further, with particular reference to Methodism in the eighteenth century.[1] This chapter seeks to show, notwithstanding some scholarly consensus to the contrary, that a significant number of early Methodists showed a keen interest in the books of Daniel and Revelation, read them in the standard historicist way and even, it seems, used them to support a premillennial eschatological expectation. These concurrent interests, interpretations, expectations and beliefs were, it is true, found in some branches of Methodism that lay off the standard beaten track (in which context the work of the early Methodist enthusiast George Bell will be noted). However, they were found also in some much more central places. Indeed, even the work of John Wesley himself seems suggestive in this context. Perhaps the most significant body of evidence for the existence within early Methodism of a strong streak of premillennial belief tied to an historicist (and traditional anti-Catholic) reading of Daniel and Revelation, however, comes from the hand of Charles Wesley. In the following chapter, therefore, it will be Charles' views which are brought into particular focus.

The extent to which the Methodist tradition has supported eschatological expectation has been questioned. In an article published in 1980, for example, D. N. Hempton suggests that among nineteenth-century interpreters of biblical prophecy, 'Wesleyan Methodists are

---

[1] An earlier version of some parts of this chapter first appeared in the *BJRULM* 78 (1996): 103–22, under the same title. I am grateful to the editor of that journal for permission to reuse that material here.

conspicuous by their absence.'[2] Such a remark encapsulates the fairly
widespread belief that eschatological fervour was not a significant force
in the development of early Methodism. Whether such a belief is the
result of the lack of research in this area or its cause cannot be determined, but certainly this particular aspect of early Methodism has
suffered surprising neglect. Even Clive D. Field's bibliographical survey
of Methodist research[3] lists only five entries in the category of 'Eschatology', the most substantial of which is an unpublished Ph.D. thesis
completed in 1960, a work which, despite its title, is almost exclusively
concerned with John Wesley.[4]

It is not the purpose of the present study to challenge Hempton's
views directly; the concern here is primarily with eighteenth- and not
nineteenth-century Methodist eschatological belief (though some brief
remarks on the 1803 commentary on Daniel by Thomas Coke (1747–
1814) are offered below). Hempton's remarks have been noted, however,
since they have obvious significance: it is widely accepted that the
beginning of the nineteenth century saw a general rise in eschatological
expectation among the Christian Churches. Henry Rack in particular
notes that in the period following the French Revolution there was a
definite, if modest, increase in such interest even in Methodist circles.[5]
If, then, as Hempton's remark suggests, evidence of eschatological
expectation is difficult to track down in nineteenth-century Methodist
sources, such material ought perhaps to be almost completely absent in
the eighteenth. As we shall see, however, that is manifestly not the case.
Rather, as this chapter seeks to show, within eighteenth-century British
Methodism a strong and recurrent streak of vivid eschatological interest,
often founded upon highly complex historicist biblical interpretative
schemes, is clearly and easily discernible. In fact, it would appear from
some of the sources here surveyed that even the rawest form of Christian
eschatological expectation, belief in the sudden, visible and physical
premillennial advent of Christ, had significant support among some in

[2] D. N. Hempton, 'Evangelicalism and Eschatology', Journal of Ecclesiastical History 31 (1980):
174–94, p. 189. Hempton makes the same basic point in his Methodism and Politics in British Society
1750–1850 (London, Hutchinson, 1984), pp. 77, 95.
[3] See Rupert Davies, A. Raymond George and Gordon Rupp (eds.), The History of the Methodist
Church in Great Britain (4 vols., London: Epworth Press, 1965–88), vol. IV, pp. 720–1.
[4] James Cyril Downes, 'Eschatological Doctrines in the Writings of John and Charles Wesley',
Ph.D. thesis, University of Edinburgh, 1960. A copy is held in the Methodist Archives and
Research Centre (hereinafter 'MARC') of the John Rylands University Library of
Manchester.
[5] Henry Rack, Reasonable Enthusiast: John Wesley and the Rise of Methodism (London: Epworth Press,
1989), p. 475.

the early Methodist societies, and that such beliefs were often tied to texts such as Revelation 19.

That eschatological speculation was an area in which some eighteenth-century Methodists actively engaged is suggested by a remark made by Luke Tyerman, one of John Wesley's earliest biographers. According to him 'there can be no doubt, that Wesley, like his father before him, was a millenarian'.[6] In fact it is clear from the context of this remark that Tyerman is suggesting that Wesley was not simply 'a millenarian', but a premillennialist, that is, that he looked for the sudden appearance of Jesus upon the clouds of heaven and the inauguration of Christ's personal reign upon earth. Such a position is in fact affirmed by John Wesley himself, who in a letter to Thomas Hartley (1764) wrote of the latter's presentation of his clearly premillennial beliefs: 'I cannot but thank you for your strong and seasonable confirmation of that comfortable doctrine: of which I cannot entertain the least doubt, as long as I believe the Bible.'[7] Note also the criticism launched by Bishop Lavington, according to whom the young John Wesley, like the French Prophets[8] and the Fraticelli[9] before him, spoke frequently and unequivocally of the nearness of Christ's second coming.[10] Similarly, though Wesley may not have agreed with all he read in the prophetic interpretative works of J. A. Bengel (who thought that the millennium would begin in 1836),[11] he seems nevertheless to have felt the work of that scholar to be sufficiently important to warrant translation and reprint in his own *Notes upon the New Testament* (1754). He even prints

[6] Luke Tyerman, *The Life and Times of the Rev. John Wesley, M.A* (3 vols., London: Hodder & Stoughton, 1870–1), vol. II, p. 523.

[7] John Wesley to Thomas Hartley, 27 March 1764, *Arminian Magazine* (hereinafter *AM*) 6 (1783): 498–500. R. A. Knox, *Enthusiasm: A Chapter in the History of Religion* (Oxford: Clarendon Press, 1950), p. 546.

[8] The French Prophets arose c. 1700. Three people, Elie Marion, Jean Cavalier and Durand Fage, came to London in 1707, where they soon gained a modest following, especially among the exiled Huguenot community. The message was the traditional one of the nearness of the end coupled with a somewhat violent premillennial agenda. See especially Hillel Schwartz, *The French Prophets: The History of a Millenarian Group in Eighteenth-Century England* (Berkeley: University of California Press, 1980). On Methodism and the French Prophets see also Kenneth G. C. Newport, 'The French Prophets and Early Methodism: Some New Evidence', *Proceedings of the Wesley Historical Society* 50 (1996): 127–40.

[9] The Fraticelli was a general term used of two distinct groups of fourteenth-century Franciscans. Both groups were heavily influenced by the thinking of Joachim of Fiore and as a result saw themselves as standing on the brink of a new world. The most substantial study on the Fraticelli is that of Decima L. Douie, *The Nature and the Effect of the Heresy of the Fraticelli* (Manchester: Manchester University Press, 1932).

[10] Bishop Lavington, *Enthusiasm of Methodists and Papists Compared* (2 vols., 1749), vol. I, pp. 80, 125.

[11] See further Brady, *Number of the Beast*, pp. 218–24.

Bengel's apocalyptic time chart.[12] This, it should be noted, is detailed indeed in its presentation of the author's understanding of the meaning and dates of fulfilment of several of the time prophecies in the Apocalypse (for example the '42 months' and the '1,260 days'). Rack correctly notes that Wesley was himself rather non-committal regarding Bengel's chronology, and was cautious in introducing the work to his audience.[13] At the very least, however, the fact that he has printed it at all surely indicates his open mind on the issue.

It appears, then, that in the works of John Wesley there is at least some indication of the author's definite if chronologically indeterminate eschatological expectation. John's brother Charles similarly gave voice to an eschatological faith. Charles' timetable of last-day events is extremely precise: the final end of all things will come in 1794, a year which will see the 'end of these wonders' spoken of in Dan. 12.6–7, that is, the conclusion of the eschatological events and the premillennial return of Christ.[14]

Another leading early Methodist whose work reflects intense eschatological concern was John Fletcher (1745–85), who was arguably third in the Methodist hierarchy, and was chosen by John Wesley as his successor, although in the event Fletcher died first. Fletcher wrote a letter to John Wesley in 1755 on the subject of the prophecies.[15] In the course of the letter he makes it clear that he expects the end of all things to come in the near future. Indeed, according to him the year 1750 may already have seen the close of the 2,300-day prophecy of Dan. 8.14 (calculated on the 'year-day' principle as equivalent to 2,300 years); the sanctuary has begun to be cleansed and the final consummation is very near. Fletcher is basically premillennialist, though in his scheme there are three advents, not two, and he criticises those who 'confound our Lord's second with his third coming'.[16] The third coming will be at the end of all things (that is, at the end of the millennium). However, in the context of discussing the final turbulence of the world's present phase of history Fletcher says (with an eye on Rev. 6.2):

Give me leave here, Rev. Sir, to propose to you, a thing that many will look upon as a great paradox, but has yet sufficient ground in Scripture to raise the expectation of every Christian, who sincerely looks for the Coming of our Lord;

---

[12] Wesley, *Explanatory Notes upon the New Testament*, pp. 932, 1051–2.
[13] Rack, *Reasonable Enthusiast*, p. 475.   [14] Charles' work will be discussed in detail in chapter 6.
[15] Letter of John Fletcher to John Wesley, 29 November 1755. Printed in *AM* 16 (1793): 370–6, 409–16.
[16] *AM* 16: 411.

I mean, the great probability, that in the midst of this grand Revolution, our Lord Jesus will suddenly come down from Heaven, and go himself, conquering and to conquer.[17]

It would seem then that Fletcher did not expect this world to slip gradually and silently into the millennial age as a result of the spreading of the gospel. Rather 'in the midst of this grand Revolution' (not at its conclusion) Christ will come suddenly and visibly to complete the work that has begun.

Who does not perceive that Christ will come to give the finishing stroke to the great work begun by the might of his spirit, to establish his kingdom upon earth, and to bring those happy days, *when ten people shall lay hold of an Israelite saying, lead us to the Temple of the Lord?*[18]

The 'happy days' to which Fletcher here refers are the millennium, though it must be noted that he reckons this period as 'thousands' of years, not *a* thousand.[19] Fletcher's letter, then, contains some variations of the premillennialist theme, but the crucial point, that the appearance of Jesus upon the clouds precedes the dawn of the millennial kingdom on earth, is plain, and his concern to match scripture with expectation no less so. It would even appear that he set a rough date for the commencement of the millennium, for in two manuscript letters written by Walter Churchey reference is made to the fact that 'Mr Fletcher' (it is assumed that John Fletcher is in mind) stated that the 'the millennium would most assuredly commence in the third generation from 1754'.[20] The first of these letters is in general a very interesting one, for it witnesses to the fact that the Methodist Welshman Walter Churchey, who was probably a convert of Thomas Coke, and is credited with suggesting to Wesley that he publish the *Arminian Magazine*,[21] himself became a follower of the prophet Richard Brothers.[22] Churchey was writing to Benson in an effort to convince him of the truth of Brothers' claims to prophetic office. Hence the letter begins 'Dear Sir, I will not

---

[17] Ibid.   [18] Ibid. The allusion is to Zec. 8.23.   [19] *AM* 16: 412.
[20] Letter of W. Churchey to Joseph Benson, n.d. The letter is uncatalogued but may be found in the MARC in a folio of letters entitled 'Letters chiefly addressed to Charles Wesley' (leather vol. 6, no. 16); Letter of W. Churchey to Joseph Benson, 28 October 1797 (MARC ref. MAM PLP 24.1.2).
[21] Tyerman, *Life and Times*, vol. III, p. 282.
[22] Richard Brothers (1757–1824) predicted that the millennium would begin on 19 November 1795. His task in these latter days, he believed, was to lead the Jews back to the Holy Land and rebuild Jerusalem. The 'Jews' in question, however, were not principally the 'visible Hebrews' but rather the descendants of the lost ten tribes, many of whom were now living in England. See further J. C. F. Harrison, *The Second Coming: Popular Millenarianism 1780–1850* (London: Routledge & Kegan Paul, 1979), pp. 57–85.

give you up in the great matter of the new prophet without one letter more.' There follows a list of events which, according to Churchey, prove that Brothers has the prophetic gift and that consequently 'the millennium is begun or beginning, or very near at hand'. In another letter to Benson, apparently written in 1801, Churchey expresses the hope, which seems to be based on Revelation 20, that he will see John Wesley again 'soon and upon the earth, when the *sufferers* for Christ are to *rise* to reign in His spiritual Kingdom on *earth* a 1000 *years*' and remarks further 'I grow *daily* a greater *Brotherite*.'[23]

More could certainly be said regarding Fletcher's and Churchey's millennialism and interpretation. This is not needed here; the concern has been to show that apocalyptic expectation, sometimes even in the form of premillennialism, was a significant and indeed fairly widespread factor in early Methodism, and was tied to complex interpretations of biblical books. The views of the three most important figures in early Methodism, John and Charles Wesley and John Fletcher, have been noted, and further examples are not difficult to find. Thus, for example, a somewhat vague but definite reference to the end is found from the hand of Vincent Perronet (1693–1785), who wrote to his son William remarking that

The season is by no means healthy: your B. Briggs has been ill at Canterbury; poor *Charles*, at the foundry; and poor *Jacky* at Shoreham. It is no wonder that *individuals* are in disorder; when all *nature* seems to be in confusion. Indeed we are only at the beginning of alarming providences; a few years will produce still greater events. Happy would it be for a sinking world if they could see that *the end of all things is at hand*; and would therefore *grow sober to watch unto prayer!*[24]

It would of course be unwise to make too much of this one reference, which may reflect a transitory period of depression induced by the sickness of loved ones, but it must surely be noted that the letter indicates a theological pessimism most often related to a premillennial rather than postmillennial faith: individuals are in 'disorder', nature is in 'confusion', the world is 'sinking', and we are but 'at the beginning of alarming providences'.

---

23 This MS letter is noted by Tyerman, *Life and Times*, vol. III, p. 579, and is found in the MARC (ref. MAM PLP 24.1.3).
24 Letter of Vincent Perronet to William Perronet. The letter is dated 9 December. No year is given, but the contents suggest between 1750 and 1755. The letter is uncatalogued but may be found among a collection of loose materials held together in the MAB section of the MARC in a folder marked simply 'VP'. The scripture allusion is to 1 Pet. 4.7.

Dr J. Robertson wrote a letter to Charles Wesley in 1747 in which he expressed the view that the millennium would begin on 'Sunday 18th June, 1836'; the letter is peppered with references to Daniel and the Apocalypse.[25] John Wesley seems to have come up against a very definite outburst of eschatological fervour when in Newcastle in 1742 he met one John Brown, who came through the town 'hallooing and shouting, and driving all the people before him; telling them that God had told him he should be a king'.[26]

The Methodist preacher and enthusiast George Bell thought that the world was going to end on 28 February 1763, and in this seems to have gained a significant following. Quite how Bell arrived at his date is unclear, but there is a hint of the process in a letter written by William Briggs to Charles Wesley on 5 March 1763. According to Briggs

Bell took a solemn farewell of Biggs a few days before Monday, saying, 'Farewell – I shall see your face no more before we hear the last trumpet'![27]

This reference to the 'last trumpet' perhaps gives a slight clue to the origin of Bell's thought, for it is possible that he is referring here to 1 Thess. 4.16 (cf. Matt. 24.31). This passage speaks of Paul's hope that 'the Lord himself shall descend from heaven with a shout, with the voice of the archangel and with the trump of God'. This is consistent with Tyerman's remark that several of Maxfield's closest followers spent the night of 28 February at Mr Biggs' house 'every moment in full expectation of hearing the blast of the archangel's trumpet'.[28]

A slightly more informative account of Bell's thinking and the possible eisegetical basis for his understanding of the timing of the end is found in a letter of John Walsh to Charles Wesley dated 11 August 1762. The letter reports that it was Bell's claim that

the millennium [sic] was begun, and he should never die, that he and several other Men had seen Satan bound and cast into the bottomless pit, and the angel had set a Seal upon him that he should not come out to deceive the nations.[29]

---

[25] John Robertson to Charles Wesley, 23 September 1747. The letter is uncatalogued, but may be found in the MAB section of the MARC in a volume of letters entitled 'Letters chiefly addressed to Charles Wesley', leather folio volume 6, letter no. 67.
[26] Nehemiah Curnock (ed.), *The Journal of the Rev. John Wesley, A.M.* (8 vols., London: Charles H. Kelly, 1909–16), vol. III, p. 54.
[27] William Briggs to Charles Wesley, 5 March 1763, JRL ref. DDWES 2:61.
[28] Tyerman, *Life and Times*, vol. II, p. 438. This is probably based on John Wesley's diary entry for 23 April 1763 (W. Reginald Ward and Richard P. Heitzenrater (eds.), *Works of John Wesley*, vols. XVIII–XXIV (Nashville, TN: Abingdon, 1988–95), vol. XX, p. 410).
[29] John Walsh to Charles Wesley, 11 August 1762. The letter is uncatalogued but may be found in the Early Methodist Folio at the MARC, no. 134.

Walsh makes reference to the fact that Bell encouraged him to sing hymns 'significant of my name being written in the Lamb's book of life'. The information given by Walsh regarding Bell's apocalypticism is slight, but it at least provides a glimpse of what Bell was thinking. The references to the millennium, immortality and the binding of Satan are all taken from Rev. 20.1–6. The 'Lamb's book of life' appears in Rev. 13.8; 21.27 (cf. Rev. 3.5; 17.8; 20.15; 22.19). Bell, then, obviously had an eye on the book of Revelation as he sought to work out his prophetic scheme. Unfortunately there is insufficient evidence to give a broader picture, but from what has survived it would seem that Bell (and with him probably the much more significant figure of Thomas Maxfield) looked to Revelation to give a preview of those events that were shortly to break upon the world.[30]

This kind of patchy information is easy to amass from the primary, usually MS, documents. Quite who the 'poor madman' was whom Charles Wesley reports as foretelling the arrival of an (eschatological?) earthquake is unclear. The message of this individual did not, however, go unheeded, for Charles reports also that many believed this man and as a consequence fled the city.[31] Similarly, in a sermon preached at the Methodist chapel in Colchester on 18 June 1797, John Stephens urged his audience to perceive clearly the 'signs of the times';[32] Antichrist (Rome) is even now falling, a clear sign of the fulfilment of prophecy. The fields are 'white unto harvest' (John 4.35) and hence at this season the business of 'king Jesus' (the preaching of the gospel) requires great haste; present labours in this field must surpass the former ones, 'as the exertions of the husbandman in autumn surpass the common toil of the year'.[33] Stephens' vision is partly cataclysmic; the process of evangelisation is a universal one. However, the world will not slip thereby into the millennial age, but face a definite eschatological rite of passage. A day of wrath is coming.[34] The sermon ends with the command to pray always '*thy kingdom come!* yea, *come, Lord Jesus, come quickly!*'[35]

An intense belief in the literal, visible second coming of Jesus is seen also in four sermons by Joseph Benson.[36] Benson (1748–1821) served

[30] See further Kenneth G. C. Newport, 'George Bell, Prophet and Enthusiast', *Methodist History* 35 (1997): 95–105; Kenneth G. C. Newport and Gareth Lloyd, 'George Bell and Early Methodist Enthusiasm: A New Source from the Manchester Archives', *BJRULM* 80 (1) (Spring 1998): 89–101.

[31] MARC ref. MAB DDCW 4.13.

[32] John Stephens, *The Signs of the Times. A Sermon: Preached in the Methodist Chapel, Colchester; on the 18th of June, 1797. With some enlargements* n.d. MARC MAW pa 1797.

[33] Ibid., p. 28. [34] Ibid., p. 29. The reference to the 'day of wrath' relates to Job 20.28 and 21.30.

[35] Stephens, *Signs of the Times*, p. 30. The reference is to Rev. 22.20.

[36] Joseph Benson, *Four Sermons on the Second Coming of Christ and the Future Misery of the Wicked* (1781).

Methodist circuits all over England and Wales, and was one of the most successful and influential of early Methodism's preachers. According to Benson, the promised second coming 'will not be long deferred' and 'will be sudden and unexpected'.[37] Indeed, he is apparently of the belief that he will see the Lord's descent himself; after describing John's vision of Christ in Rev. 19.11ff., he writes

But ah! how much more will the representation strike us when it is made by Christ in person, and we shall see him as he is! – Shall see heaven open, and the Son of God in the pomp of Majesty ineffable descending![38]

Not surprisingly, then, the first sermon ends on a note of warning:

Awake! awake! ye sleepy sinners! shake off your fatal slumbers! Arise from the bed of sloth, and the lap of enchanting pleasures! Haste, haste, and flee for shelter from this day of wrath and unrelenting fury![39]

Again we note the pessimism; the day that is coming is a day of wrath and fury. This world, then, is not on the threshold of a golden age to be brought about by the spreading and acceptance of the gospel. Rather it is on the brink of an apocalyptic abyss.

It seems clear, then, that there was a definite streak of eschatological fervour within early Methodism, which was often reflected in the understanding of the interpretation of biblical prophecy. It is apparent also that premillennial theological pessimism (rather than enthusiasm for postmillennial missionary endeavour) finds expression in a number of sources. Whether this streak was strong enough to warrant the criticism made by Richard Hardy in 1753 that one of the chief errors 'into which the *Methodists* are zealously running . . . is their confidently asserting, that the *Millennium* is at hand' is less apparent,[40] but that it was there seems indisputable. Further, though in several places the evidence is rather patchy, from what has survived it appears quite clear that the early Methodists who did adopt an (often premillennial) eschatological expectation did so in parallel with a basically historicist reading of the books of Daniel and Revelation, with which several other passages of scripture were integrated.

In the remainder of this chapter the works of several early Methodist figures relating to the millennium and the end of the world are examined in finer detail. The purpose here is to attempt to show that

---

[37] Ibid., p. 11.   [38] Ibid., p. 15.
[39] Ibid., p. 23. The reference appears to be loosely to Isa. 51.17.
[40] Richard Hardy, *A Letter from a Clergyman to one of his Parishioners who was Inclined to Turn Methodist* (1753), p. 73.

Methodist millennial expectation was not only widespread, as has been argued to this point, but also far more than skin deep. In some early Methodist writers, it seems, there was a serious, scholarly and calculated attempt to discern the future. The focus of this attempt, as might be expected, was the biblical books of Daniel and Revelation. Once again there will be good cause to note just how flexible the text is. Eisegesis rather then exegesis is clearly the activity in which these authors, this time Methodist, are engaged.

JOSEPH SUTCLIFFE (1762–1856)

Joseph Sutcliffe was born in Baildon, Yorkshire. His Methodist credentials cannot be disputed: in 1786 he was appointed by John Wesley to the Redruth Circuit and appears fifth on the list of preachers at the Bristol conference in 1790. He was the author of a number of works, including an English grammar, several works related to geology, an introduction to Christianity and a commentary on scripture.[41] The work in focus here is a twenty-five-page pamphlet entitled *A Treatise on the Universal Spread of the Gospel, the Glorious Millennium and the Second Coming of Christ* (1798), which gives vivid expression to an historicist-based, eschatological faith.

Sutcliffe's work, like many other works of prophetic interpretation written after the events of the French Revolution, finds a place for these events in the eschatological providence of God. He sees the Revolution as the fulfilment of the prophecy in Rev. 11.13 regarding the 'great earthquake' which was to strike a tenth part of the city. The earthquake, he argues, is a political one, and the 'tenth part of the city' is France, a tenth of the empire of the Roman Catholic Church. The striking of the tenth part of the city is accompanied in Rev. 11.11 by the raising up of the two witnesses. This Sutcliffe takes as a reference to the breathing anew by God of spiritual life into the lungs of the Church (Joel 2). This spiritual infusion empowers the Church to preach the pure unadulterated gospel to the whole world, a task which must be accomplished before the end can come (Matt. 24.14).

Not surprisingly, then, an air of excitement runs through Sutcliffe's work. God has in very recent times acted in the destruction of the 'tenth part of the city', and will now continue to act until the final events of the world's history are played out. Sutcliffe is reluctant to give precise dates,

---

[41] Details of Sutcliffe's life given here are taken from Nolan B. Harmon (ed.), *Encyclopedia of World Methodism* (2 vols., Nashville: United Methodist Publishing House, 1974), vol. II, p. 287.

but a careful analysis of his interpretation indicates that he did have a fairly definite timetable in mind.

According to Sutcliffe, in about 1790 the 1,260-day prophecy of Rev. 11.3 (= the 42 months of Rev. 11.2; 13.5 and the 'time, times and the dividing of time' of Rev. 12.14) ended. This period of 1,260 days is taken by him to equal the same number of years. This 1,260-year period is that of the reign of Antichrist (Sutcliffe took the standard Protestant view that the Antichrist was the Roman Catholic Church). On the basis of the two further time periods of Dan. 12.11–12 (the 1,290 days and 1,335 days), Sutcliffe calculates that there will be a period of about thirty years after the first blow has been struck against Antichrist (the Roman Catholic Church) before its final demise, therefore in about 1820, we may conjecture. This period is characterised also by the beginnings of the spread of the gospel throughout the world (Matt. 24.14 = Rev. 14.6–8). This period will extend for a further forty-five years beyond the close of the thirty-year period (the difference between the 1,290 days and the 1,335 days of Dan. 12.11–12) given for the destruction of Antichrist, and thus will come to an end in about 1865.[42] (Sutcliffe does not give dates, but his logic is obvious.) According to Sutcliffe, the Jews play a special role during this time (it should be noted that the view that the Jews would be converted before the end was a commonplace of eigtheenth-century English eschatological thought).[43] Working with Romans 11 and several OT texts Sutcliffe argues that the Jews have been prepared by God for tremendous work. They have been spread throughout the world and have a good grasp of the countless languages and cultures, and are thus in a prime position to work for the conversion of the heathen. Soon God will take the veil from their eyes, they will see that Isaiah 53 relates to the events of Jesus' life and work, and they will become Christians. The Jews will then fulfil their eschatological role as the converters of the heathen.

At the close of this process, which, as has been noted, Sutcliffe expects in about 1865, the Jews are to be found again in Jerusalem. Revelation 20 appears to be very much in view from this point in Sutcliffe's thinking. Satan launches one last attack on the holy city, but it fails because of the sudden appearance of Christ in visible form to slay his enemies.

---

[42] Sutcliffe, *Treatise*, p. 21.
[43] See Christopher Hill, 'Till the Conversion of the Jews', in Richard H. Popkin (ed.), *Millenarianism and Messianism in English Literature and Thought 1650–1800* (Leiden: E. J. Brill, 1988), pp. 12–36.

The happy age before us, which has so long been the cheering theme of prophecy, and the support of the church in all her struggles with the pagan and papal beast, shall be ushered in by a personal, though transient manifestation of the Son of God.[44]

There follows the eschatological slaughter of the wicked, who have not listened to those who have called them to repentance. The righteous martyrs, who have throughout the ages given up their lives for the defence and propagation of the gospel, will, however, be raised at this time and return with Christ to the celestial realms. The millennium now begins, and for 1,000 years Christ and the righteous martyrs rule the earthly Church from the celestial court (cf. Rev. 20.4). The earth is transformed; war and famine are no more. Wild beasts are domesticated, the wolf lying down with the lamb and the leopard with the kid (Isa. 11.6). Perfect worship will be restored and the 'immense congregations be overshadowed with the Divine presence'.[45]

At the end of the 1,000 years there is one last releasing of Satan, who tries again to mislead the faithful. These events, says Sutcliffe, are distant and hence not open to full view, but there will be, it seems, one last battle. Satan succeeds in ensnaring again some of those who are alive at this time and raises an army against the faithful. However,

Short indeed will be this last struggle of the common enemy; for the Lord Jesus shall be revealed from heaven in a flaming fire, to surprise and punish the apostate multitudes. 'As it was in the days of Noah, so shall the coming of the Son of Man be. They were eating and drinking, marrying and giving in marriage, and the flood came and destroyed them all.' Luke xvii.27

There follows the general resurrection (the previous resurrection being only of the faithful martyrs) and the final judgement. The wicked are destroyed.

The scene shall close by the accession of the righteous to the new and everlasting kingdom of our Lord and Saviour Jesus Christ. Their bodies shall be inconceivably beautiful, perfect and luminous, like the glorified humanity of Christ . . . The mediatorial kingdom shall cease, and be delivered up to God, even the Father. Then shall we see, – and O that God may count us worthy to see,– the Lord Jesus, who is above every name that is named, at the head of his church, which is his body and the fulness of him that filleth all in all.[46]

This is an interesting mixture of pre- and postmillennialism. Christ comes visibly prior to the 1,000-year reign, and in this sense Sutcliffe is premillennial in his expectation. However, the millennium, which 'will

---

[44] Sutcliffe, *Treatise*, p. 15.   [45] Ibid., p. 19.   [46] Ibid., p. 23.

not be wholly free from wickedness',[47] is followed by yet another advent and the final destruction of the wicked.[48] It is clear, then, that Sutcliffe is here giving expression to a very definite eschatological hope. His conception of heaven and the afterlife seems rooted in a basically terrestrial (at least in the first instance) and time-bound framework. The resurrection is a literal raising of the body and takes place at a definite future time and not upon the death of the individual. The millennium takes place on earth and is a wholly physical experience. The precursory period of the preaching of the gospel in all the world will not result in total conversion and a gradual slipping of this world into the kingdom of God. Rather this transition will be accomplished by the appearance of Christ. Neither should it go unnoticed that though Sutcliffe does not give a firm date for this premillennial (and 'transitory') manifestation of Christ, he does appear to have an opinion on the matter. Indeed, his exegetical remarks on Dan. 12.10–12 lead uncompromisingly to the conclusion that the end will come some time very close to 1865.

In the Methodist writer Sutcliffe, then, we find a complex eisegetical system that, while focused centrally upon Revelation 20 and Daniel 12, takes in much more. Sutcliffe has looked to the text for the information he requires and, not surprisingly, finds it. The text has once again yielded to the interests of the reader. While many of the points made by Sutcliffe are relatively new with him (and indeed that must be the case as he seeks to make space for the events of the French Revolution and hence engages in the continual task of updating the paradigm in the light of contemporary events), his fundamentally historicist, anti-Catholic modified premillennial understanding of the material runs along fairly standard Protestant lines.

JAMES KERSHAW (1730?–97)

James Kershaw was converted to the Methodist cause in c. 1760 and soon afterwards took upon himself the life of an itinerant preacher.[49] He

---

[47] Ibid., p. 21.

[48] A similar pattern of things is presented in a short article entitled 'Of the Renovation of all Things' printed in *AM* 7 (1784): 154–5, 209–11. The author is not named, but Tyerman implies that the article is the work of John Wesley (Tyerman, *Life and Times*, vol. II, p. 524). Like Sutcliffe, the author argues that there are numerous texts in the Bible which seem

> to denote middle state betwixt the present pollution, corruption, and degradation of this terrestrial mansion; and that of a total, universal restoration of all things, in a purely angelical, celestial, ethereal state. (p. 155)

[49] *DNB*, vol. XI, p. 70.

is mentioned by John Wesley in at least three letters, all addressed to Charles,[50] and in his journal John Wesley records also how on 29 April 1765 he rode with Kershaw 'through a fruitful country to Kilmarnock, and thence to Ayr'.[51] In about 1770 Kershaw settled down in Gainsborough, where he continued to preach. In 1780 he published a two-volume work entitled *An Essay on the Principal Parts of the Book of the Revelations*.[52] It is this publication which is in focus here. The title page of this work is reproduced as figure 5.

Kershaw's interpretation of Revelation is complex, his dating of the dawn of the millennium distant, but his calculations extremely precise: the end of the present age will come in the year 2000. This year will see the transition of the present age into the literal 1,000-year period of peace upon earth. The transition itself, according to Kershaw, will not be a silent one, but rather one which can be observed. Indeed, according to Kershaw, in AD 2000 Christ himself will come again and there will be a literal, bodily resurrection of the dead.

Kershaw's prediction that the year AD 2000 would see the dramatic intervention of God in the world of human affairs was by no means new. Indeed, Kershaw himself refers to the tradition found in both Jewish and Christian circles that 'at the end of 6000 years the Messiah shall come, *and the world shall be renewed*'.[53] In this context, for example, the work of William Whiston, discussed in chapter 3 above, might be further noted. Whiston in his *Essay on the Revelation of Saint John* similarly predicted that the end of all things would come in AD 2000. The reasoning behind this thinking is reasonably plain: the world was created in six days followed by a day of rest; scripture says that 'one day is with the Lord as a thousand years, and a thousand years as one day' (2 Pet. 3.8); therefore there will be 6,000 years of toil followed by a Sabbath-millennium. Kershaw himself appeals to such reasoning.[54]

---

[50] *The Works of John Wesley* (14 vols., London: Wesleyan Conference Office, 1872; reprint, Grand Rapids, MI: Zondervan, n.d.), vol. XII, pp. 306–8.

[51] Ward and Heitzenrater, *Works*, vol. XXI, p. 505.

[52] James Kershaw, *An Essay on the Principal Parts of the Book of the Revelations; in a Series of Dialogues between Didascalos and Phylotheos* (2 vols., 1780), vol. II, pp. 181–2.

[53] Kershaw is quoting Thomas Newton at this point. See Thomas Newton, *Dissertation on the Prophecies*, 18th edn, (1834), p. 696. The work was originally published in 1754.

[54] For a discussion of belief in the Sabbath-millennium, see further John Jarick, 'The Fall of the House (of Cards) of Ussher: Why the World as We Know it Did not End at Sunset on 22nd October 1997 (and Will not End at Midnight on 31st December 1999/1st January 2000)', in Stanley E. Porter, Michael A. Hayes and David Tombs (eds.), *Faith in the Millennium* (Roehampton Institute London Papers, 7; Sheffield Academic Press, forthcoming, 2000).

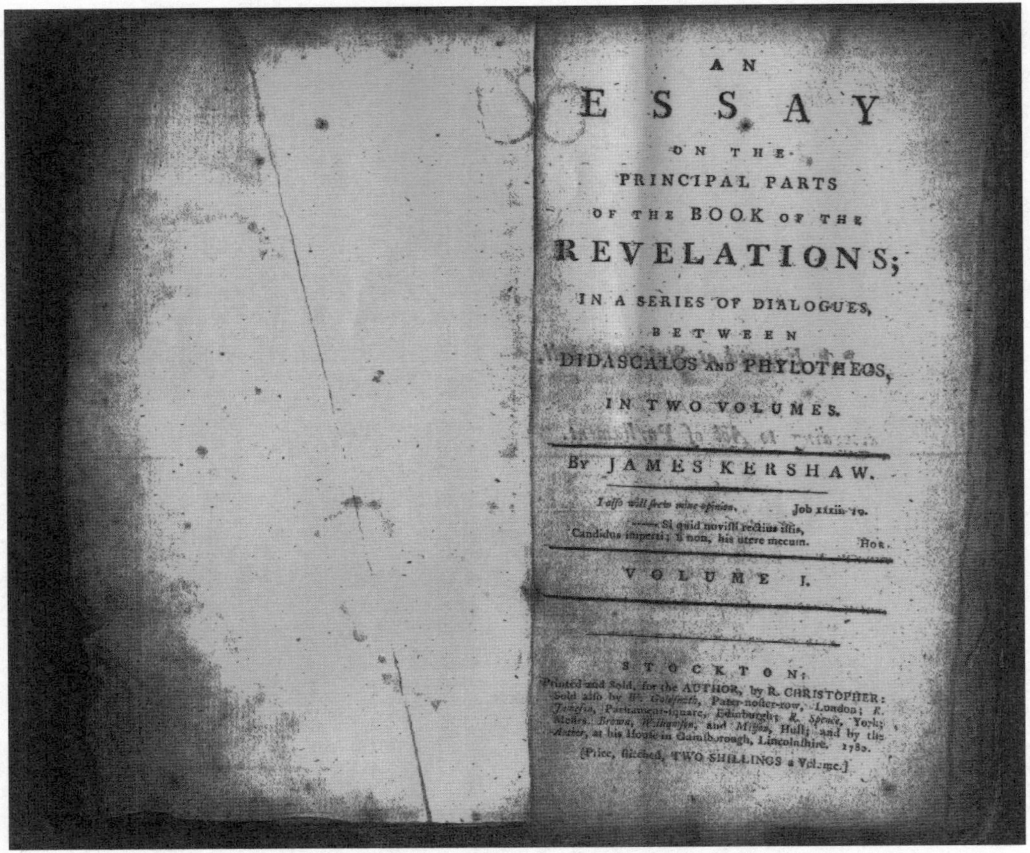

AN

ESSAY

ON THE

PRINCIPAL PARTS

OF THE BOOK OF THE

REVELATIONS;

IN A SERIES OF DIALOGUES,

BETWEEN

DIDASCALOS AND PHYLOTHEOS,

IN TWO VOLUMES.

By JAMES KERSHAW.

Tessâ will facto mine officio.   Job xxiii. 10.
——— Si quid novisti rectius istis,
Candidus imperti; si non, his utere mecum.   Hor.

VOLUME I.

STOCKTON:

Printed and sold for the AUTHOR, by R. CHRISTOPHER:
Sold also by W. Goldsmith, Pater-noster-row, London; E.
Todd, York, J. Wilson, Edinburgh; R. Spence, Waghorn &
Nicholl, Newcastle; ——, and Messrs. Hull; and by the
Author, at his House in Gainsborough, Lincolnshire. 1780.

[Price, in sheets, TWO SHILLINGS a Volume.]

Figure 5   Title page of Kershaw's *An Essay on Revelations* (1780)

It is immediately apparent from Kershaw's *Essay*, however, that his reasoning is far more complex than simply a restatement of this older view. It is not necessary for present purposes to examine his eisegetical methodology in detail; however, it will be useful to give at least an outline of how he arrives at his date, since this will make it apparent that this Methodist preacher for one (and he was certainly not alone) invested a considerable amount of time and not a little intellectual energy in seeking to ascertain the very year of the Lord's return. It is true that in Kershaw's case the resultant date was a distant one, but even so it demonstrates clearly enough the more general point that some Methodist preachers were of the opinion that Christ would return visibly to this earth, that this event would precede the millennium, and that through careful analysis of the relevant parts of scripture the event could be dated with precise accuracy. One may not know the day or the hour (Matt. 24.36); the year, however, might be discerned.

Kershaw notes that in the books of Daniel and Revelation frequent mention is made of various numbers. These numbers are sometimes of days (for example the 1,260 days of Rev. 11.3) and sometimes of months (for example the 42 months of Rev. 11.2), but in Rev. 13.18 it is the 'number of a man' that is mentioned. Kershaw spins a highly complex eisegetical web around these numbers, but what he says in effect is that the number 666 refers to the word '*Lateinos*' (Λατεινος) and also (in Hebrew script) to '*Romiith*', (רומיית), the letters of both of which add up to 666. This marks out the Roman Catholic Church as the Antichrist himself.[55] Such reasoning was absolutely standard for Kershaw's day. He begins to deviate from the standard exegetical comments on Rev. 13.18, however, when he goes on to note that the number 666 also holds the key to the date when the millennium will dawn.

Kershaw argues that the number 666, as well as referring to the number of the name of the beast, also refers to the period of his reign. However, according to him, the number cannot be taken at face value, for it is linked to the other numbers mentioned in connection with the beasts in Revelation 13 and the dragon in Revelation 12. These numbers include the *ten* horns and *seven* heads on the first beast (Rev. 13.1), the *two* horns on the second beast (Rev. 13.11) and the *ten* horns of the dragon in Rev. 12.3. The 'grand Key to unlock this Treasury of Wisdom' is the observation that in Rev. 7.4ff. a multiplication is performed ($12 \times 12,000 = 144,000$). This suggests to Kershaw that multiplication is

---

[55] Kershaw, *Essay*, vol. II, pp. 232–3.

the first rule by which to 'count' these numbers. He thus sets about his calculations.

His first point of mathematical call is the dragon of Rev. 12.3ff. This individual is none other than Satan himself, the originator of all that is opposed to God. He will last, according to Kershaw's reckoning, for 6,660 years (= 10 (horns) × 666). This is the total number of years he is to deceive mankind, not including the literal 1,000-year period during which he is the captive of God (Rev. 20.2). See further the appendix to this chapter, in which Kershaw's extremely detailed reasoning is quoted at some length.

Kershaw's scheme relates to his general reading of Rev. 20.2–3, which reads:

And he laid hold on the dragon, that old serpent, which is the Devil, and Satan, and bound him a thousand years, And cast him into the bottomless pit, and shut him up, and set a seal upon him, that he should deceive the nations no more, till the thousand years should be fulfilled: and after that he must be loosed a little season.

This is an interesting and relatively unusual scheme. Kershaw is arguing that this age will spill over into and indeed outlast the millennium. In the year 2000 Christ will return visibly to this earth. His belief in the literal, visible advent of Jesus in the year 2000 emerges several times in the course of his work. On page 247, for example, he writes, 'Now the first Resurrection, as I take it, will take place immediately at the conclusion of the six thousandth year of the world, when Christ will come a second time without sin unto salvation.' According to Kershaw, when this resurrection happens, Satan will be bound and the literal 1000-year millennium will begin. In the year 3000, however, Satan will be loosed for a period so that he may once again deceive the nations for a 'little season'. This little season will last, according to Kershaw, for 660 years, so the final end of all things, which will be marked by the casting of Satan and his cohorts into the lake of fire (Rev. 20.10), will come, it may be calculated, in 3660. Such precise dating of the eschatological timetable is unusual, though by no means unique even among Methodist writers.

Over the course of the next several pages Kershaw seeks to strengthen his argument that the dawn of the millennium will come in AD 2000. Among other evidence he brings to bear is his belief that the temple of Jerusalem was destroyed 'utterly' in AD 74. Add to this date the number 666 (Rev. 13.18) and the number 1,260 (Rev. 11.3) and again the year 2000 is reached. Even leaving aside the question of the accuracy of this date of AD 74, one might well object that there seems no good reason why the 'utter' destruction of the temple should be of particular prophetic significance. However, to this Kershaw would reply that key events in the history of the Jewish temples put down definite markers in the progress of the history of the world leading up to the renovation. Indeed, according to Kershaw Solomon's temple was completed in the 3000th year of the world, that is, its completion marked the mid point in the history of this present age.

Kershaw points also to Dan. 8.14, where it is said that there will be 2,300 'days' (Kershaw notes that the phrase is actually 'evenings and mornings') before the sanctuary is cleansed. The beginning of this prophecy, says Kershaw, coincided with the beginning of the reign of King Ptolemy, since it is he, together with the other three successors to Alexander the Great, who is referred to in the vision of the four horns in Dan. 8.8.[56] This event Kershaw dates to 'the year of the world 3700'. Add to this the 2,300 year-days of Dan. 8.14, and 'the cleansing of the sanctuary' is seen once again to fall in the year of the world 6000 (= AD 2000).

Kershaw is particularly ingenious regarding the three time periods mentioned in Daniel 12.7, 11–12. The first of these, the 'time, times and half a time' Kershaw takes as $3\frac{1}{2}$ years of 360 days each, which equals 1,260 days/years. This period begins in the year of the world (AM) 4734. It will therefore close in AM 5994, that is, just six years before the end of the present age. The second period, the 1,290 days (Dan. 12.11), writes Kershaw, is to be dated to the time when the 'abomination which makes desolate' (Dan. 9.27) was set up. The date for this is the establishment in AD 658 of 'Mohammedism'. This 1,290-year period will close in AM 5952, at which time the vials of God's wrath will begin to fall and continue to do so until AM 6000, the dawn of the millennium. The importance of the 1,335 days (Dan. 12.12), according to Kershaw, is to be discerned in another way. Jesus was born in AM 4000; add to this the mystical number 666 and the number 1335 and the result is 6001, the first year of the millennium. No wonder, says Kershaw, that Daniel said 'blessed is he that waiteth, and cometh to the 1335 days', for 'such will have part in the first resurrection, &c. at Christ's next coming'.

There is much more in Kershaw in this vein; however, his work need not be explored futher here. However, what should be noted carefully is

[56] Ibid., vol. II, p. 246.

that Kershaw, a minister intimately connected with the Methodist movement, was clearly of the opinion that this world was operating to a definite chronological schedule. The end was coming, and it was his work to help others prepare for that inevitability. The energy he has expended upon the text of Daniel and Revelation is quite obvious, and the ingenuity with which he sought to decipher the numbers of the beasts and the references to various time periods is equally apparent. Kershaw was a premillennialist, though, as we have seen, his millennium is followed by another period of sin and a third advent of Christ.

THOMAS TAYLOR (1738–1816)

Taylor was one of the more influential and certainly one of the more successful early Methodist preachers.[57] John Wesley spoke well of his work in Ireland, and indeed Taylor was to become one of his closest and most trusted associates. Taylor was elected president of the Wesleyan conference in 1796. He was by no means on the fringes of Methodism, and consequently his work *Ten Sermons on the Millennium or, the Glory of the Latter Days: and Five Sermons on what Appears to Follow that Happy Aera* (1789) deserves to be seen not as the ravings of an obscure fanatic (as might be argued in the case of John Brown and perhaps Bell), but rather the careful reflections of a respected religious leader and self-taught biblical scholar. His work is representative of at least 'a' Methodist viewpoint.

It has been noted that both Sutcliffe and Kershaw seem to have espoused a basic, if modified, historicist premillennial faith. In the work of Thomas Taylor, however, a variation on this theme is encountered, for Taylor's work is more akin to postmillennialism. In the preface to his work he expresses the view (but not the firm conviction) that the approach of the kingdom may 'perhaps' be gradual.[58] Taylor's work is interesting, however, in that though he does put forward the view that the kingdom of God is 'invisible' and will advance slowly on earth, he nevertheless gives vivid expression to the belief that this process represents the playing out of the fulfilment of a definite eschatological timetable which is found already in the scripture prophecies. Taylor's work, then, like those others mentioned above, gives voice to a vibrant eschatological faith. The details are different, but even Taylor seems to expect and long for the eventual literal second advent. In the course of

---

57 For the life of Taylor see John Telford (ed.), *Wesley's Veterans* (7 vols., London: Charles H. Kelly, 1912), vol. VII, p. 126.
58 Taylor, *Ten Sermons*, p. v.

discussing the 'Kingdom of God' in Matt. 6.13, for example, Taylor makes the following remark (Rev. 19.6 is clearly in view):

Sweet time of refreshing from the presence of the Lord! O, hasten, hasten it, blessed Lord, when thou wilt mount thy white horse, and be followed by thy shining hosts, and display thy now concealed name, – KING OF KINGS AND LORD OF LORDS.[59]

Taylor states in the preface of his book that the subject of the millennium had been of interest to him for a considerable number of years, and that through his reading of the scriptures he had come to the conclusion that the millennium was yet to come. His reading of the secondary sources on the topic did not satisfy him, and thus his own quest for truth on the matter began. The fifteen sermons he published in this area encapsulate the results of his enquiries.

Taylor's key texts on the topic of the millennium are far ranging and cannot all be discussed here. He notes among other passages many of those commonly discussed by Protestant interpreters such as 2 Thess. 2.8, Matt. 24 and Rom. 11. From such passages he deduces that Rome is the great Antichrist, that Antichrist must fall and that the Jews will be gathered in before the end. Such themes were commonplace in eighteenth-century English eschatological thought.

Taylor's vision of the last things is complex and not easily categorised. He is clearly of the opinion that his world is on the brink of eschatological renewal. However, before the climax of history, i.e. the appearance of Jesus as Lord, certain conditions must be met. These include the destruction of Antichrist (Sermon 1 (2 Thess. 2.8)), the chaining of the dragon (Sermon 2 (Rev. 20.11–12)), the cessation of strife (Sermon 3 (Isa. 11.4)), the universal spread of the gospel (Sermon 4 (Mark 13.10)), the outpouring of the spirit (Sermon 5 (Joel 2.28)), the gathering of the Jews (Sermon 6 (Romans 11.23)) and the bringing in of the full number of the Gentiles (Sermon 7 (Isa 11.11)).

When all these have been accomplished, Christ will come visibly to establish his literal kingdom upon earth. In Sermon 10, entitled 'The Glory of Christ seen by all', Taylor expounds the Lord's Prayer. 'The Kingdom' of Matt. 6.13, he argues, is a spiritual one which has been advancing upon earth since the time of Christ's first advent. However, that which is now invisible and spiritual will in the climax of all things becomes visible and literal.

The spiritual kingdom was foreseen by Adam and Eve and also by the

---

[59] Ibid., p. 242.

patriarchs and prophets, but it is Daniel in Dan. 2.44 who gives clearest expression to the hope. It was symbolised in the various secrecy parables of Jesus (for example the Hidden Treasure in Matt. 13.44). Like the mustard seed of Matt. 13.31 it has continued to grow and is, according to Taylor, now nearing its fullness. The process of evangelisation will continue and Antichrist (Rome) will be overthrown; with the downfall of Antichrist comes that also of the 'false prophet' (Rev. 19.20), which Taylor thinks is 'Mohammedism'. According to Taylor the instrument by which these two satanic powers will be overthrown is the 'breath of his mouth' mentioned in 2 Thess. 2.8.[60] This Taylor takes to be 'effective preaching' and such preaching has, states Taylor, been going on since A.D. 1100, when the Albigenses and Waldenses, who he thinks are symbolised by the first vial of Revelation 16, launched the attack upon Antichrist by the preaching of the pure gospel of Christ. The process will continue until (in the not too distant future) Antichrist is defeated.

The personal consequence of Taylor's thinking on this point is obvious. Taylor, a tireless and successful preacher of the Methodist message, sees himself as far more than just a preacher. He is rather an instrument in God's hands, a divine weapon used by the Almighty to deliver another withering, perhaps the last, blow against Antichrist. Little wonder then that Taylor set about his work with rigorous and life-long enthusiasm. The words of James Montgomery written in Taylor's memory perhaps catch this point well. Taylor preached just a few hours before his death, and on this and Taylor's other preaching Montgomery wrote:

> His sword was in his hand,
> Still warm with recent fight
> Ready that moment at command
> Through rock and steel to smite.
> It was a two-edged blade
> Of heavenly temper keen;
> And double were the wounds it made
> Where'er it glanced between.[61]

According to Taylor, the destruction of Antichrist and false prophet is followed by the binding of Satan (Rev. 20.1–3). This he takes to refer to the process by which God ensnares Satan and prevents him from working his evil on earth. Again Taylor seems to think that the event is not far distant

---

[60] Taylor appears to be using his own translation here. The KJV has 'spirit' for πνεῦμα.
[61] Telford, *Wesley's Veterans*, vol. vii, p. 126.

and warns all his readers to be aware of the fact that just prior to Satan's binding will come a time of great trouble for mankind. Taylor draws attention to Rev. 12.12 and sees there a prophetic description of his own day. Satan knows that his time is short and will use whatever time he has left to the best of his satanic abilities. But the battle goes on and victory is assured. The imagery, this time Taylor's, is again military:

O blessed period! much longed for moment! gird thy sword upon thy thigh, O thou most mighty, and in thy glory and in thy majesty ride on prosperously! let thine arrows be sharp in the king's enemies! let the grand Abaddon fall; let the prisoners come forth, and such as sit in the prison-house show themselves.[62]

Taylor's fifteen sermons continue in this general vein. They need not be explored further here, except to note his conviction that after all the preparatory steps have been taken, the millennial kingdom will dawn. This kingdom may have its centre in Jerusalem. There will be a burning of the earth and the final judgment. The wicked will be condemned and the saints taken to heaven.

For Taylor, then, as for the other Methodist preachers mentioned above, the end is in sight. However, unlike some others in the early Methodist movement, for example George Bell and John Robertson, who were discussed above, and Charles Wesley, whose views will be considered in chapter 6, Taylor is wary of setting precise dates. He is concerned to avoid the pitfall of setting a date lest he be proved wrong on the question of timing, and this should raise doubts also concerning what he has to say about the nature of the millennium.[63] It is apparent in the preface, however, that while he may be less confident that he has the timing right than he is about his ability to discern in scripture lessons regarding the nature of the millennium, he nevertheless has at least a rough date in mind. Indeed, he says as much quite clearly in the following words:

Whatever, therefore, my thoughts may be, touching the time when the glorious scene of Christ's millennial reign will take place, I deem it quite prudent to keep them to myself. The thing, I am certain, will take place, because God hath said it; but, as to the time, it seems to be one of the secrets which belong to himself alone.[64]

Later in the sermons Taylor expresses the view that the end may not be far away; in fact 'perhaps we are upon the dawn of that blessed day; several things seem to encourage us to hope so'.[65]

---

[62] The references are successively to Ps. 45.3–5; Rev. 9.11; and Isa. 42.7.
[63] Taylor, *Ten Sermons*, pp. v–vi.   [64] Ibid., p. v.   [65] Ibid., p. 251.

In the course of this study it has been noted that eschatological speculation focused upon biblical eisegesis was by no means unknown in early Methodist circles. Kershaw's scheme was extremely precise and the detail with which he argued for it exhaustive. Sutcliffe's work, though less detailed than that of Kershaw, similarly gives voice to a modified but basically premillennial faith. Both Kershaw and Sutcliffe appear to have had dates firmly in mind: Kershaw is clear on this point and commits himself to the year AD 2000; Sutcliffe falls short of giving the precise year, but has a scheme which leads inevitably to 1865. Taylor is noncommittal, but more than once expresses the view that the dawn of the millennium is not at a great distance. All three read the relevant texts from an historicist point of view and in all three, it is suggested, the modern reader can see clearly enough the eisegetical process at work. Paradigms are updated in the light of contemporary events, and in each case the text is made to have particular relevance in the context (religious, geographical and chronological) in which the interpreter himself is living.

Sutcliffe, Kershaw and Taylor were by no means unusual among the early Methodist communities. It has been noted that a list of Methodist worthies who at one time or another gave voice to a vivid, historicist-eisegetical, often premillennial, eschatological faith is easily drawn up. These include John and especially Charles Wesley, together with several others such as Fletcher, Perronet, Benson and Robertson. This list could easily have been extended. Note might have been taken, for example, of the work of David Simpson, an individual closely connected to the Methodist work in Macclesfield.[66] Simpson wrote a highly detailed work on the prophecies which appeared posthumously in 1839 (he died in 1799).[67] Simpson warns against speaking too assuredly on the matter of exact chronology, but nevertheless thinks that 'this desirable event' (the destruction of the Roman Antichrist) is 'near at hand ... and it is not very improbable, that this generation shall not pass away before most of these things be fulfilled'.[68] In fact, like Kershaw, Simpson edges towards the year AD 2000 as the dawn of the millennium and discerns in his own day the taking of the last premillennial steps; Antichrist is falling, the Jews are soon to be converted,[69] and the Mahometans will fall with the

---

[66] Benjamin Smith, *Methodism in Macclesfield* (1875), p. 236.

[67] David Simpson, *A Key to the Prophecies, or a Concise View of the Predictions Contained in the Old and New Testaments, which have been Fulfilled, are now Fulfilling, or are yet to be Fulfilled in the Latter Ages of the World* (1839); Smith, *Methodism in Macclesfield*, p. 236.

[68] Simpson, *Key to the Prophecies*, pp. 319–20.   [69] Simpson, *Key to the Prophecies*, p. 256.

Roman Antichrist.[70] Mention might also have been made of the surprising report written by Charles Wesley in 1739 in which he describes the considerable impact upon the fledgeling society made by Mrs Lavington. Lavington was a French Prophetess and hence heir to a definite millennial (and often quite violent) message. According to one of Charles' sources 'many' even of the strongest of the brethren were much taken with her pronouncements.[71]

Attention might also have been given to Thomas Coke's *Commentary on the Holy Bible*, the fourth volume of which appeared in 1803. In his remarks on Dan. 12.11–12 Coke is indeed cautious in seeking a precise date for the end. 'But', he says, 'of this the people of God may be sure, that the end of all the sufferings of his church hastens apace; that we are called with patience to wait for the blessed day; and that our happiness will then be complete and everlasting.'[72] Elsewhere he is somewhat less cautious; the 'time, times and an half' of Dan. 12.7 is to be understood as the 1,260 year-days of Antichrist's rule. According to Coke this rule began in 606 and will come to an end (it may be conjectured – Coke does not spell it out) in 1866.[73] At the close of this period, says Coke,

a great and glorious revolution will follow, which, I verily believe, refers to the destruction of Antichrist, and the restoration of the Jews. But another still greater and more glorious will succeed; and what can this be, but the full conversion of the Gentiles to the Church of Christ, and the beginning of the Millennium, or reign of the saints upon earth?[74]

Again care must be taken not to press upon Coke a scheme to which he did not subscribe, but his logic seems plain. The 1,260 year-days began in 606 and ended in 1866; there follows a period of 30 years (i.e. the difference between the 1,260 year-days of Dan. 12.7 and the 1,290 year-days of Dan. 12.11) during which the Jews are converted and the full number of the Gentiles come in. At the close of a further period of 45 years (note the 1,335 year-days of Dan. 12.12) 'the enemies of Christ' will be utterly destroyed. Did Coke think that the millennium was to begin in 1911? He warns against such certainty, but his own arguments lead logically to this conclusion.

[70] Charles Wesley, 'Lavington's Case' (n.d.; probably June 1739). MARC ref. MAB DDCW 8.12. A shorter form is found in Thomas Jackson (ed.), *The Journal of the Rev. Charles Wesley, M.A.* 2 vols., [London: John Mason, 1849], vol. I, p. 152. The apparent attraction of the message of the French Prophets to some in the early Methodist societies is discussed in Newport, 'The French Prophets and Early Methodism'.
[71] Simpson, *Key to the Prophecies*, p. 254.
[72] Thomas Coke, *A Commentary on the Holy Bible*, vol. IV, (London, 1803), p. 456.
[73] Ibid., vol. IV, p. 455.   [74] Ibid., vol. IV, p. 454.

Despite the rather limited scope of the study presented, however, the situation is fairly clear. Some early Methodists, like the Baptists noted in chapter 2, the other established and Free Church Protestants of chapter 3 and the Catholics of chapter 4, seem to have had an interest in prophetic speculation and the interpretation of biblical-prophetic books. They looked forward to the coming of Christ and the dawn of the millennium. Details differ from one writer to another as the text is moulded to suit the needs of the individual interpreter, but it has been noted that within early Methodism there was a distinct tendency towards premillennialism, which is itself rather strange when seen in a broader eighteenth-century history of interpretation framework. It has been noted also that several Methodist writers were prepared to work hard at the prophetic numbers and to give dates. It is hoped, then, that this survey has at least demonstrated reasonably clearly that Methodism could and indeed did support intense eschatological speculation and that that speculation was often wedded to historicist eisegesis. We are still not in a position to judge the fairness of Richard Hardy's criticism that one of the most obvious examples of Methodist folly was the Methodists' recurrent and confident claim that the millennium was at hand. More work is needed. However, initial findings suggest that Hardy might not have been completely wide of the mark.

APPENDIX[75]

To this division of time, and to this way of reckoning it, I make no doubt but St. John alluded to and found all his mystic numbers.

1. With him one day stands for one year.
2. One month stands for 30 days or years.
3. One year stands for 360 days or years, and is called a Time: and I doubt not, my dear Phyl. but the diagrams below will abundantly illustrate and prove it, all which are founded upon, and flow from my very easy method of counting the Enigmatical number 666.

For many years it appeared to me as clear as the light, that, as Bengelius says, '*This wisdom* consists in our apprehending the comparison of the Prophetical Numbers, *as the true Key of our mediations on the Divine Administration thro' all ages of the World. The periods of time predicted in the Revelations, are always so formed, that they must be added to those periods that were past, from the Creation to the date of the Prophecy.* Beng. Ib. page 200.

Phyl. As the number of the Beast is accompanied with a command to calculate,

[75] From Kershaw, *An Essay on the Principal Parts of the Book of the Revelations*, vol. II, pp. 239–43. Three footnotes marked with symbols such as asterisk and dagger have been brought into parentheses in the text. Spelling, punctuation and italic are reproduced without alteration.

reckon, or count, and as every calculation requires at least two numbers, pray where do you find them in the text?

Didas. The Enigmatical number 666 itself is one, but this number is only an adjective number, and wants a substantive to determine what the 666 are, whether years, or days, or months, &c. Now as St John says, that it is the number of a man, or *the number of man*, and as years are the periods by which man measures his life upon earth, why may not the ellipsis be supplied by the word years?

Phyl. I see no reason to the contrary; in that it informs us that the number is the *number of man*, and as man's life is counted by years, &c. it seems rational to suppose that years are intended.

But tho' the ellipsis be thus supplied, and the word years be understood, so that we read it 666 years, yet this does not supply a second number to reckon by. The principal difficulty as it appears to me, is, to find out another number that is essential to the Beast, or that necessarily belongs to him as such, by which to form a proper calculation: or, as the number 666 supplies us with the numerous numerans, we want a numerous numeratous belonging to the Beast to calculate by.

Didas. True: but we need not be at a loss for that, for the Vision supplies us with three such numbers, all of which belong to, or are essential to the Beasts mentioned in this Chapter: they are the ten horns – the two horns, and the seven heads, and these, together with the number 666, will supply us with sufficient numbers to calculate by.

Phyl. True: but then have these any reference to his duration?

Didas. Why not? It is certain that the seven heads have, for the angel plainly represents them as successive, when he says, *five are fallen, one is, and the other is not yet come*, &c. (Ch. xvii. 10, 11)

Phyl. But I observe the Dragon has seven heads, and ten horns, as well as the Beast.

Didas. He has so; and the Dragon is that old Serpent, &c. Now *old* is a relative term, whose correlative is *young*; the *life* of the Dragon or Serpent, as such, is measured by *days*. (Gen. iii. 14.) This Serpent, *as a beast of the field*, (ib. ver. 1) the Lord God made him when he made other beasts; here was the *beginning* of his *days of life* or living; and St. John informs us of his imprisonment, and the term of it, viz. 1000 years: and that at the end of *a little season* he shall afterwards be cast into the lake of fire, which is the second death – here then we have the *ending* of the days of his life.

Within the term of the Dragon's life, the life of the Beasts are contained. The first Beast rose out of the sea, *and the Dragon gave him His power, &c.* so that he is the Dragon's deputy or co-partner, of which his ten horns are the ensigns – but He will be cast into the lake of fire long before the Dragon, yea, before the Dragon is bound; see Chap. xix. 20 and xx. 1, 2. The second Beast rose *out of the earth* long after the first rose out of the sea; yet they both perish together.

Now it is of the greatest concern to be acquainted with these several important periods, all of which, I doubt not, but that the above numbers, when rightly counted, will precisely fix, and plainly acquaint us withal.

Phyl. But what operation of arithmetic will you first perform with these mystic numbers, for *to count* signifies to number – add – subtract – multiply – divide, &c.

Didas. The book itself is it's own best interpreter. Now the book supplies us with one *remarkable* operation of Arithmetic, and but one; this is multiplication. 12 time 12 are 144, by which rule the twelve Tribes are counted in Chapter vii. 4, and twice mentioned elsewhere, Ch. xiv. and xxi.

Phyl. Does not this afford a sufficient presumption, that *multiplication* is the first rule, and Grand key to unlock this Treasury of Wisdom?

Didas. It seems so; and as the ten horns of the Dragon occur before the Beast rises, we will begin with them, and multiply the ten horns by the number 666. To make it the plainer, I shall cast it into the following form, and call it

DIAGRAM I

Or, the Dragon's ten Horns counted.

6 }		{ }		{ 60
60 }	times	{ 10 }	makes	{ 600
<u>600</u> }		{ }		{ <u>6000</u>
666 }			Total	6660

I presume this diagram shews, first, the duration of the Dragon as such; that is, from the Serpent's deceiving Eve in Paradise, to the time the Dragon is bound: and from the time of his loosing, to his utter destruction in the lake of fire. As to the time that he is imprisoned, or the 1000 years that he will be bound, they do not come into the account, because all that time he neither acts the part of the Serpent to deceive the Nations, nor that of a Dragon to force and persecute.

Phyl. How long then do you suppose it will be from his deceiving Eve to his binding and imprisonment?

Didas. I apprehend exactly 6000 years; or ten times 600. And as you see the total is 6660, so I suppose that the 660 years is the space of time that St. John allots for him to deceive the Nations in after he is loosed. I apprehend that these 6000 years are exactly the space of time from the Creation to the Renovation of all things. And the 660 years of deceiving the nations are certainly but *a little season* when compared with 6000 allowed him before his imprisonment. 'There is an old tradition both among Jews and Christians, that at the end of 6000 years the Messiah shall come, *and the world shall be renewed* – the reign of the Wicked One shall cease, and the Reign of the Saints upon earth shall begin.' Again, 'About that period, according to an old tradition which was current before our Saviour's time, and was probably founded upon the Prophecies, great changes and revolutions are expected: and particularly, as *Rabbi Abraham Sebah* saith, Rome is to be overthrown, and the Jews are to be restored.' Dr. Newton's Diff. Vol. ii. page 77.

St *Barnabas*, St Paul's companion, saith, 'And God made in six days the work of his hands: this signifies that the Lord God will *finish all things* in 6000 years. For a day with Him is as a thousand years: therefore Children, in six days, that is in 6000 years shall all things be consummated.' Epis. St. Barnab. Cap. 15. *Lactantius* also says, 'Because all the works of God were finished in six days, it is necessary that the world should remain in this state six ages, that is 6000 years. Because having finished the works He rested on the seventh day, and blessed it; it is necessary that at the end of the six thousandth year, *all wickedness should be abolished out of the earth*, and righteousness should reign for 1000 years. At the same time the Prince of Devils shall be bound by chains. *This is the Doctrine of the holy Prophets, which we Christians follow, this is our Wisdom.*' See much more in Cap. 14, 24, and 26, of his works. To strengthen this supposition, it is very probable that the Jewish Temple or Temples, were intended to mark out this important period.

CHAPTER 6

Charles Wesley: prophetic interpreter

It has been shown in the preceding chapters that apocalyptic expectation, often reflected in highly complex readings of biblical texts, was very much alive in the period from c. AD 1550 to 1800. This expectation and the concurrent eisegetical process are found widely in the literature from the period. They are not limited to a particular religious tradition, nor are they found only among those whose intellectual integrity could be questioned. Individuals such as Goodwin, Whiston, Newton and Priestley, all able scholars, turned their hands to the task of prophetic interpretation and all used the text to suit their own individual and ever-changing ends. In the previous chapter an apparently quite strong streak of premillennial historicist eschatological expectation was noted among Methodist interpreters. The level of that expectation, and the concurrent concern with the books of Daniel and Revelation in particular, it was argued, were both widespread and more than skin deep.

In this chapter the study of the Methodist tradition is continued through a detailed examination of the eschatological views of Charles Wesley (1707–88).[1] Since, however, this is a book that is concerned primarily with the use and/or influence of biblical texts and not with the broader history of eschatological expectation in general, the focus is on his views on the correct interpretation of biblical prophecy, although some more general remarks are offered in order to sketch in the broader context of his historicist, premillennial, anti-Catholic understanding of the biblical texts. Not surprisingly the sections of the Bible that come most clearly into view in this context are the books of Daniel and the Apocalypse of St John. Charles, however, was a man well acquainted

---

[1] Some parts of this chapter first appeared in the *BJRULM* 77 (1995): 31–52, the *Wesleyan Theological Journal* 32 (1997): 85–103 and the *Proceedings of the Charles Wesley Society* 3 (1996): 33–61 under various titles. I am grateful to the editors of those journals for permission to reuse some of that material here.

with the Bible as a whole, and as a result his remarks are not limited to reflections upon those parts of the scriptures.

The evidence from Charles' works supportive of the view that premillennial, historicist eschatological expectation was a significant force in his theological world view is set out below. In this a particular attempt has been made to avoid placing undue stress upon any single period of his life. (It would, for example, be easy to amass material from the period immediately following the earthquakes of the early 1750s)[2]. Rather a general survey is here presented, in an attempt to answer the question 'What were Charles' general views regarding the interpretation of biblical prophecy?' Obviously, since his literary career lasted more than fifty years, it would be unwise to expect absolute consistency. However, it is argued here that some general picture does seem discernible in the surviving literary deposits, and that that picture is on the whole fairly self-consistent. In the period c. 1750–60 in particular there is substantial evidence to suggest that Charles' eschatological views and understanding of biblical prophecy were a very distinctive and vibrant force in his overall theological development. His views in the period before 1750 seem to have included a less obvious, but still identifiable, eschatological element. The situation in the period after 1760 is difficult to judge since much of the necessary documentary evidence is lacking.

Despite the need to be highly selective (a process which carries obvious dangers and of which the reader is here warned), an attempt has been made to give at least a broadly representative sample of the materials available. One point, however, must be made by way of disclaimer: Charles' hymns and other poetical compositions do not here receive the kind of attention they deserve. This comparative neglect is partly due to the sheer quantity of the poetical material. In part, however, it is also a deliberate attempt to highlight the indisputable value of his surviving prose materials, which, in comparison with the hymns and poems, have generally been significantly under-researched. Almost all the prose material falls into three basic categories – the journal, the letters and the sermons – and material relevant to the

---

[2] An account of the earthquake is found in John Wesley's journal for 8 March 1750 (Ward and Heizenrater, *Works of John Wesley*, vol. xx, pp. 323–4), with a briefer note on the earlier shake on 8 February (vol. xx, p. 320). Charles records on 8 February simply that 'there was an earthquake in London' (Jackson, *Journal*, vol. ii, p. 67). His journal has no entry for 8 March, but that for 10 March records how he preached on Isa. 24 'a chapter I had not taken much notice of, till this awful providence explained it' (Jackson, *Journal*, vol. ii, pp. 68–9). See also Tyerman's account of the events and their effect on the Wesleys (Tyerman, *Life and Times*, vol. ii, pp. 71–4), and that of Jackson (Thomas Jackson, *The Life of the Rev. Charles Wesley, M.A.* (2 vols., 1841), vol. i, pp. 549–56).

present discussion is found in each. (He also wrote a small number of prose pamphlets, and also tracts, but these are of little relevance in the present context).[3]

A fair number of Charles' journal entries could be explored here with profit. Some have been discussed elsewhere,[4] but to these may be added several more. For example, part of the long entry for 25 March 1736 reads:

About noon, in the midst of a violent storm of thunder and lightning, I read the eighteenth Psalm, and found it gloriously suited to my circumstances. I never felt the Scriptures as now. Now I need them, I find them all written for my instruction and comfort. At the same time I felt great joy in the expectation of our Saviour thus coming to judgement, when the secrets of all hearts shall be revealed, and God shall make my innocency as clear as the light, and my just dealing as the noon-day.[5]

The point of the passage seems plain enough: Charles has been falsely accused (of various forms of misconduct, including sexual improprieties[6]), but looks forward to the time when the Saviour will come and make the truth known. He is seeking consolation from the text and finds there words which 'gloriously' apply to his situation. His attention is turned to Psalm 18, a text which needs to be kept in mind as the journal entry is read. Ps. 18.7–10 reads:

Then the earth shook and trembled; the foundations also of the hills moved and were shaken, because he was wroth. There went up a smoke out of his nostrils, and fire out of his mouth devoured: coals were kindled by it. He bowed the heavens also, and came down: and darkness was under his feet. And he rode upon a cherub, and did fly: yea, he did fly upon the wings of the wind.

Care must of course be taken not to press the journal entry too far. However, when the passage is read in the context of the psalm to which Charles refers, his thinking seems plain enough. He thinks that the psalm relates to some event as yet distant. It is one of the many passages which he seeks to integrate into his general understanding of last-day events as he works them out from the books of Daniel and Revelation. Christ, so Charles read in this psalm, would one day return to this earth as judge, and that coming would be a literal, magisterial and terrible event.

3 See further Thomas R. Albin, 'Charles Wesley's Other Prose Writings', in ST Kimbrough (ed.), *Charles Wesley: Poet and Theologian* (Nashville, TN: Kingswood Books, 1992), pp. 91–3.
4 Kenneth G. C. Newport, 'Premillennialism in the Early Writings of Charles Wesley', *Wesleyan Theological Journal* 32 (1997): 85–103.
5 Jackson, *Journal*, vol. 1, p. 10.   6 Ibid., vol. 1, pp. 6–12.

Several further examples of this kind of eschatological hope could be given. For example, in part of the journal entry for 24 July 1743 Charles relates how he and his colleagues 'longed for his last glorious appearing, and with an eye of faith saw the Son of man, as coming in the clouds of heaven, to confess us before his father and the holy angels'.[7] The entry for 1 February 1745 might also be noted. Here Charles writes, 'At our watchnight I described the new Jerusalem; (Rev. xxi.;) and great was our rejoicing before the Lord.'[8] On 31 October 1747 he preached on 'These are they that came out of great tribulation, and washed their robes, and made them white in the blood of the Lamb' and records that 'it was a time of solemn rejoicing in hope of His coming to wipe away all tears from our eyes'.[9] This last entry is particularly illuminating for the present purposes. Charles is clearly preaching from the book of Revelation; the allusions are to Rev. 7.14 and 21.4.

Charles preached again from Revelation on July 24, 1754. He wrote 'My congregation at night was considerably increased by market-folk out of the country. I preached repentance from Rev. i. 7: "Behold, he cometh with the clouds; and every eye shall see him," &c.'[10]

It is thus quite noticeable in the journal that the book of Revelation was a source upon which Charles appears to have reflected constantly and drawn often. It is therefore perhaps not surprising to discover that he was later to write that while Luther might well say in times of trouble[11] 'Come, let us sing the forty-sixth Psalm', Charles would rather say 'Let us read the Revelation of Jesus Christ.'[12]

A number of the letters from the early part of Charles' ministry are also of importance in this context. The lengthy letter written to him by John Robertson in 1737 has already been referred to briefly in chapter 5. In this the detailed apocalyptic-exegetical scheme of Bengel is critically discussed in such a way as to suggest that Robertson knew of Charles' interest in such matters (and it should be recalled that Robertson was of the opinion that the millennium would begin on Sunday 18 June 1836). Here, then, is a letter to Charles suggestive of the recipient's apocalyptic interests. Ten years later he wrote from Dublin on 18 December (1747) to assure the recipient, Sarah Whitham, that 'Yet a little while, and he

---

[7] Jackson, *Life*, vol. I, p. 327. The references (in this typically dense tissue of scriptural allusions and echoes) are successively to Titus 2.13; Dan. 7.13 and Matt. 24.30; and Luke 12.8 and Rev. 3.5.
[8] Jackson, *Life*, vol. I, p. 393.   [9] Ibid., vol. I, p. 464.   [10] Ibid., vol. II, p. 104.
[11] The trouble in question, in Charles' case, was the severe sickness of his brother, who was 'far gone in a galloping consumption' and of whose recovery he was far from confident (Jackson, *Life*, vol. II, p. 96).
[12] Jackson, *Life*, vol. II, p. 98.

that shall come, will come, and take us all into everlasting habitations.'[13] This reference is short but to the point, and its implication unmistakable. Charles is expecting the return of the Lord in 'yet a little while'.

A few further letters from this period are worth noting. On 29 January 1750 Charles wrote to his friend Mrs Jones of Fonmon Castle, at a time when she was evidently suffering some 'fresh troubles' and afflictions. His advice, which he gives in the first line of the letter, is simple enough and linked to an expected chronological framework: 'bear up under your burthen, till the everlasting comforter comes'.[14] Also from 1750 (10 August) is a letter to one of the early Methodist preachers, John Bennet, where again his premillennial views seem plain enough: 'We see our calling', he writes, 'which is to suffer all things; disrespect and ingratitude in particular from those we serve in the Gospel. But we expect no reward, "till the great shepherd comes".' (The expression 'the great shepherd' is from Heb. 13.20, although the context there is not at all eschatological.) Only the coming of Christ, then, will bring the reward. Does Charles perhaps have in mind Matt. 16.27, 'For the Son of Man shall come in the glory of his Father with his angels; and then he shall reward every man according to his works'? On the same MS as this letter to Bennet, Charles adds a note to Bennet's wife Grace which includes the words

Fear not: in six troubles the Lord hath saved you. A little more suffering, and the end cometh, and the Lord and bridegroom of our souls.[15]

Similarly, in 1756 Charles wrote to another early Methodist, William Perronet, urging him to 'watch and pray always that you may be counted worthy to escape the judgments coming on the world, and to stand before the Son of Man',[16] words which again seem to voice a premillennialist position. The words 'watch and pray' are part of a biblical injunction which appears more than once in Charles' writings. There are several possible references; those in Mark 14.33 and Luke 21.36 seem the most likely. The exhortation to Perronet is almost verbatim Luke 21.36. However, whichever text is in view, the point of the injunction is much the same: the believer must be always vigilant since the return of Christ will occur when least expected (cf. Mark 13.35, 14.36; Matt. 24.42–3, 25.13; Luke 21.34, 36).

[13] MARC ref. DDCW 1/16. The first part of this quotes Heb. 10.37; the 'everlasting habitations' are from Luke 16.9.
[14] MARC ref. DDCW 1/32. This is a photocopy; the original is held at Glamorgan County Record Office.
[15] MARC ref. DDCW 1/37. The 'six troubles' are an allusion to Job 5.19.
[16] MARC ref. DDCW 1/15a.

The case, then, seems reasonably clear: the letters strongly suggest that in the 1740s and 1750s at least Charles' eschatology was imminent and premillennial and focused upon the reading of certain parts of scripture. This world will not get better. The end to troubles will not come in this present age and rewards should not be expected. Rather it is when 'the great shepherd comes' that rewards will be given, and at the coming of the Lord and bridegroom that troubles will cease. The main beams of the premillennial theological structure therefore seem to be in place in the letters discussed above. Things will get worse rather than better, and the end to trouble will come instantaneously with the literal advent of Christ, not gradually with the spread of Christian social-ethical standards. This letter evidence confirms and complements that gleaned from the contemporary journal entries.

By far the most important letter from Charles on this topic, however, comes from 1754. This is a letter of great significance, for it sets out the basic historicist, premillennial and anti-Catholic context of the less definite remarks found in those letters to which reference has just been made. The 1754 letter has been reproduced in its entirety in the appendix to this chapter, and should be consulted at this point. A copy of the first page is shown as figure 6. The letter is at once highly informative and annoyingly short on detail. Indeed, one of the most frustrating aspects of it is the reference in §15 to a book which Charles is either planning to write himself or expects another to publish in the near future. This planned work, it seems, will deal much more fully with the topics addressed only briefly in the letter. If the reference is to a work that Charles was planning to write himself, then it never appeared. However, even in the relatively short space of the letter a significant insight into Charles' interpretation into several key prophecies can be gained. A detailed analysis therefore follows.

The letter begins with a common enough theme. The kingdom of the Lord, says Charles, is rapidly approaching in all its fullness. It emerges in the rest of the letter that what he means by this is that the literal kingdom of God is approaching, a process which will reach its consummation in 1794. Like many before him, Charles rejects the view that the kingdom of God is merely a spiritual realm; for him it is a literal spatial kingdom which God will usher in. The day is coming when Christ himself, the Lord of hosts, shall reign in Mount Sion, and in Jerusalem (§3). Elsewhere in the letter it becomes plain that the writer was a premillennial-ist, that is, he looked forward to the appearance of Christ and the executing of the great judgement before the onset of the millennium

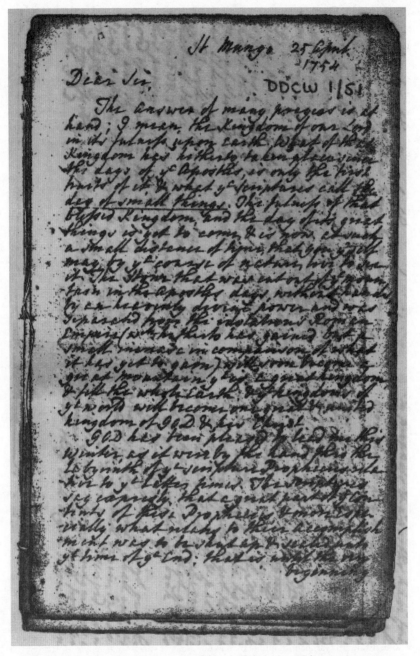

Figure 6 Front page of Charles Wesley's 1754 letter

depicted in Revelation 20. Following this appearance of Christ, the millennium, a period of 1,000 years during which Christ would reign upon earth, would begin.

The immediate reference in §1 is to the vision of Daniel 2. That chapter describes an image of a man with a head of gold, a chest of silver, loins of brass and legs of iron. The whole image is supported, rather precariously, by feet compounded of a weak mixture of iron and clay. At length, a stone, which has been cut without hands, strikes the bottom of the image and the whole statue collapses. The stone grows into a mountain and fills the whole earth.

The meaning of this vision, according to such commentators as Sir Isaac Newton, whose work Charles recommends to his reader (§15), is fairly plain. The statue represents four kingdoms: Babylon, Persia, Greece and Rome. The feet represent the divided kingdom which was to follow the fourth kingdom, namely the individual states into which the empire of Rome eventually disintegrated. The stone, which has been 'cut out without hands' (Dan. 2.34), represents the kingdom of God which will destroy the kingdoms of this world, replacing them as an everlasting kingdom.[17] This was a scheme with which Charles evidently agreed.

Charles, like some others of his day, divides the arrival of the 'kingdom of our Lord' or 'kingdom of God' into two basic phases. In the vision of Daniel 2, commentators noted, the kingdom of God arrives as a 'stone' but grows into a 'great mountain' which fills the whole earth (Dan. 2.35). Some rather naturally took this to mean that the growth of the kingdom of God was to be gradual; as the stone 'grew' into a mountain, so the kingdom of God, which arrived in its infancy with the first advent of Jesus, would eventually grow into a utopia upon earth. Others, however, argued that while the kingdom had arrived in a small measure with the first advent of Jesus, the final consummation of the kingdom would be marked by an eschatological rite of passage. The latter was the opinion of, among others, Priestley, who argued that the little stone represents the beginning of the kingdom of God, which, at its inception, was but 'inconsiderable'. However, it will become a mountain at the second advent when all empires will be overturned and 'some infinitely better state of things' be introduced in their place.[18]

A third view on Dan. 2.35, 45 is found in the works of one of Priestley's associates, Robert Edward Garnham.[19] Garnham argued

---

[17] Newton, *Observations upon the Prophecies*, pp. 24–7.   [18] Priestley, *Works*, vol. XII, pp. 309–43.
[19] Robert Edward Garnham, 'An Enquiry into the Time, at which the Kingdom of Heaven will commence', in Joseph Priestley (ed.), *Theological Repository* (6 vols., 1769–88), vol. VI, pp. 244–84.

that the stone in no way represents the kingdom established by Jesus at his first advent, for the kingdom established at that time was only spiritual and thus differs not in degree, but in kind from the kingdom that will be set up when Christ comes with power. Garnham's conception of the kingdom of God is quite clear. For him it is literal, not spiritual, and its arrival will coincide with the visible coming of the Son of Man.[20] Indeed, according to Garnham the phrase 'kingdom of God' conveys 'the uncompounded idea of the government to be set up, when he shall hereafter come in the clouds'.[21]

In this letter Charles comes close to Priestley's opinion, for it later becomes quite clear that the kingdom which he is expecting is not of a spiritual, but a literal nature and its arrival is preceded by the terrible punishments sent by God upon the unjust. It is after these climactic events, and only then, that the 'kingdoms of the world will become one great and united kingdom of GOD and his Christ' (§1 cf. Rev. 11.15).

Charles' reference to the 'idolatrous Roman Empire' (§1) and the 'Romish Antichrist' whose destruction is foretold in the prophecies (§3) similarly reflects the view widely held among eighteenth-century Protestants, and discussed extensively in chapter 3, that the Roman Catholic Church was the incarnation of Antichrist. Charles does not mention here any particular prophecies which lead him to identify Antichrist with Rome, but, as has been noted, those most commonly cited were Dan. 7.8 together with its interpretation in Dan. 7.24–5, and especially Revelation 13. Similarly, many commentators of the period identified 'the man of sin' mentioned in 2 Thess. 2.8 with the Pope.[22]

The second paragraph of the letter is of particular interest. Throughout, Charles makes it clear that he considers the days in which he is living to be the 'latter times' spoken of in scripture. For Charles, the end of the present world order is near indeed. The reference to the shutting up and sealing of the prophecies until the time of the end is again taken from Daniel, who right at the end of the book is told 'But thou, O Daniel, shut up the words and seal the book, even to the time of the end: many shall run to and fro, and knowledge shall be increased' (Dan. 12.4). Those who were living, as they believed, in this 'time of the end' naturally saw in this passage a promise that at this time the contents of the book of Daniel, together with those of Revelation, were to become plain to those who were wise (Dan. 12.10). The knowledge that was to be

[20] Ibid., p. 253.   [21] Ibid., p. 245.
[22] See, for example, G. Benson, *A Dissertation on 2 Thess II:1–12 in which 'tis Shewn that the Bishop of Rome is the Man of Sin . . .* (1748).

increased is knowledge of the book of Daniel. Charles is clearly of this opinion, for he says later in the letter that neither Newton nor Mede, skilled as they were in interpreting the prophecies, could really gain an accurate insight into all truth since God's time, for the unsealing of the book had not come in their lifetimes. The time has now come, however, and a full knowledge of the prophecies is therefore possible. This had been said before Charles, and it was to be said again after him (see especially the work of William Miller, discussed in the next chapter). Indeed, it is generally the case that interpreters of the prophecies imagine that they are living in the closing stages of the world's history and that this being the case, they alone may witness the unsealing of Daniel's book.

Charles here is perhaps reiterating also another fairly common theme: the identification of Daniel's book with the 'scroll' of Revelation 5. In that chapter we read of a book which has seven seals and the question is asked 'Who is worthy to open the book, and to loose the seals thereof?' (Rev. 5.2). The only one judged worthy is 'the Lion of the tribe of Juda, the Root of David' (Rev. 5.5; cf. Charles' remark that the prophecies have been open to 'unworthy me'). Christ, then, can open the sealed book of Daniel and reveal the mystery of its prophecies. Newton certainly identified Daniel and the scroll, stating that 'John *saw, in the right hand of him that sat upon the throne, a book written within and on the backside, sealed with seven seals, viz.* the book which *Daniel* was commanded to seal up'.[23] This may have been Charles' thinking also. The description of Christ as the one who has the key of David is from Rev. 3.7; the reference to the one 'who shuts so as no man can open, and opens so as no man can shut' is from Isa. 22.22 (cf. Rev. 3.8). Charles, then, is in confident mood here; it is to him that the secrets of the prophecies have been revealed. Living as he does in the 'time of the end', he may now gain full knowledge.

In the final words of §2 there comes a most remarkable statement. Not only has the nature of the prophecies been revealed to Charles, but even the time of their accomplishment. This is not a remark to be passed over lightly, for it goes beyond a mere statement that the last days have arrived. Charles' timing of last-day events was unusually precise. The conversion and restoration of the Jews to their own land would take place in about 1761 (§4). About the year 1771 or 1772 they will have 'an Anointed Prince of their own over them' (§14). They will be invaded in

23 Newton, *Observations*, p. 259. Italic in the original.

their own land and 'their prince be cut off and their city and sanctuary once more demolished' in about 1777 (§14), and the end of all things will come in 1794 (§14). Such precise date fixing is not unique, but it is unusual.

The catena of events listed in §3 outlines Charles' expectations for the future. Like many of his contemporaries, he thought that before the end could come, the Jews must first be converted to Christianity. This expectation was based in part upon the numerous predictions found in the Old Testament relating to God's final gathering of dispersed Israel (e.g. Deut. 30.1–5; Isa. 11.11–12).[24] But perhaps most importantly of all, Paul, the great apostle to the Gentiles, clearly expected that the Jews would one day be restored to their rightful place as God's people; this is the point of Romans 9–11. Indeed, given that Charles here mentions also the 'the inbringing of the fulness of the Gentiles', it seems that he may well have had his eye on Rom. 11.25–6.

Charles links the predicted restoration of the Jewish people with another prophecy which stated that one day the Jewish sanctuary would be restored (Dan. 8.14). This 'cleansing' of the sanctuary Charles understood quite literally; the 'sanctuary' was not, as some others had argued, the earth which would be 'cleansed' at the great eschaton (the view that William Miller was later to take), but the literal rebuilt sanctuary in Jerusalem. Charles predicts that this event will take place in the year 1761 or 1762.

That the Pope and his minions were Antichrist was almost a given among Charles' contemporary Protestant interpreters. Antichrist's days were, however, numbered and again Charles predicts the final destruction of this evil beast with precision: Antichrist will fall in the year 1794. The basis of this calculation is examined below.

In the second half of §3 Charles refers to 'that long and blessed Period when peace, righteousness and felicity, are to flourish over the whole earth'. It is at this time that 'Christ the Lord of hosts shall reign in Mount Sion, and in Jerusalem and before his Elders gloriously'. The 'long and blessed period' is surely the millennium, the period of peace and joy which was the hope of many (cf. Revelation 20).

Charles' apocalyptic vision of the future is thus outlined in §3 and over the course of the rest of the letter he fleshes out this skeletal frame. The millennial reign of Christ is coming, but before that event God's judgement must be poured out on the unrighteous. Chief of all sinners is

---

[24] See, for example, the comments on these texts made by Priestley (*Works*, vol. XI, p. 296; vol. XII, p. 164).

the mystical 'Babylon' of Revelation 17 *et passim* (§5, 9). This 'Babylon' was no other than Rome, the great Antichrist himself. However, Charles warns, the destruction of Babylon is not quite yet, and before it does come, she must gain the full measure of her increase (§1) and 'distress the Protestant Churches by wars and persecutions' (§6). But the faithful need not fear, for despite such afflictions, which might even include a martyr's death, they will be 'made white' by God (§6–7; cf. Rev. 3.4, 7.14).

Charles looks again to the book of Revelation for information concerning the nature of the judgements. He is not clear on how long this period of judgement and punishment is to last, although he does know that the period will end in the year 1794. He says also that the judgements will have begun by 1761 at the latest (§8).

The judgements themselves consist of the events outlined in the seven trumpets and seven vials of Revelation. The first six of the seven trumpets are found in Revelation 8–9 and the seventh in 11.15. The blowing of these seven trumpets announces the coming of various calamities upon the earth. At the blowing of the first trumpet, for example, hail, fire and blood rain down upon the earth; when the second trumpet is blown a great mountain burning with fire is cast into the sea and a third of the sea is turned into blood. The next two trumpets continue in this vein, but worse is yet to come, for when the fifth angel blows, a pit is opened and monstrous creatures, half locust, half scorpion, swarm out across the earth stinging men as they go. The sixth trumpet issues forth an army of 200,000,000 horsemen of terrible appearance. As far as we can tell, for Charles these terrible events were all still in the future and part of the awful judgements and punishments that God was to send upon the earth. His interpretation of the trumpets is somewhat unusual, for the norm among writers of the period was to interpret them symbolically. Further, most commentators located the trumpets, at least the first six of them, in the past. So, for example, Priestley thinks that the first trumpet represents the invasion of the Goths under Alaric in 395; the second the coming of the Vandals (with Burgundians and Alans) c. 407–55 etc. The locusts are the Saracens under Mahomet and the period of 'five months' mentioned is from c. 612 to 762 (i.e. 150 day/years; Priestley shares the standard year/day view).[25]

The seven vials (Revelation 15–16) are no less terrible, though Charles draws some comfort from the fact that Rev. 16.2 suggests to him that the first vial is poured out upon 'the men which had the mark of the beast, and upon them which worshipped his image'. Further, in Rev. 17.1 it is said that one of the seven angels who had the vials came over and talked to John and showed him 'the judgement of the great whore'. This 'great whore' is Babylon, that is, to Charles, Rome. Charles is therefore inclined to think that at least the first six of the seven last plagues are designed mainly as a punishment to be inflicted upon Rome and her followers. Charles' reference to the 'mark of the beast' is taken from Rev. 13.16, though quite what he understood this mark to be is not clear. However, the beast is surely Rome.

Charles does not expect that the righteous will be immune from all the terrible things that come upon the earth during the final judgements, but rather that they will be tried and refined by the experience. They will come through it victorious.

But let not them who fear GOD and tremble at his word be afraid beyond measure of these days of judgement which are coming, for many are the promises scattered up and down the word of GOD, for their encouragement. Yea, they will be sealed in their foreheads, with the seal of the living GOD, so that the preternatural judgements will scarsely, if at all, be allowed to touch them; and as to the natural ones of famine, sword and pestilence, they will only be allowed to touch the people of GOD so far as may be for their vastly greater good. (§11)

It is not surprising given the nature of these terrible events that many will perish. Indeed, Charles is expecting that some 'two thirds of the whole number of mankind on the face of the earth will be cut off' (§10). The one-third that remains is a mixed group: some, though they suffer now, are destined for salvation, while others are to be destroyed.

Those destined for final salvation are, then, among the one-third still alive at the end of the sixth plague. The seventh plague is, however, different from the rest and none can survive it. It is the sending of hail made up of stones each weighing 'a talent' (Rev. 16.17–21). It is in this passage that we meet the phrase 'the cup of the wine of the fierceness of his wrath' which is given to Babylon as mentioned by Charles in §5. From this final plague none can escape, and hence those who are to be saved are spared its fury. It is not only for the beast and his followers, but 'extends to the wicked in general over the whole earth' (§8).

Before the outpouring of this last judgement, then, God will intervene directly to save his own. His angels will take them away to a place of safety. In support of this claim Charles refers to what he considers the complementary prophecy of Jesus in Luke 18.26 (*sic:* he is actually referring to Luke 17.34ff.). According to this text there will come a time when some of the population will simply disappear; there will be two men in one bed, one shall be taken, the other left. There will be two men at work in the field, one shall be taken the other left. There will be two women at the mill, one shall be taken, the other left. Charles integrates this into his vision of the end. During the course of the first phase of the last judgements (the seven trumpets and the first six vials) two-thirds of humankind shall perish. Of the one-third that is left, some are destined for salvation and these will be taken by God before the concluding part of the judgement, the outpouring of the seventh vial, is begun. This rescue or 'rapture' of the righteous is accomplished by angels 'whom GOD will send forth to gather his elect from the 4 corners of the earth, unto a place of safety on the earth, where he will provide for them' (§10).

The drama is almost complete. The final destruction, which is to be accomplished by the seventh plague, now takes place. Babylon, Antichrist, is destroyed. The millennium, 'that long and blessed Period when peace, righteousness and felicity, are to flourish over the whole earth' (§1), may now begin and 'Christ the Lord of hosts shall reign in Mount Sion, and in Jerusalem and before his Elders gloriously' (§1).

Enough has now been said to indicate that this letter is a work of some significance. It gives us a glimpse of an aspect of Charles' thought that has hitherto received only slight attention.[26] Perhaps the most interesting aspect of the letter is, however, not the predictions of the abovementioned events themselves, but the way in which Charles sets about calculating when they are to take place. He is prepared to set precise dates, and the methodology he employs to set them is highly unusual.

It is clear from the letter that Charles had been interested in date setting for some time. He refers back to 1746, in which year, he says, he had begun to study the prophecies and had come close to the truth. However, it was only in 1754, on 21 March of that year to be precise, that the full picture had come to him, and by the time he wrote the letter a little over a month later his confidence is obvious:

The numbers and periods mentioned in Daniel and the Revelation, when rightly understood and compared together, do point out the time when these

---

[26] The only substantial study of Charles Wesley's eschatology is Downes, 'Eschatological Doctrines'. Downes is more concerned with John than with Charles, and did not have access to the letter under consideration here. Consequently his treatment of Charles' eschatology is limited and, in places, inaccurate (e.g. his remark, p. 125, that Charles rejected date setting absolutely).

things shall be fully accomplished, so as it may be calculated without hazard, and without erring above a year or so. (§11).

It is unfortunate that Charles does not say a little more about the methods he employed to arrive at his apocalyptic timetable, for there is much in the letter that is left unclear. However, he himself warns in §12 that 'I can only now just give you a glimpse of the first step of the calculation, without giving you the proofs.' Nevertheless, the thinking which lies behind some of what is said in the letter is relatively easy to track down.

The clearest prophetic date in the letter is the year 1794, the date given for 'the accomplishment of all these things' (§13 cf. §4). Charles arrives at this date in a highly unusual way. The basis of the prediction is Dan. 12.6–7, a verse near the very end of Daniel, where we read of two men standing on either side of a river. One man says to the other 'how long shall it be to the end of these wonders?', to which the other replies 'it shall be for a time, times and half a time'. For Charles this statement is crucial. Daniel's vision of the entire course of world history is almost completed, and the question 'how long shall it be to the end of these wonders?' is, for Charles, a question about the end of the present world order.

If Charles is to figure out when the prophecy of the time, times and half a time ends, and thus know the date for 'the accomplishment of all these things', he must have two pieces of information: he must know when the period begins and how long it is to last. It is the first of these problems that prevented his full understanding of the prophecies before 21 March 1754 (§12), but he now understands that the period begins in 538 BC. He states:

I am able to shew that the scriptures do expressly point out the first year thereof to have been the year 538 before the first of the Christian Aera, being the first year of Darius the Mede, who was made king over the realm of the Chaldeans. (§13)

This date is probably taken from Dan. 11.1–2, which introduces the vision of which Dan. 12.7 is a part. Alternatively, since Charles links the vision of the seventy weeks in Daniel 9 with the 'time, times and half a time' of Daniel 12, he may have taken the reference to the 'first year of Darius the Mede' from Dan. 9.1. In either case the conclusion is the same: the period begins in 538 BC. The start of the period, then, is known to Charles, but what is the meaning of the 'time, times and half a time'?

Charles' understanding of the phrase is extremely interesting, for he takes the unusual (though not unknown) step of linking the phrase to the number of the beast mentioned in Rev. 13.18.[27] He writes:

The first step then toward the finding out the time fixed by scripture for the accomplishment of all these things is the observing that the number 666, assigned Revelation 13.18 for determining the time of the final destruction of the Beast, hath a relation to the *time*, *times* and *half a* time, assigned in Dan. 12 for bringing all the events spoken of in that and the preceeding chapters, to an accomplishment. (§13)

It was Charles' view that a 'time' is equal to 666 years and that a 'time, times and half a time' is therefore 2,331 years (§13). The end of this period will mark 'the end of these wonders', that is, the end of the present world order.

Charles now has both pieces of the puzzle: the period begins in 538 BC and lasts for 2,331 years. The answer to the question 'how long shall it be to the end of these wonders?' asked by the man in Dan. 12.6 has, for Charles, been deciphered; the end will come in 1794. Charles has left a little room for doubt since he says that the years 'may be calculated without hazard, and without erring above a year or so' (§11), but he expects the end by 1795 at the very latest.

The date 1794 is thus firmly fixed as the point at which the judgements will end and the period of great peace begin; the reason for Charles' adoption of this date, even if imaginative, is nevertheless relatively clear. A second date, 1762, is also reasonably easy to pin down, though again there may be an error of not more than one year. This is the date mentioned by Charles in §4 where he states that 'the conversion of the Jews and their restoration to their own land, [shall be] within the short space of seven or eight years time'. Charles arrives at it on the basis of Dan. 8.14, 'unto two thousand and three hundred days; then shall the sanctuary be cleansed'. This period, says Charles, begins in 538 BC (§14). He is of course working on the basis of the year-day principle, and hence the period of 2,300 days is understood by him (as it was later by William Miller) as 2,300 literal years. Working on this assumption and knowing as he does that the starting point for the 2,300 days/years is in 538 BC, Charles must therefore have calculated that the period came to an end

---

[27] It is quite possible, perhaps even probable, that Charles has drawn here from the works of Bengel, who similarly linked the number 666 to the 'time, times and half a time' period. Bengel's reasoning is ingenious, and involves an interpretation which is a good deal more complex than the relatively simple one proposed by Charles. A summary of Bengel's views may be found in Brady, *Number of the Beast*, pp. 218–21.

in 1762. This ties in with his 'seven or eight years time' statement in §4. It is in this year that the 'sanctuary', apparently taken by Charles as a literal sanctuary which is to be restored by the converted Jews in their own land, will be cleansed. Again, his thinking is fairly plain. The Jews will be converted and restore the sanctuary in about 1761. The end of all things will come in 1794.

The dates 1794 and 1761 are, then, relatively clear. From this point on, however, things become less plain. Charles has obviously given attention to the seventy-week prophecy in Dan. 9.24–7, and it is this prophecy which underlies his remarks in the first half of §14. The prophecy reads:

Seventy weeks are determined upon thy people and upon thy holy city, to finish the transgression, and to make an end of sins, and to make reconciliation for iniquity, and to bring in everlasting righteousness, and to seal up the vision and prophecy, and to anoint the most Holy. Know therefore and understand, that from the going forth of the commandment to restore and to build Jerusalem unto the Messiah the Prince shall be seven weeks, and threescore and two weeks: the street shall be built again, and the wall, even in troublous times. And after threescore and two weeks shall Messiah be cut off, but not for himself: and the people of the prince that shall come shall destroy the city and the sanctuary; and the end thereof shall be with a flood, and unto the end of the war desolations are determined. And he shall confirm the covenant with many for one week: and in the midst of the week he shall cause the sacrifice and the oblation to cease, and for the overspreading of abominations he shall make it desolate, even until the consummation, and that determined shall be poured upon the desolate.

It was generally accepted by commentators of the period that this was a prophecy relating to the incarnation of Christ. Details varied, but the thrust of this majority opinion was that the seventy weeks were to be calculated as 490 years (the year-day principle being once again invoked). The 'Prince' mentioned in the prophecy is Jesus, and the prophecy relates to the period of his incarnation. The 'going forth of the commandment to restore and to build Jerusalem' takes place c. 457 BC and ends in c. AD 34 with the crucifixion. Newton, for example, adopts this scheme.[28] Another view was that the seventy weeks ended with the destruction of Jerusalem in AD 70. It was at this time, so commentators argued, that the seventy weeks determined for 'thy [Daniel's] people' finally came to an end. This view was taken by, among others, the highly influential Joseph Mede.[29] Charles' interpretation, however, is quite

---

[28] Newton, *Observations*, pp. 128–43.
[29] Joseph Mede, *Daniel's Weekes. An Interpretation of Part of the Prophecy of Daniel* (1643). It is also argued for by Richard Parry in his *An Attempt to Demonstrate the Messiahship of Jesus from the Prophetic History and Chronology of the Messiah's Kingdom in Daniel* (1773).

unusual. He proposes that the prophecy is related to the end time, and not to the time of the incarnation. Unfortunately he does not say much in this letter relating to how he has interpreted this prophecy and no pattern is immediately obvious. The only part of Charles' interpretation that does seem plain is that he has taken the 'one week' during which the Prince confirms the covenant with many as a period of seven years from c. 1771 to 1778. How the rest of the prophecy fits together in Charles' mind is far from clear. However, it seems relatively certain that he took the unusual views that the seventy-week prophecy relates to the events surrounding the second and not the first advent, and that the 'Prince' mentioned in the prophecy is someone other than Christ.[30]

The remainder of the letter seeks to encourage the reader to engage in an independent study of the prophecies. The promised book mentioned at the beginning of §15 (if indeed it was one that Charles planned to write himself) never appeared. The references to Newton and Mede have been explained, though it is worth pointing out that there is much in their works that Charles disagrees with in this letter. The reference to Fletcher's work is less clear. This cannot be the John Fletcher of Madeley, whose role in early Methodism was briefly commented on in the previous chapter, since it appears that the Fletcher in question is already dead. Who this other Fletcher may be is unknown, and the work 'Fulfilling of the scriptures' has so far proved untraceable.

In the very last paragraph the sectarian note is very noticeable. Charles turns this time to Malachi 3, seeing in the reference to a special group which God would preserve when all else is reduced to stubble for burning a reference to those who are of 'the concert for prayer for the coming of the Kingdom of Christ'. This little group, he says, will be preserved during the last judgements. The picture we are left with is of a small band of faithful believers miraculously saved by God just before the final destruction of the wicked.

This letter from 1754 is, then, quite detailed and indicates that on several key points Charles takes an unusual, at times unique, line in his interpretation of biblical prophecy. This is especially apparent in his understanding of the number 666 and its link to the 'time, times and half a time'. His conviction that the whole of Daniel 9 relates to the eschatological events and not to the incarnation is also relatively uncommon,

---

[30] Priestley also argued that the 'Prince' in Dan. 9.25 is someone other than Jesus; see *Works*, vol. ii, p. 368, vol. xii, pp. 438–41; vol. xx, pp. 230–1; cf. Clarke Garrett, *Respectable Folly: Millenarians and the French Revolution in England and France* (Baltimore: The Johns Hopkins University Press, 1975), p. 132.

as is his apparent identification of 'the Prince' of Dan. 9.25 as someone other than Jesus. His view that the Seven Trumpets are still in the future is also at variance from the norm. Neither is the clear premillennialism in this letter typical of the age, for, as was discussed in the introductory chapter, the more common view during this period was that Christ would return only after the millennial period of 1,000 years. The letter is therefore of importance not only in that it gives us a picture of Charles that has seldom before come into view, but also in that it demonstrates his imaginative freedom from the norms of prophetic interpretation. The letter provides good insights into his mind regarding the interpretation of Daniel and the Revelation in particular. Here again we see someone whose intellectual ability is unquestionable engaging in what would appear to many as nothing more than wild, perhaps even irrational, speculation. However, Charles' views on the prophecies, while they may look odd to the modern-day academic, would clearly have made sense to his own contemporaries. Some Protestants (and presumably all Catholics) of the eighteenth century would no doubt have wished to challenge him on a number of key points. However, his basic historicist reading of the relevant texts would have raised little question. He reflects and works within the basic paradigm of his day.

In addition to this highly informative letter, there are several other sources that deserve attention, for example Charles' sermons. Assessing the evidence of the surviving sermon corpus is, however, rather difficult. This problematic situation is partly the result of the confusion that surrounds the sermon MSS. A collection of twelve sermons attributed to Charles was edited (anonymously) and published in 1816,[31] but it is now clear that at least seven of these were not in fact written by him, but were copies made from his brother's MSS.[32] On the other hand, two of Charles' sermons are found in John Wesley's works, and of these only one, that on Eph. 5.14,[33] is clearly labelled as being by Charles. (The other is 'The Cause and Cure of Earthquakes', which will be considered

[31] *Sermons by the Late Rev. Charles Wesley, A.M. Student of Christ-Church, Oxford. With a Memoir of the Author, by the Editor* (London, 1816).

[32] See Richard P. Heitzenrater, 'John Wesley's Earliest Sermons', *Proceedings of the Wesley Historical Society* 37 (1969–70), pp. 112–13.

[33] 'A sermon preached on Sunday, April 4th, 1742, before the University of Oxford. By Charles Wesley, M.A., Student of Christ Church' (London, n.d.). The second edition indicates that it was printed by W. Strahan in 1742. It was included as sermon 3 in John Wesley's *Sermons on Several Occasions* from the 1746 edition of volume I onwards (*Sermons on Several Occasions. In Three Volumes. By John Wesley M.A., Fellow of Lincoln College, Oxford. Vol. 1* (London, 1746)) and is reprinted in Albert C. Outler (ed.), *The Works of John Wesley*, vols. I–IV (Nashville, TN: Abingdon, 1984–7), vol. 1, pp. 142–58.

below.) In addition, several other MS sermons have fairly recently come to light. The six shorthand sermons are now well known;[34] some few other MSS, including one completely unpublished sermon on John 4.41, have, however, received less attention. This is not the place to discuss in detail these problems of authorship and authenticity.[35] However, in this corpus there is material that seems to be of direct relevance here.

In a sermon either preached, written, or both on 21 October 1735,[36] for example, Charles several times urges his hearers to 'watch and pray', but does not finish the quotation, though its context is significant ('... for you know not the hour in which your Lord cometh'; cf. Mark 13.35; Matt. 24.42–3; Luke 21.36 etc.). In one passage, however, his thinking does emerge. The relevant section reads:

Caution and watchfulness is a necessary characteristic of a true Xtian. It is enjoined by our blessed Lord himself frequently to his disciples, and by them the obligation to it extended to all mankind; 'what I say unto you I say unto all, watch'. None you see excepted from the duty, no excuse can be urged for not performing it. Watch therefore for the coming of your Lord, for you know neither the day nor hour of his coming. 'Let your loins be girded, your lamps burning and ye yourselves like unto men that watch for their Lord that they may be ready to enter in with him when he cometh. For blessed are those servants whom his Lord when he cometh shall find so doing.'[37]

Such words seem fairly plain. Charles has picked up a number of biblical passages and woven them together into a statement on the need for constant vigilance in the light of eschatological expectation. In what is the only Charles Wesley sermon in fairly wide circulation, that on Eph. 5.14, he makes a number of similar remarks. Indeed, the theme of

---

[34] Oliver A. Beckerlegge and Thomas R. Albin, *Charles Wesley's Earliest Evangelical Sermons: Six Shorthand Manuscript Sermons Now for the First Time Transcribed from the Original* (Ilford: Wesley Historical Society, 1987).

[35] For a full discussion see Kenneth G. C. Newport, *The Sermons of Charles Wesley: A Critical Edition with an Introduction and Notes* (Oxford: Oxford University Press, forthcoming), chapter 4.

[36] The sermon is printed as number 11 in the 1816 edition (pp. 186–206). The MS of this sermon (which has been edited significantly in the 1816 edition) is now held in the MARC, ref. cw Box v. As noted briefly above, it is difficult to assess the probability that this sermon was composed by Charles himself. Thomas Albin, for example, thinks that the case is 'exceedingly weak' (Albin, 'Charles Wesley's Other Prose Writings'), arguing that the only evidence is that the MS is in Charles' own hand. However, this evidence is surely not to be ignored. The fact that Charles took care to indicate (in Byrom's shorthand) that he had copied some of the sermons from his brother, or some other unspecified source (as is the case with a sermon on Luke 16.8 (MARC ref. cw Box v; printed in Outler, *Works*, vol. iv, pp. 361–70)), suggests that, evidence to the contrary being lacking, those that are not specifically said to be copies are original compositions.

[37] I have used the original here (MARC ref. cw Box v). The form in the 1816 edition is a little different (pp. 196–7). The direct scripture quotations are from Mark 13.37 and Luke 12.35–7; the reference between them is to Mark 13.32 and its parallels.

judgement runs throughout the sermon as he calls the sinner to awaken. Elaborating on the message of John the Baptist, Charles warns those who disregard 'the warning voice of God "to flee from the wrath to come"'.[38] Elsewhere in the sermon the threat of the coming judgement hangs heavy. Towards the end of the sermon Charles is speaking of the deplorable condition into which mankind has slipped and the need for Christians to rise above it. It is in this context that he warns, in language soaked through with biblical allusions,

And 'shall not I visit for these things?' saith the Lord. 'Shall not my soul be avenged on a nation such as this?' Yea, we know not how soon he may say to the sword, 'Sword, go though this land!' He hath given us long space to repent. He lets us alone this year also. But he warns and awakens us by thunder. His judgements are abroad in the earth. And we have all reason to expect that heaviest of all, even 'that he should come unto us quickly, and remove our candlestick out of its place, except we repent and do the first works'.[39]

And the whole sermon is rounded off with a passage which begins with the words

My brethren, it is high time for us to awake out of sleep; before 'the great trumpet of the Lord be blown', and our land become a field of blood. O may we speedily see the things that make for our peace, before they are hid from our eyes! 'Turn thou us, O good Lord, and let thine anger cease from us.' 'O Lord, look down from heaven, behold and visit this vine'; and cause us to know the time of our visitation.[40]

Taken together and within the more general context of the sermon as a whole and especially in the light of the materials from other sources that have been noted, these passages from 'Awake thou that sleepest' provide an interesting insight into Charles' expectations. This world, for Charles, was not set to improve with a gradual spreading of the kingdom of God through the preaching and acceptance of the gospel. Rather the future has a definite apocalyptic climax which will itself bring the age to a close. Things are bad and will get worse. Even professed Christians are slipping into perdition unawares. But though the Lord has spared the earth 'this year also' (Luke 13.8), the space to repent is getting ever smaller. Indeed, the time will come when 'the things that make for our peace' will be hidden and it will be too late. Then the Lord will say

[38] Outler, *Works*, vol. I, p. 143. The quotation is taken from Matt. 3.7 and parallel.
[39] Outler, *Works*, vol. I, pp. 157–8. The scripture references are successively to Jer. 5.9 (=Jer. 5.29; 9.9); Ezek. 14.17; Luke 13.8; 1 Chr. 16.14; and Rev. 2.5.
[40] Outler, *Works*, vol. I, p. 158. The scripture references are successively to Rom. 13.11; Isa. 27.13; Matt. 27.8; Luke 19.42; Ps. 85.4; Ps. 80.14; and Luke 19.44.

'Sword, go though this land.' The 'wrath to come' will have come and unpleasant indeed will it be for those who have not fled from it. While the whole eschatological scheme is not spelt out in detail in this sermon, the general picture is distinctly and unmistakably premillennial.

Charles' sermon on earthquakes also needs brief mention here.[41] The earthquakes which hit London in 1750 gave rise to a general upsurge in warnings of impending apocalyptic doom, and Charles was not alone in seeing in them the hand of God and the fulfilment of biblical prophecy.[42] Throughout this sermon there is a noticeable air of typically premillennial pessimism regarding the short-term future of the world and humankind. Charles issues a call for repentance before it is too late:

> In the name of the Lord Jesus, I warn thee once more, as a watchman over the house of Israel, to flee from the wrath to come! I put thee in remembrance (if thou hast so soon forgotten it) of the late awful judgement, whereby God shook thee over the mouth of hell![43]

> He hath spared thee for this very thing; that thine eyes might see his salvation. Whatever judgements come in these latter days, yet whosoever shall call on the name of the Lord Jesus shall be delivered.[44]

With regard to Charles' preaching, there is one further scrap of information to be considered. The full content of the sermon which Thomas Illingworth heard him preach in October 1756 is unknown. However, Illingworth's report is worth noting. He writes:

> He [Charles Wesley] spoke much concerning the end of the World, telling us the Signs foretold were so fully accomplish'd as demonstratively shew'd its Dissolution near.[45]

The sermon evidence, then, in so far as it can be reconstructed from the small amount of homiletic material that has survived, seems to point in the same direction as the journals and letters. Charles, it seems,

---

[41] This sermon was printed in *Works of John Wesley* (1872), vol. vii, pp. 386–99.
[42] Brief details of this eighteenth-century interest are found in Outler, *Works*, vol. i, p. 357 n. 6.
[43] *Works of John Wesley*, vol. vii, pp. 397–8. The scripture allusion is to Ezek. 3.17 (= 33.7).
[44] *Works of John Wesley*, vol. vii, p. 399. The scripture allusion is to Luke 2.30.
[45] As quoted in Frank Baker, *William Grimshaw 1708–1763* (London: Epworth Press, 1963), p. 195. Cf. Charles' journal entries for October 1756, many of which could be quoted here with profit. On 7–9 October, for example, he appears to have spoken several times to different audiences on Luke 21 (the apocalyptic discourse) and concluded 'I have no doubt but they will be counted worthy to escape, and to stand before the Son of Man' (cf. Luke 21.36). Later on 9 October he warned his audience of the 'impending storm'. On 10 October, he wrote, 'between four and five thousand were left to receive my warning from Luke xxi' and later he judged those to whom he spoke to be 'like men prepared to meet the Lord'. The remainder of the journal continues in this vein right up to the last few entries.

expected the coming of the judgements of God in the not too distant future. He frequently appeals to scripture in support of this, and even more frequently uses biblical language to express it. In the light of the 1754 letter these other materials come together to give a picture of an individual concerned with the fulfilment of biblical prophecies in his own day.

In this chapter some of the evidence has been presented which supports the suggestion that Charles' views regarding the end of the world were definite, reasonably consistent, and historicist-premillennial. Charles was concerned with the interpretation of biblical prophecy, especially Daniel and the Revelation; however, as has been seen throughout, he was thoroughly acquainted with the biblical text, and it is no surprise to find him reflecting quite widely on passages which were not commonly used in an eschatological context. Thus in support of his premillennial vision he quotes from passages such as Psa. 18, Heb. 10.37 and Titus 2 as well as the more common texts. Often, of course, it is difficult in Charles' work to distinguish between his use of biblical language and his understanding of the actual biblical text. However, even allowing for a margin of error in the attempt that has been made here to disentangle the these two aspects of the prose writings, the overall picture that has emerged is a fairly consistent one and, when it is seen in the context of the 1754 letter, some unity of thought becomes apparent.

Charles' premillennial historicist interest in the biblical texts was not a passing one. Rather, the evidence from the journal and the letters suggests that his concern in this area is discernible from an early stage and ran throughout the course of his documented career. While there does seem to have been something of an increase in the height of expectation in the 1750s (perhaps explained by the earthquakes), Charles was interested in such matters well before that time. We know for certain that he had been attempting to interpret 'the scripture prophecies' since at least 1746 because he says so in the 1754 letter. He writes:

The first time I began to attempt the scripture calculations relating to the conversion of the Jews, the fall of Antichrist and the introduction of the fulness of the Gentiles was in the year 1746. And having made myself master of an antient Chronology, I did then make such calculations as happened become pretty near to what I now find to be the truth.

Further, the 1754 letter itself suggests that he had spent considerable time in his attempt to interpret the prophecies; he speaks of other prophetic interpreters, whose works he has evidently read, and seems to have been acquainted even with the highly influential, and highly complex, prophetic scheme proposed by Bengel. In 1754, then, his interest is fairly intense.

This study could have been extended. For example, it would have been very easy to have peppered this chapter with references to some of Charles' 9000 or so hymns and other poetical compositions, several of which confirm what has become apparent from the prose material: 'Lo he comes with clouds descending'[46] and 'He comes! He Comes! the judge severe'[47] are relatively well known and the view of 'the end' expressed in them is clear. Similar is 'Lift your heads, ye friends of Jesus', which is worth quoting as one among many possible further examples.[48] Allusions to the book of Revelation are woven throughout.

> 1. Lift your heads, ye friends of Jesus,
> Partners in his patience here,
> Christ to all believers precious,
> Lord of Lords, shall soon appear:
> Mark the tokens
> Of his heavenly kingdom near!
>
> 2. Hear all nature's groans proclaiming
> Nature's swift-approaching doom!
> War and pestilence and famine
> Signify the wrath to come;
> Cleaves the centre,
> Nations rush into the tomb.
>
> 3. Close behind the tribulation
> Of these last tremendous days,
> See the flaming revelation,
> See the universal blaze!
> Earth and heaven
> Melt before the judge's face!
>
> 4. Sun and moon are both confounded,
> Darken'd into endless night,
> When with angel-hosts surrounded,
> In his Father's glory bright
> Beams the saviour,
> Shines the everlasting light.

---

[46] Osborn, *Poetical Works*, vol. VI, pp. 143–4.   [47] Ibid., vol. VI, p. 141.
[48] Ibid., vol. VI, pp. 144–5.

5. See the stars from heaven falling;
Hark on earth the doleful cry,
Men on rocks and mountains calling,
While the frowning judge draws nigh,
Hide us, hide us
Rocks and mountains from his eye!

6. With what different exclamation
Shall the saints his banner see!
By the monuments of his passion,
By the marks received for *me*
All discern him,
All with shouts cry out, 'Tis he!

7. Lo! 'tis he! our heart's desire
Come for his espoused below,
Come to join us with his choir,
Come to make our joys o'erflow:
Palms of victory,
Crowns of glory to bestow.

8. Yes, the prize shall now be given,
We his open face shall see;
Love, the earnest of our heaven,
Love our full reward shall be,
Love shall crown us
Kings through all eternity.

It is also worth noting that Charles was well able to argue a distinctive case. For example, his interpretation of the mystical number 666 and his view that the 'Prince' of Dan. 9.25ff. was someone other than Jesus are quite unusual. As one follows Charles along his exegetical pathways one is aware that he was well conversant with the prophetic-exegetical thinking of his day. In places his exegesis is unusual, even novel. He can appeal to standard eighteenth-century exegetical logic in support of his views and not religious sentiment, and the reader of the 1754 letter is asked not so much to hear the whisper in the heart as to discern with the eye of reason the self-evident, logically derived truth on the basis of the exegesis that Charles has presented. However, while Charles' own interests and concerns were unique and while he was able to develop his thinking in ways which were quite novel, it is once again quite plain that the dominant Protestant-historicist anti-Catholic eisegetical paradigm is operative.

Charles Wesley was a man of significant intellectual ability and great poetical skill, a skill almost unmatched in the area of specifically religious verse. He was a man esteemed by his peers; he enjoyed significant status, had a happy marriage and was relatively well to do. His work on biblical prophecy needs to be seen in this light. These are not the ravings of an apocalyptic fanatic or the cries of the marginalised or underprivileged. The dominance of the Protestant historicist paradigm was such, however, that even Charles fell under its influence and reflected it throughout his work. This paradigm included the year-day principle, armed with which Charles was able to ascertain the very year of the end (and we have noted just how mathematically ingenious he was on this specific issue). It included also the view that Antichrist had his incarnation in the Roman Catholic Church. Charles too reflects that anti-Catholic stance.

Quite how he would have dealt with the non-arrival of the kingdom in 1794 cannot be known, for he died some six years previously. William Miller, however, the subject of the next chapter, did not escape by death the inglorious non-fulfilment of his apocalyptic predictions and, as Miller discovered, living in the afterglow of a failed prophecy is not a happy experience.

APPENDIX: LETTER OF CHARLES WESLEY TO AN UNKNOWN CORRESPONDENT[49]

St Mungo, 25 April 1754[50]

Dear Sir

1   The answer of many prayers is at hand; I mean the kingdom of our Lord in its fulness upon earth. What of that Kingdom has hitherto taken place since the days of the Apostles, is only the first fruits of it, and what the scriptures call *the day of small things*.[51] The fulness of that blessed kingdom, and the day of its great things, is yet to come, and is now at such a small distance of time that you yourself may, by the course of nature, live to see it. The stone that was cut out of the mountain[52] in the Apostles' days, without hands, by an heavenly divine power and was separated from the idolatrous Roman Empire (which hitherto has gained but a small increase in comparison of what it has yet to gain) will soon become a great mountain, that is a great kingdom and fill the whole Earth; and the kingdoms of the world will become one great and united kingdom of GOD and his Christ.[53]

---

49 Spelling, punctuation and italic are reproduced without alteration.
50 The reference to 'St Mungo' is problematic, for it is not apparent where this place was.
51 Zech. 4.10.   52 Cf. Dan. 2.45.   53 Cf. Rev. 11.15.

2 GOD has been pleased to lead me this winter, as it were by the hand, thro the labyrinth of the scripture Prophecies relative to the latter times. The scriptures say expressly that a great part of the contents of these Prophecies, and more especially what relates to their accomplishment, was to be shut up and sealed unto the time of the end; that is, until the very beginning of those days when they are to be fulfilled. And now these days are begun. He who hath the key of David, who shuts so as no man can open, and opens so as no man can shut,[54] hath taken off the seals, and opened to unworthy me in a very great, tho' not yet in a full, measure, not only the nature of these awful and glorious events which the scriptures say are to be brought to pass in the latter times, but also the very times which the scriptures point out for their accomplishment.

3 As for the events themselves it is only proper at this time to mention in general, that they are the conversion of GOD's antient people the Jews, their restoration to their own land; the destruction of the Romish Antichrist and of all the other adversaries of Christ's kingdom; the inbringing of the fulness of the Gentiles, and the beginning of that long and blessed Period when peace, righteousness and felicity, are to flourish over the whole earth. Then Christ the Lord of hosts shall reign in Mount Sion, and in Jerusalem and before his Elders gloriously.

4 It will appear a Paradox to affirm that all these events will be accomplished in FORTY years time counted from this present year 1754; and the first and second of them, viz the conversion of the Jews and their restoration to their own land, within the short space of seven or eight years time; but what with men is impossible, is both possible and easy with GOD.

5 But O! dreadful days that are coming on the earth before the last of the above mentioned events, I mean before the long and blessed period take place. There is a long train of dreadful judgements coming on the earth, more dreadful that ever it yet beheld; more especially upon these nations, upon whom Christ's name is called, for their neglect and contempt of his glorious gospel. And above all, Babylon shall have her double cup, and be made drunk with the wine of the fierceness of the wrath of GOD as his holy prophets and apostles foretold long ago.[55]

6 Howbeit, before she shall be brought to her final Ruin, power shall be given her to distress the Protestant Churches by wars and persecutions, and many of Christ's faithful ones in those days shall be tried and purified and made white.[56]

7 O the blessed meaning of that expression *made white*! It means no less than that in these trying times they shall be enabled to stand with firmness and constancy to the cause of Christ and the testimony of his word; and shall be honoured to die the martyr's death and get the martyr's Crown and those white robes and palms mentioned in the book of the *Revelation*[57] and be made partakers of that glorious reward which the same inspired book calls the First Resurrection.

---

[54] Rev. 3.7.   [55] Cf. Rev. 16.19 and 18.6.   [56] Dan. 12.10.   [57] Rev. 7.9.

8   The Scriptures point out the time when the judgements shall end and when the blessed days shall begin, but do not, so far as I have yet observed, point out the precise year when the judgements are to commence; only it is clear from scripture that they will begin before the end of SEVEN years hence. And tho' they should commence this very year, it woud be no way inconsistent with the scripture-prophecies, but when once they are begun, they will go on in a continued train of one judgement on the back of another, till the end of the FORTY years, counting from this present year. Wars, famine and pestilence shall be but the beginning of sorrows;[58] for besides and on the back of all these, shall follow all the woes contained under the Seven Trumpets[59] and Seven Vials;[60] only that the Vials (the last excepted which extends to the wicked in general over the whole earth) seem chiefly, if not only, for the beast and his followers.

9   The whole prophecies relating to the latter times, (which make up by far the largest part of the prophetical books of the Old Testament), are full of judgements which are to be executed upon the earth in these days, and of the blessings which are to be poured forth upon the earth and its inhabitants, and more especially upon GOD's antient people, when once these judgements are over: and when that people are to be made blessed themselves, all the nations of the earth are at the same time to be blessed in them, and along with them, in their national capacity. Read over the prophets once more and you will find them full of the judgements and blessings that are to be poured forth in the latter times; and you will be led at the same time to take notice that generally there is some passage or circumstance which points out the judgement to be about the time of the deliverance of GOD's antient people. The year of his redeemed, the day of his great wrath, and the year of his recompense for the Controversy of Sion,[61] and the destruction of Babylon, go together; and the blessings are to be made good at that time when Israel's Light is come, and the glory of the Lord arisen upon them. Then, say the scriptures, shall the Gentiles come to Israel's Light and kings to the brightness of their rising.[62] And the Apostle expressly says, that GOD's receiving again of the Jewish people shall bring the world and its inhabitants, as it were, life from the dead.[63]

10 But to return to the judgements: the scriptures expressly say that by these judgements which are coming on, two thirds of the whole number of mankind on the face of the earth will be cut off, and that a third part will be made to escape and will be refined as silver and be tried as gold is tried.[64] Yet the last judgement that is to be executed on the earth in these times shall be of such a dreadful and extraordinary nature, that none can escape being cut off by it, but by the preternatural assistance of angels, whom GOD will send forth to gather his elect from the 4 corners of the earth,[65] unto a place of safety on the earth, where he will provide for them. And where that place is to be is also expressly mentioned in scripture, and then shall be

---

[58] Cf. Matt. 24.8.   [59] Rev. 8.2 *et passim*.   [60] Rev. 15.7 *et passim*.   [61] Isa. 34.8.
[62] Cf. Isa. 60.1–3.   [63] Cf. Rom. 11.15.   [64] Cf. Zech. 13.9.   [65] Cf. Rev. 7.1.

fulfilled that word of the Lord Luk. 18.26 etc, that two men shall be in one bed, the one shall be taken and the other left; and the one shall be taken to a place of safety by the angels of GOD, and the other left to destruction. And two women shall be grinding together at the same mill, and in like manner, the one shall be taken and the other left; and two men shall be working together in the field, at one and the same work, the one shall be taken and the other left.

11 But let not them who fear GOD and tremble at his word be afraid beyond measure of these days of judgement which are coming, for many are the promises scattered up and down the word of GOD, for their encouragement. Yea, they will be sealed in their foreheads,[66] with the seal of the living GOD, so that the preternatural judgements will scarsely, if at all, be allowed to touch them; and as to the natural ones of famine, sword and pestilence, they will only be allowed to touch the people of GOD so far as may be for their vastly greater good. The 46 and 91 Psalms are intended in a particular manner for the comfort of GOD's people in these times. Let them also comfort themselves in this, that the days of judgement, distressful as they are, yet are nothing when compared with the long and glorious period of universal peace, righteousness and blessedness which is to follow immediately on the back of the judgements. And as by the oeconomy of nature, silver cannot be brought out of ore, but by means of the furnace, so by oeconomy of Providence, the day of blessedness cannot be brought about, but by the means of the preceeding days of judgement. 'Tis quite vain and inconsistent with the word of GOD, to expect the blessings to be poured forth upon the earth in any other shape. The numbers and periods mentioned in Daniel and the Revelation, when rightly understood and compared together, do point out the time when these things shall be fully accomplished, so as it may be calculated without hazard, and without erring above a year or so.

12 The first time I began to attempt the scripture calculations relating to the conversion of the Jews, the fall of Antichrist and the introduction of the fulness of the Gentiles was in the year 1746. And having made myself master of an antient Chronology, I did then make such calculations as happened to become pretty near to what I now find to be the truth: but I afterward saw that my then calculations could not be depended upon, because I did not then observe any scriptures which seemed to fix the year from whence any of the periods assigned in Daniel, or in the Revelations, were to be computed. However, by means of these calculations, and by the predictions of some good men, I was impressed with a notion that these events were at no great distance of time. But on the 21 of March last, after I had by an accurate examination of in the scripture prophecies, both of the Old and New Testament, been enabled to penetrate into the nature of the great and awful events that are to be brought about in the latter days, I was enabled also to penetrate into the passages of scripture, which determine

[66] Cf. Rev. 7.3.

the time of their fulfilment. I can only now just give you a glimpse of the first step of the calculation, without giving you the proofs.

13   The first step then toward the finding out the time fixed by scripture for the accomplishment of all these things is the observing that the number 666, assigned Revelation 13.18 for determining the time of the final destruction of the Beast, hath a relation to the *time*, *times* and *half time*, assigned in Dan. 12 for bringing all the events spoken of in that and the preceeding chapters, to an accomplishment, and particularly, for the bringing the end of Antichrist spoken of in the end of the last verse of the 11 chapter; and the final deliverance of the Jews spoken of the 1 and 7 verse of chapter 12. And so the said period of *time* and *times* and *half* a time is made up of 666 – 666 – 666 – 333 amounting in all to 2331 years, concerning which 2331 years I am able to shew that the scriptures do expressly point out the first year thereof to have been the year 538 before the first of the Christian Aera, being the first year of Darius the Mede, who was made king over the realm of the Chaldeans.

14   I am also able to produce another concurring Prophecy which assigns the same number of years and divides them into different parts, from which Division it appears that the Jews will have returned to their own land, and have an Anointed Prince of their own over them about the year 1771 or 1772; that they will be invaded in their own land and their Prince cut off and their city and sanctuary once more demolished, about the year 1777 or 1778; that they, as well as the whole people of Xt, will remain under a Cloud for a time. But all will be brought to rights again by the pouring forth of the last plagues on the adversaries of Christ, and at length by that total final Destruction which the Prophet calls *The great day of* GOD's wrath[67] about the year 1794. Herewith also concurs the prophecy in Dan. 8.14, which foretells that the Jewish sanctuary is to be cleansed (or justified, as in the Hebrew) that it shall be made fit for divine service at the end of 2300 years, which I am able to shew commences from the same year before Christ 538, being the first year of the Mede-Chaldean or Mede-Persian monarchy prophecied of in that same 8 chapter of Daniel under the vision of the Ram which had two horns, viz the Medean and Chaldean empires and whose higher horn, the Chaldean, came up last.

15   What I have now hinted is only a small part of the scripture-evidences relating to the subject, which you must be content with till the book comes out. Meantime let me commend to you to read over again Fletcher's Fulfilling of the scriptures, and remark the places referred to[†]. Let me also recommend to you to look into the passages of Sir Isaac Newton on Daniel and the Revelations[+], and into Mead's commentary on the Revelations[‡], both of whom come very near the truth. And the only thing that hindered them from penetrating more thoroughly into it, was because GOD's time for taking off the seals was not fully come; but had any of these three men been alive at this day, they might in the Divine Providence have made it plain.

[67] Rev. 6.17.

16 Show this to any who have been of the concert for prayer for the coming of the Kingdom of Christ. I am well assured in my own mind that that very Society, tho' not the only persons, yet are among the persons especially pointed at by the Spirit in those remarkable words [in] Malachi 3.16–17: 'Then they that feared the Lord, spoke often one to another, and the Lord hearkened, and heard it, and a book of remembrance (i.e. a register) was written before him for them that feared the Lord, and that thought on his name, and they shall be mine, saith the Lord of hosts, in that day when I make up my jewels (i.e. my special treasure or my peculiar and proper people) and I will spare them as a man spareth his own son that serveth him.' The time when he will more especially spare them is mentioned in the beginning of the 4 chapter: 'For behold the day cometh that shall burn as an oven and all the proud and all that do wickedly shall be as stubble, and the day that cometh shall burn them up, saith the Lord of hosts, that it shall leave [them neither root nor branch]'.

† Edit 1671. p. 29, 32–38, 122–125, 190, 193, 194, 354, 360, 371, 513, 514
⁺ The 8th edit. 1733 p. 12, 15, 247–251 also p. 245, 246
‡ On chap 20 [shorthand note][68]

[68] The meaning of this brief shorthand note is unclear.

CHAPTER 7

William Miller, the book of Daniel and the end of the world

The studies so far presented in this book have been focused primarily, though not quite exclusively, upon the interpretation of the book of Revelation, and upon literature produced and/or published in England during the period c. 1550 to 1800. In the last three chapters, however, the focus changes. The most obvious shift is geographical, for attention is now turned from England to North America. However, there is also a chronological shift. In the present chapter the period 1830–44 comes particularly into focus, while in the following two the eisegetical trajectory of one particular millennial movement, the Seventh-day Adventist Church, together with one of its offshoots (the Shepherd's Rod/ Davidians/Branch Davidians) is traced through the latter half of the nineteenth and into the twentieth century.

In this chapter there is also a shift in textual focus. As we have seen, the books of Daniel and Revelation often go together in millennial eisegesis, and numerous commentators wrote works dealing with both.[1] This same integration is seen also in the work of William Miller, but the most revealing insight into Miller's hermeneutic can be gained by focusing upon his understanding of the book of Daniel. It is primarily from his work on that book, and specifically Daniel 7–9, that he came to the view that Jesus was to return to this earth in 1843 (later adjusted to 1844) – though he did think that the date could be deduced also from the book of Revelation and even, in part, from Luke 13.32.[2] In this chapter, then, it is the book of Daniel rather than Revelation which takes centre stage.

---

[1] E.g. Newton, *Observations*; R. Clark, *A Warning to the World; or the Prophetical Numbers of Daniel and John Calculated* (1759).
[2] See further Arasola, *The End of Historicism*, p. 220; Miller's own summary of his 'Time Proved in Fifteen Ways' (1843) has been reproduced in Arasola, *The End of Historicism*, pp. 222–5 and earlier in Steen Raabjerg Rasmussen, 'Roots of the Prophetic Hermeneutic of William Miller', MA thesis, Newbold College, Bracknell, Berkshire (1983), pp. 96–103.

The shift in geographical, chronological and textual focus evident in these final chapters in part demonstrates that the process of eisegesis is not confined by boundaries: nineteenth-century American Protestants or twentieth-century 'sectarians'[3] can be no less skilled in the art than sixteenth-century continental Catholics or eighteenth-century English Methodists. This shift also demonstrates again, through the use of the extreme example of Waco, that the afterlife of a biblical text is not always positive. The genesis of the Waco tragedy can be traced back through the Shepherd's Rod movement into Seventh-day Adventism and to Millerism itself. Some of that story is told here.

Given the focus of this book the emphasis is, of course, upon Miller's eisegetical trajectory, though the element of continuity between Miller, Seventh-day Adventism and the Branch Davidians will also be demonstrated in other ways. Perhaps most importantly the Waco chapter, for which both this present one and the next are essential preludes, also demonstrates again the importance of the study of eisegesis as a way into the thought world of others. An appreciation of the centrality of the book of Revelation (and other parts of the Bible) in the thought world of Koresh and the Branch Davidians was fundamentally missing during those fateful days in early 1993, and it is the suggestion here that had an attempt been made to enter into that thought world, a less disastrous outcome to the Waco stand-off might been possible. The study of eisegesis might have had very real benefits.

While this chapter is a prelude to that on Waco, it is nevertheless important in its own right. Once again in the case of Miller there will be cause to note just how malleable a text, this time the book of Daniel, becomes in the hands of a determined eisegete. Miller's interpretation of the book of Daniel was highly imaginative, but also, it must be said, very clearly and logically set out. From the perspective of the modern critical reader it is plain that the text of Daniel has had imposed upon it an eisegetical structure that is quite foreign to the original intention of the author(s).[4] However, when one reads Miller on his own terms, this scarcely appears to be the case. His is a careful analysis of the text from a

---

3 The word 'sect' is used here in the way defined by Rodney Stark and William Sims Bainbridge, *The Future of Religion: Secularization, Revival, Cult Formation* (Berkeley: University of California Press, 1985), pp. 24–5, i.e. to refer to a group which has split off from another. No negative connotation is implied.

4 While most scholars would accept that the book was composed in the wake of the events of c. 167–164 BC, many would argue that some of the material, especially that found in chapters 1–6, comes from an earlier period. See, for example, Louis F. Hartmann and Alexander A. di Lella, *The Book of Daniel*, Anchor Bible, vol. 23 (New York: Doubleday & Co., 1977), p. 13.

traditional Protestant historicist perspective, and seen in this context it is a masterpiece of eisegetical reasoning. It is only as one appreciates that reasoning and follows Miller through his very carefully worked out scheme that the phenomenon of Millerism can be understood.

This chapter therefore demonstrates again, using a different text, a different interpreter and a different cultural context, the way in which the millennial mind works with the biblical material. It demonstrates also the importance of the study of eisegesis as a way into the thought world of individuals such as Miller. It is also noted in this chapter that the treatment of this text by Miller did lead, for some at least, to unfortunate results, 'The Great Disappointment' and its aftermath, of which more will be said below. Millerism's negative legacy was not on the same scale as that of the Branch Davidianism of Koresh; neither was it as widespread as the anti-Catholicism to which attention has already been paid in chapter 3. Nevertheless, the eisegesis of Miller and his followers clearly did not result in only good effects.

On Wednesday 16 October 1844 *The Advent Herald*, a weekly newspaper published as a medium for the propagation of the belief that the Lord was soon to return to this earth, printed the following statement:

As the date of the present number of the *Herald* is our last of publication before the tenth day of the seventh month, we shall make no provision for issuing a paper for the week following . . . We feel called upon to suspend our labors and await the result.[5]

This statement is startling in the confidence with which it gives voice to the advent hope: no plans need to be in place for the issuing of the paper on 23 October 1844, since before that day arrives, the Lord himself will have come in glorious majesty to redeem his own and inaugurate the perfect millennial age. To the editor and many of the readers of the *Advent Herald* this hope was not a distant dream: it would happen next Tuesday.

It was in accordance with this same premillennial advent hope that Henry B. Bear made ready:

I got rid of all my money except eighty dollars; this I laid on the table, in our house; locked up the house, and gave the key to our neighbor, (a tenant in my father's house, near by,) to give to some of my folks. We now left, as we believed, never to return to that house: and went to one of the advent believers about

---

5 *The Advent Herald*, 16 October 1844, p. 81 (as quoted in Francis D. Nichol, *The Midnight Cry: A Defense of William Miller and the Millerites* (Washington, DC: Review and Herald Publishing Association, 1944), p. 243). The reference to the seventh month will be examined below.

three miles distant, where all the Millerites had agreed to meet and await the coming of the Lord within twenty-four hours.[6]

Bear's account relates to the build-up to the lesser disappointment of 22 September 1844, a date upon which some Millerites expected Jesus to return. When this failed to occur, hope was refocused on 22 October 1844, the date upon which the majority expectation was centred. This was the position taken by Bear himself, who states 'My idea then was, that if the time was not correct as to September, it would be the more certain to come in October.'[7]

Bear's hopes, like those of the editor of the *Advent Herald*, even if misguided, had real substance.[8] His millennial hope determined his actions, and Bear gave up his worldly possessions in the firm belief that the Lord would do what he had (as the Millerites thought) revealed in scripture. For Bear the future was bright, for history was moving unalterably towards its predetermined and premillennial goal. What were the riches of this world when compared to those of the world which was shortly to come?

Bear was not the only one who gave up his wealth, believing, and acting upon the belief, that this age was soon to disappear and be replaced by the glorious millennial reign of Christ. Contemporary newspapers report believers throwing money in the streets, and while some of the details of these stories may be challenged (journalistic imbalance in favour of the more extreme is not a modern phenomenon), they doubtless carry a substance of truth.[9] Similarly, the case records of

---

[6] Henry B. Bear, *Henry B. Bear's Advent-Experiences* (Whitewater, OH: n.d) as reprinted in Ronald L. Numbers and Jonathan M. Butler (eds.), *The Disappointed: Millerism and Millenarianism in the Nineteenth Century* (Bloomington and Indianapolis: Indiana University Press, 1987), pp. 217–26, 220.

[7] Numbers and Butler, *The Disappointed*, p. 220.

[8] It was the same kind of very real belief that, according to some accounts, drove a Mr Shortridge to climb up, and subsequently to fall from, an apple tree on 22 October in an effort to meet the Lord marginally sooner. The story of Mr Shortridge's arboreal endeavours is much discussed in the literature dealing with the connection between Millerism and madness, and it is probably now impossible to get at the truth. The original story printed in the *New York Observer* suggested that he had died of a broken neck when he fell to the ground after leaping heavenward from an apple tree. A series of further letters on the incident were forthcoming, including some reportedly from Mr Shortridge himself making no reference to his death – a circumstance which, the editor of the *New York Daily Tribune* reasonably enough remarked, 'could hardly have escaped his notice' (Nichol, *Midnight Cry*, p. 378). The story ranks alongside those about the ascension robes as one of the principal pieces of evidence for the connection between Millerism and madness. According to this latter story the Millerites dressed themselves in white robes (the commonest versions of the story say, made of muslin) in preparation for their ascension to join the Lord. See further Nichol, *Midnight Cry*, pp. 370–426, who argues with some plausibility against the truth of these and other stories, although allowance must be made for the fact that his stated aim is to defend Miller and his followers from charges such as these.

[9] Nichol, *Midnight Cry*, pp. 322–3.

two Millerite patients in the Utica State Lunatic Asylum report that the abnormal behaviour they exhibited included the reckless spending and giving away of money, actions which might normally be classed as manic.[10] However, in the circumstances such actions were entirely understandable. They represented the logical conclusion of the belief that the present world order was shortly to come to a close and the final hopes of Christianity were about to be realised with the glorious return of Christ. As another Millerite, Hiram Edson, put it:

[W]e confidently expected to see Jesus Christ and all the holy angels with him; and that his voice would call up Abraham, Isaac and Jacob, and all the ancient worthies, and near and dear friends which had been torn from us by death, and that our trials and sufferings with our earthly pilgrimage would close, and we should be caught up to meet our coming Lord to be forever with him to inhabit the bright golden mansions in the golden home city prepared for the redeemed.[11]

Edson, Bear and all their Millerite co-believers (and there may have been as many as 50,000 of them)[12] were of course disappointed: Jesus did not return on 22 October as expected. The scale of that disappointment is, like the hope which undergirded it, difficult for the outsider to grasp. The quotation from Hiram Edson continues:

Our expectations were raised high, and thus we looked for our coming Lord until the clock tolled 12 at midnight. The day had then passed and our disappointment became a certainty. Our fondest hopes and expectations were blasted, and such a spirit of weeping came over us as I never experienced before. It seemed that the loss of all earthly friends could have been no comparison. We wept, and wept, till the day dawn.[13]

The anticlimax of 23 October 1844 was the culmination of the work of William Miller (1782–1849), a New England farmer turned prophetic interpreter, who had come to the belief that the visible, apocalyptic return of Christ to this earth was to take place on 22 October 1844. This date was not the only one that Miller had set, but it was the one upon

[10] Ronald L. Numbers and Janet S. Numbers, 'Millerism and Madness: A Study of "Religious Insanity" in Nineteenth-Century America', in Numbers and Butler, *The Disappointed*, pp. 92–117, 103.

[11] Hiram Edson, undated MS fragment. As printed in Numbers and Butler, *The Disappointed*, p. 215.

[12] David L. Rowe, 'Millerites: A Shadow Portrait', in Numbers and Butler (eds.), *The Disappointed*, p. 7. Rowe is commenting on the work of Nichol (*Midnight Cry*, p. 204), but states that his own work on the Millerites in upstate New York (*Thunder and Trumpets: Millerites and Religious Dissent in Upstate New York, 1800–1850* (Chico, CA: Scholars Press, 1985)) is broadly supportive of Nichol's estimates.

[13] Numbers and Butler, *The Disappointed*, p. 215.

which the hopes of his followers became most prominently centred. Thus while the Millerite movement was able to survive intact the earlier disappointments of March and September 1844, this final prophetic failure fragmented the movement beyond all possible repair. It is true that a number of other religious movements, some of them, as will be seen, very significant, were to arise from the Millerite ashes, but with the dawn of 23 October came the simple and unavoidable conclusion that Miller himself had been wrong. Millerite hopes had been dashed and their expectations left unfulfilled. Consequently Miller and his movement lost all credibility and the relatively small Advent Christian group that continued to hold to his teachings, with, of course, the necessary abandonment of the precise date for the Lord's return, was but a pale reflection of what Millerism had once been.

It would of course be easy to dismiss Miller and his followers as, at best, holy fools, and such an interpretation of the movement has been voiced before. Indeed, it was largely this kind of understanding of them that inspired Nichol to write his defence of the movement, *The Midnight Cry*.[14] However, for the academic researcher such an interpretation is scarcely adequate, for it fails to grasp the integrity of the system when seen from the point of view of the individual Millerite believer, and lacks proper historical and cultural sensitivity. In fact, in common with the views of so many of the commentators already noted, William Miller's prophetic interpretative scheme did not lack clarity or logical persuasiveness, given the presuppositions upon which it is based. Miller, who once described the Bible as a 'feast of reason',[15] can in no way be charged with incoherent religious ranting. What he had to say was entirely coherent, though in order to grasp his arguments an attempt must be made, difficult as this process might be for the average (i.e. non-fundamentalist) twentieth-century reader, to take into account his broader history-of-eisegesis framework. It is only in the context of that framework that the connections between Miller's evidence (i.e. his proof texts) and the deductions he made from it can be seen. Similarly, it is only as he is seen within in the context of nineteenth-century American religion, with its enthusiasm, supernaturalism and biblical authoritarianism, that a rounded picture of the Millerite movement can be gained. As Nichol has observed,[16] it is all too easy to take out the old family photographs and snigger at the strange clothing and hairstyles of

[14] See also 'Millerism and Madness', in Numbers and Butler, *The Disappointed*, pp. 92–117.
[15] William Miller, *William Miller's Apology and Defence* (Boston, MA 1848), p. 6.
[16] Nichol, *Midnight Cry*, p. 288.

one's grandparents; but the photograph is a window on a world which was not strange to those who lived in it. As has been shown, Miller's hope was vivid and real and had very practical consequences. Further, Millerism's trajectories have made a lasting, if modest, contribution to the development of American (and indeed world) religious history. For several reasons, then, Miller deserves to be studied and what he had to say needs to be carefully analysed rather than summarily dismissed.

At the outset of this chapter it was emphasised that the remainder of this book deals with interpretations generated in a period and context which is quite different from that of chapters 2–6. This is certainly not to say, however, that there is a lack of continuity in the basic eisegetical paradigm. It is not necessary to enter here into a fully detailed discussion of the extent to which the kind of interpretation explored in previous chapters was exported to nineteenth-century America and found its way into the work of William Miller. Suffice it to say that the approach to the biblical-prophetic literature already sketched out did continue in Britain up to the end of the eighteenth century and into the nineteenth. Protestant historicism was also a significant factor in America during the early years of the nineteenth century (though there was during this period on both sides of the Atlantic a shift towards postmillennial interpretations). Here too the Bible continued to be seen as literally true and accurate in all that it said, and this included the portion of the scriptures which contained 'things which must shortly come to pass' (Rev. 1.1) and those which related to 'the time of the end' (Dan. 8.17). The historical-critical approach to scripture, which insists that the Bible must be seen in its own historical and cultural context, had scarcely emerged, and where it did exist was largely the preserve of a small number of mainly German academics. In any case, despite his undoubted learning, most of it self-taught, Miller can hardly be described as an academic; he was probably not even aware of, let alone influenced by, the emerging criticism of a few European biblical scholars.

The exact extent to which Miller was influenced directly by interpreters such as Mede, Brightman, Newton, Priestley or Gill is debated, but Rasmussen in particular has argued the case at some length that he was.[17] A case for Miller's dependence upon the classic Protestant historicist tradition can certainly be made. The argument has three strands. First, the presence and availability of historicist works in America during

---

[17] Rasmussen, 'Prophetic Hermeneutic', *passim*; see especially the summaries on pp. 2–3 and pp. 85–8.

the period in which Miller was active; second, Miller's own statements regarding his acquaintance with the tradition; and third, the many examples of substantial overlap in both method and detail between Miller and those who had gone before him. Only the second of these is reasonably water-tight since the first assumes that Miller read the available literature and the third that parallel schemes cannot emerge independently. Neither of these is unquestionably the case. However, the cumulative effect of these three strands of argument does amount to something more than the balance of probability.

Reprints of a number of the standard historicist works on Daniel and Revelation were produced in America during the period that saw Miller's most formative work.[18] These include works by Thomas Newton, Adam Clarke and Joseph Priestley, whose contributions to historicism have been mentioned in previous chapters. In addition Miller would have been able to access, had he wished to do so, the widely distributed work of William Jenks (1788–1866), whose *Comprehensive Commentary on the Holy Bible* (1834–8) was openly dependent upon much of the traditional British historicist exegesis and reprinted sections of it.[19] That Miller knew such works and, it seems, others of a similar persuasion on matters prophetic is seen in a remark he made to his follower Joshua V. Himes (1805–95) in a letter dated 10 November 1844: 'And, even to this day', wrote Miller, 'my opposers have not been able to show wherein I have departed from any rule laid down by our old standard Protestant writers.'[20] Even allowing for the fact that Miller is here on the defensive (the letter comes not quite three weeks after the Great Disappointment), the implication is clear: Miller had read the 'standard Protestant' works, which, given those that were available to him and taking into account the context in which he wrote, must have included the historicism of Mede, Newton, Gill, Priestley et al.

Perhaps the most persuasive argument in favour of Miller's dependence upon the Protestant historicist tradition, however, is the actual content of his work, which has an entirely historicist flavour throughout. All the standards of the genre are in place. As will be seen in the detailed analysis which follows, the year-day principle was the backbone of Miller's understanding of Dan 8.14 and the means by which he arrived at his date for the return of Christ. He argued also that the Pope/Roman Catholic Church is Antichrist and that the 1,260 days (years) are

[18] For details see Froom, *Prophetic Faith*, vol. IV, pp. 108–33, 392–5. [19] Ibid., vol. IV, pp. 125–6.
[20] Letter of William Miller to Joshua V. Himes, 10 November 1844, published in Sylvester Bliss, *Memoirs of William Miller* (1853), pp. 277–8.

the length of his rule.[21] The 'two witnesses' of Rev. 11.3 are, according to Miller, the Old and New Testaments, which testify of Christ down through the ages, including the 1,260 years of Antichrist.[22] The statue of Daniel 2, says Miller, in common with his Protestant historicist forebears, outlines the history of world empires from Babylon (head) through Medo-Persia (breast and arms), Greece (belly and thighs) and Rome (legs).[23] Further parallels are too numerous to mention but will be obvious to anyone who reads Miller's work.

It is of course theoretically possible that Miller developed this entire system without recourse to the standard Protestant works of the earlier centuries; but it is hardly likely. And as Rasmussen has noted (following Harrison), it is not the detail as such that is important, but the basic historicist methodology that runs throughout.[24] In the adoption of this methodology, if not in all the individual results it threw up, Miller was treading a very well-worn path.

Miller, then, came at Daniel (and indeed the rest of scripture) as an historicist. He also came at it as a pre- rather than a postmillennialist, and the strongly premillennial stance he adopted continued beyond the failure of his precise dating of the coming of Christ. (It must be noted, however, that not all Millerites showed the total lack of social concern which characterised most premillenialism.[25]) This premillennialism is again something that Miller may have imbibed via the standard Protestant-historicist tradition. Harrison has argued already that it was predominantly from Britain that the premillennial historicist reading of Daniel and Revelation was exported to the United States of America.[26] It is perhaps not surprising, then, given this combination of historicism and premillennialism, that Miller, and indeed some other American interpreters, sought to get at least a rough idea of when Christ would return. Perhaps the day and the hour are hidden to all but the Father (cf. Matt. 24.36), but the year or at the very least the decade or century might be known. The Millerites were relatively unusual in setting so

---

[21] William Miller, *Evidences from Scripture and History of the Second Coming of Christ about the year A. D. 1843, and of His Personal Reign of 1000 Years* (Brandon: Vermont Telegraph Office, 1833), pp. 33–4 (p. 34 is misnumbered as '31' in the original).

[22] Ibid., p. 44.   [23] Ibid., p. 7.

[24] Rasmussen, 'Prophetic Hermeneutic', p. 86; Harrison, *Second Coming*, p. 195.

[25] See Ronald D. Graybill, 'The Abolitionist–Millerite Connection', in Numbers and Butler, *The Disappointed*, pp. 139–52. The appendix to the next chapter illustrates the abolitionist concern of one of Miller's early followers. The Seventh-day Adventist Church today continues to be involved in humanitarian activity ranging from health care to education and disaster relief.

[26] Harrison, *Second Coming*, pp. 163–206. See also Froom, *Prophetic Faith*, vol. IV, pp. 387–403 *et passim*.

precise a date, though by no means unique.[27] However, in the basic exercise of seeking to discern the signs of the times (cf. Matt. 24.32–3) they were in good and multitudinous company among their predecessors and contemporaries. 'The Revelation of Jesus Christ' promises to show 'to his servants what must soon take place' and 'what must take place after this' (Rev. 1.1; 4.1),[28] and Daniel too contains a series of visions which stretch down to 'the time of the end' (Dan. 12.9). If, therefore, the Bible is literally and timelessly true, as Miller and his contemporaries thought, an examination of the relevant prophecies might well reveal God's plans for the future and give at least a rough indication of the time of Christ's glorious return.

It was, then, with this basic premillennial, historicist understanding that Miller approached the Bible. His interpretative scheme is detailed indeed, and was expounded in numerous writings over a lengthy period. Kai Arasola's work, *The End of Historicism*, cites and discusses many of these writings. An extract from the one already quoted, *Evidences from Scripture and History of the Second Coming of Christ*, is given as an appendix to this chapter, and could profitably be read at this juncture. It demonstrates at once the detail, the intended integrity, and the imaginative leaps with which Miller approached his task.

Given the volume of Miller's writings, considerable space, much more than is available here, would need to be set aside for a complete unpacking of his theories. However, one text in particular, Dan. 8.13–14, holds the key to the 1844 date, and a good insight into his thinking can be gained by an examination of his remarks on those two verses. The verses read:

Then I heard one saint speaking, and another saint said unto that certain *saint* which spake, How long *shall be* the vision *concerning* the daily *sacrifice*, and the transgression of desolation, to give both the sanctuary and the host to be trodden under foot? And he said unto me, Unto two thousand and three hundred days; then shall the sanctuary be cleansed.

It was this text which, for Miller, held the key to the discernment of the future and the hope of a better world to come. As Miller understood them, the verses did not relate to any event in the lifetime of Daniel, and

---

[27] For example, chapter 5 noted the views of George Bell, who thought that Christ would return on 28 February 1763.

[28] It was often argued that Revelation 1–3 was a description and prophecy of events contemporaneous with or chronologically immediate to John's own time. With Rev. 4.1, however, so it was argued, a new section began which charted the subsequent history of the Christian Church down through the ages.

still less to any event in the period of the Maccabees. Rather, they related to the question of the end of time itself. The complex eisegetical web woven by Miller in order to relate this text to the end of time cannot be entered into in any detail here. However, it may be noted that the contents of Daniel 8 clearly overlap with the contents of Daniel 12, and that this latter chapter does claim to address the question of the events of the last days when 'many of them that sleep in the dust of the earth shall awake' (Dan. 12.2; cf. 1 Thess. 4.16).

In Miller's interpretation, the text indicates that after 2,300 'days' the 'sanctuary' (which he understood as the earth) would be 'cleansed'. That is to say, after 2,300 'days' Christ would return to the earth to set things finally aright. Miller was convinced not only that the Bible made sense, but also that that sense was deducible through the application of a clearly set out series of exegetical rules, of which he worked out fourteen.[29] He therefore determined to ascertain from this statement in Dan. 8.14 and related biblical statements[30] the time of Christ's (premillennial) coming. His conclusion was that Christ would return in 1843, a date which he and his followers later amended to 1844 – March, September and finally October. Much of the remainder of Miller's life was given over to propagation of this advent message. Even after the Great Disappointment of 1844 he continued to hold on to the hope that the end was near.

The stages by which Miller came to his views on the dating of Christ's return were several. As we have seen repeatedly throughout this book, it was almost universally accepted among Protestant scholars that a 'day' in prophetic time periods should be understood as a literal year. For Miller, then, there would be a time gap of 2300 years from a particular event after which Christ would return. This provided the timescale and potentially a date for the second advent. All that was left to be done was to pinpoint the event from which the 2,300 days were to last, and this he did by reference to Dan. 9.24–5.

Miller spent at least two years working out his basic hypothesis and another twenty-six years fine-tuning it.[31] It is therefore no surprise to

[29] Arasola, *The End of Historicism*, pp. 51–3.
[30] In addition to Dan. 8.14 Miller found some fourteen other 'proofs' of this date for the Lord's return or other events related to the prophetic timetable. These included such standard views as the 6,000 + 1,000-year cycle reflecting the seven days of creation. A summary can be found in chart form in Arasola, *The End of Historicism*, p. 220.
[31] In Miller's words

I was thus brought, in 1818, at the close of my two years' study of the Scriptures, to the solemn conclusion, that in about twenty-five years from that time all the affairs of our present state would be wound up. (*Apology and Defense*, pp. 11–12)

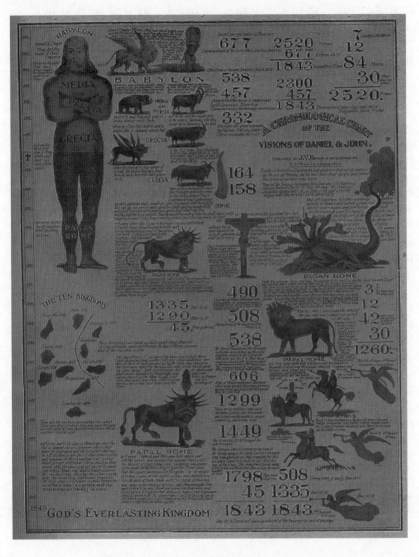

Figure 7   The 1843 Millerite prophetic chart

find that the system is complex, detailed and well worked out. An illustration of the extent of that complexity can be seen in the chart reproduced as figure 7.[32] However, the main point he made on Dan. 9.24–5 and its relationship to Dan. 8.14 seems relatively clear, and at the risk of gross oversimplification, a summary of it may be given.

Miller argued that Daniel 8 and 9 must be interpreted together (and in this he was not alone).[33] He noted that at the end of Daniel 8 the prophet plainly did not understand the content of the vision he had been given in the chapter. Indeed, so troubled had Daniel been by the vision that he had fallen sick. (Dan. 8.27 reads 'And I Daniel fainted, and was sick certain days; afterward I rose up, and did the king's business; and I was astonished at the vision, but none understood it.') Miller then argued that God would not allow this situation to remain, especially after Daniel's prayer of supplication in Dan. 9.3–19. Consequently, according to Miller, Dan. 9.21ff. relates how God sent the angel Gabriel to explain the vision of Daniel 8 to him. Gabriel instructs the prophet to 'understand the matter, and consider the vision' (Dan. 9.23). Miller argued that 'the vision' which is referred to here must be 'the vision' of Daniel 8, since that is the vision closest to Dan. 9.21–3. Thus what we have in Dan. 9.24ff. is, according to Miller, an explanation of Daniel 8.[34] (Miller also noted that 'the vision' is mentioned again in Dan. 9.25 and again argued that this was the vision of Daniel 8.) This is a vital link that is to be made if Miller's reasoning is to be followed through. Had Miller not made that link, the editor of the *Advent Herald* would not have shut down his presses on 18 October 1844, and Mr Shortridge might never have climbed up, or fallen out of, his tree – if indeed he did.[35]

Dan. 9.24–5 reads:

Seventy weeks are determined upon thy people and upon thy holy city, to finish the transgression, and to make an end of sins, and to make reconciliation for iniquity, and to bring in everlasting righteousness, and to seal up the vision and prophecy, and to anoint the most Holy. Know therefore and understand, *that* from the going forth of the commandment to restore and to build Jerusalem

---

[32] This chart was designed by Charles Fitch and Apollos Hale and adopted by the Millerites in May 1842. See the notes accompanying Nichol's reproduction of the chart between pages 208 and 209 of *Midnight Cry*.

[33] See Arasola, *The End of Historicism*, pp. 123–4, where the views of John Tillinghast and Johann Petri, writing in 1654 and 1768 respectively, are summarised. Fuller information on Tillinghast may be found in Froom, *Prophetic Faith*, vol. II, pp. 570–3.

[34] Miller's remarks on this point are reproduced in Arasola, *The End of Historicism*, p. 122.

[35] See n. 8 above.

unto the Messiah the Prince *shall be* seven weeks, and threescore and two weeks: the street shall be built again, and the wall, even in troublous times.

Miller, then, argued that 'the vision' mentioned in verse 24b was the vision of Daniel 8. His attention was also drawn to the word נֶחְתַּךְ in verse 24, which the KJV translates 'determined'. It may also be translated 'cut off', and this is the way in which Miller took it.[36] The question was, of course, from what had these seventy weeks been 'cut off'? The answer, for Miller, was simple: from the 2,300 days. The Jews ('thy people') had been allotted 70 weeks (= 70 × 7 'days' = 490 literal years according to the year-day principle) 'to finish transgression'. This meant, and in this Miller reflects again a widely held view in pre-critical Protestant eisegetical literature, that the Jews were given 490 years to repent and return to God.

Still Miller has no starting point. The vision of Daniel 8 speaks of 2,300 days (= 2,300 years) after which the sanctuary would be cleansed. That period, according to Miller, was to include a shorter period of 70 'weeks' (= 490 years) which had been allotted to the Jews as the time during which they should repent and return to God. But there is still no marker, no *terminus a quo* from which to date the start of the periods. The key, however, according to Miller, is to be found in Dan. 9.25.

The 70-week period, and therefore the 2,300-day period, argued Miller, is itself related to the 69 weeks of Dan. 9.25 (the 'seven weeks, and three score and two weeks') which begins, so the text says, with the command to 'restore and rebuild Jerusalem' (Dan. 9.25a). Miller argued that this gives the starting point of all three periods, the 69 weeks, the 70 weeks and the 2,300 days; and hence contains the key which unlocks the secret of the year of Christ's return. Thus the basic framework is in place. 'The vision' of the 2,300 days (Dan. 8.14) has within it another of 70 weeks, (Dan. 9.24) which has within it another of 69 weeks (Dan. 9.25). All three begin with the going forth of the command to restore Jerusalem (Dan. 9.25). If the date of that command can be discovered, all will fall into place. This question exercised the minds of many historicist interpreters; Miller's conclusion was that the command was that of Artaxerxes Longimanus (cf. Ezra 7.11–26), which was given in the seventh year of the reign. Like most commentators he followed Ussher in taking this year as 457 BC.[37]

---

[36] It was Miller's close follower Josiah Litch who conducted a study of the Hebrew word. His thoughts were published in the *Midnight Cry* 4, no. 25. See further Arasola, *The End of Historicism*, pp. 122–3.

[37] Arasola, *The End of Historicism*, p. 124.

Miller, of course, was at this point involved in eisegesis rather than exegesis. It was a widespread, though not universal,[38] belief that the events of Dan. 9.24–5 related to the first coming of Christ, so the prophecy must terminate at some key point either in the life of Jesus or with his death. According to Miller, who is probably following Ussher at this point also, Jesus died in AD 33.[39] If one then deducts 490 years from AD 33, one arrives at 457 BC. (This is only so if no allowance is made for the fact that there was no year zero.) Hence, according to Miller, in AD 33 the seventy weeks which had been 'determined' for the Jews came to an end when as a nation they committed deicide. The remarkable accuracy of the 70-week prophecy, as Miller saw it, confirmed 457 BC as the date for the start of the 2,300 days of Dan. 8.14 also.

Hence came Miller's initial conclusion that the end would come in 1843. As with the 70-week (= 490 years) time period mentioned above, he failed to take into account the fact there was no year zero, a mistake which he later spotted and corrected, with the result that the year for the return of Christ was reset at 1844.

Miller, then, had the year, but not as yet the month or the day. He was at first very reluctant to fine-tune his calculations to the point of fixing the precise date of Christ's expected return, perhaps heeding the warning of Matt. 24.36 (Mark 13.32), but did eventually fall victim to this temptation to greater chronological precision. It is apparent that he did not understand the complexities of the Jewish calendar, and he appears to have accepted uncritically the view that the last day of the Jewish year equivalent to AD 1843 would fall on 21 March 1844. Hence according to his later reckoning Jesus would return on 22 March (i.e. 'after' the 2,300 year-days of Dan. 8.14 which began in 457 BC). This is the first precise date.

However, there grew up within Millerism what became known as the 'seventh month movement'. This movement gained the following of a significant number of the Millerites, though Miller himself was not an early exponent of it. The supporters of the seventh-month movement drew on Miller's general argument that the Jewish feasts prefigured key events in the life of Christ. So, for example, the Passover pointed forward to the passion and the Passover lamb prefigured Christ (an

[38] As was noted in chapter 6, Charles Wesley was of the opinion that Dan. 9.24–5 referred to some event other than the first coming of Christ, a case also argued by Priestley (*Works*, vol. II, p. 368; vol. XII, pp. 438–41; vol. XX, pp. 230–1).

[39] Ussher put the date of the crucifixion at AD 33, the date adopted by Miller. This is probably the result of thinking that Jesus was thirty years old at the beginning of his ministry (Luke 3.23) and that his ministry lasted three years (as it probably does in the Johannine scheme).

argument which is in fact put forward in John's gospel). It was then argued that the Day of Atonement, which had not found its antitype during the life of Christ, was a type of the second advent when, like the high priest coming out of the most holy place, Christ would come from heaven. The movement therefore took the view that Jesus would return on the Jewish Day of Atonement, a feast which fell on the tenth day of the seventh month. The question was, then, when was the tenth day of the seventh month in the Jewish year equivalent to 1844? According to some (including the Mr Bear quoted above) it was in September, but the majority of Millerites, following the Karaite[40] rather than the Rabbinical Jewish calendar, took the view that it fell on 22 October. The details of such thinking were largely worked out by Miller's follower Samuel Sheffield Snow, but Miller himself eventually came to accept the date of 22 October for the Lord's return.[41]

The Millerites were wrong: Jesus did not return on 22 March, or on 22 September or on the final date on which so many hopes had been pinned: 22 October 1844 came and went, and with the passing of the date the whole eisegetical edifice which Miller had build up over the course of nearly thirty years came crashing to the ground. He had proposed a definite and testable hypothesis and the evidence had convincingly proven him wrong. There was no safeguard built into the Millerite system, no fine print or possibility of further qualification, and when the clock struck midnight on 22 October Miller, his system and his followers were seen to be in unqualified, irredeemable error. Despite this failure, however, Miller himself continued in his hope that Jesus' return would be soon, although he avoided setting so precise a date again. Similarly some of his followers did manage to deal with the disappointment and through various means keep alive the hope of the early return of Christ. Nevertheless, by daybreak on 23 October 1844 the Millerite boat had quite clearly been sunk and it took some imaginative theology (not to mention, as will be seen in chapter 8, a vision or two) to refloat it.

It has been claimed that 'at least 33 American religious bodies can be traced back to the Great Disappointment of October 22, 1844, when [contrary to Miller's predictions] the millennium failed to occur'.[42] Not

---

[40] This calendar was adopted by the Karaite Jews, an eighth-century Jewish sect which rejected the Oral Law. According to this the festival of New Year may fall on any day of the week, and as a consequence the Karaite and Rabbinate calendars may differ on the celebration of the Day of Atonement. See further *Encyclopaedia Judaica* (17 vols., Jerusalem: Keter Publishing House, 1972–82), vol. x, pp. 778–9.

[41] See further Froom, *Prophetic Faith*, vol. iv, pp. 810–26.

[42] Stark and Bainbridge, *The Future of Religion*, p. 487.

all of the trajectories of that splintered movement are easy to follow. However, in two well-known cases, the Jehovah's Witnesses and the Seventh-day Adventists, a fairly clear line is discernible. The Jehovah's Witnesses can be traced back to the work of Charles Taze Russell (1852–1916), a significant influence upon whom was Nelson H. Barbour, a follower of William Miller. Barbour accepted the broad outline of Miller's scheme, including the 1843 terminus for the 2,300 days of Dan. 8.14. Building further on the work of Miller and of the early nineteenth century prophetic interpreter John A. Brown,[43] Barbour eventually came to the conclusion that the end of the period of the Gentiles (cf. Luke 21.24) was due to fall in 1914. The outbreak of the First World War in that year was then understood as the fulfilment of the prophecy in Matt. 24.7 that 'nation shall rise against nation', which marked the dawn of the final stage in world history. In accordance with their understanding of Matt. 24.34 ('this generation will by no means pass away until all these things occur' (*New World Translation of the Holy Scriptures*)), the Jehovah's Witnesses remain convinced that not everybody who was alive in 1914 will die before the second advent. Thus the premillennial hope of Miller, while less clearly focused, lives on.[44]

The line of descent of the Seventh-day Adventist Church is clearer, and it may be seen as one of the principal descendants of the Millerites, and perhaps the chief. It was this movement, more than any of the others in the immediate wake of the collapse of Millerism itself, that managed eventually to salvage something from the Millerite wreck. What became Seventh-day Adventism grew from a movement which was but a tiny fraction of the total group of disappointed Millerites. Some have put the figure as low as 0.2 per cent.[45] However, from this unpromising start on the extreme margins of disappointed Millerism, there grew up a movement which had a real claim to the inheritance. These early Adventists took the view that Miller was in fact right about the date, but had misunderstood the event. Christ had clearly not come to this earth on 22 October 1844; rather, the early Seventh-day Advent-

---

[43] See Froom, *Prophetic Faith*, vol. III, pp. 404–8 for a summary of Brown's work. Froom had not been able to find any biographical data on Brown.

[44] See further M. James Penton, *Apocalypse Delayed: The Story of the Jehovah's Witnesses* (Toronto: University of Toronto Press, 1985), pp. 18–22, 44–6.

[45] This figure is based upon the statistics given in Malcolm Bull and Keith Lockhart, *Seeking a Sanctuary: Seventh-day Adventism and the American Dream* (San Francisco: Harper & Row, 1989), pp. 4–6. The authors there state that of the c. 50,000 Millerites, about 100 became 'shut door' Adventists. The reference to the 'shut door' is to Matt. 25.10; these early Adventists believed that the door to salvation (symbolised by the door to the marriage feast in Matt. 25) had been shut on 22 October 1844.

ists argued, he had entered into a new phase of his high priestly ministry in heaven. The Seventh-day Adventists, then, took the view that Dan. 8.14 speaks not, as Miller has suggested, of the return of Christ to this earth, but rather of the entry of Christ into the celestial antitypical equivalent of the earthly temple's 'most holy place'. The theology is complex, but the result is that the Seventh-day Adventist Church continues to express Miller's premillennial faith. As with the Jehovah's Witnesses, the Adventist hope is less clearly focused, but it is still there. The emergence of Seventh-day Adventism and the continuation of the premillennial historicist reading of Daniel and Revelation which Miller advanced are taken up more fully in the following chapter.

What, then, of the whole Millerite episode? It would of course be easy enough to dismiss it as of no real significance. Miller had put all his theological eggs in the one proverbial basket and had dropped the lot. Consequently he and his movement are an unimportant byway, and are best forgotten.

That, however, would not be an appropriate response from the academic guild. This book is not addressing social or religious history, but even without engaging in the necessary supporting discussion of those areas it seems certain that Miller and Millerism are important in such contexts. Miller's dissatisfaction with his own probably quite comfortable lot and his view, as a nineteenth-century American, that the kingdom of God was about to dawn need some explanation. The kind of feelings and consequent expression of eschatological hope so clearly seen in Millerism have often been understood as the particular preserve of the underprivileged and socially disadvantaged, who see the world to come as the place where present injustices will be put right. Millerism, however, drew adherents from all walks of life (we may recall, for example, Mr Bear's eighty dollars, his house, and the fact that his father had at least one tenant). Indeed, Miller himself was no pauper. Millerism, then, like the premillennialism which gained a foothold among the socially advantaged and respectable elite in nineteenth-century Britain,[46] suggests that millennial dreams are not always founded on economic deprivation. Things are not as they should be on a spiritual, ethical or social plane, and the desire for a better world is a hope not limited to any one class of persons or directed towards purely pecuniary ambitions.

---

[46] The increasing appeal of premillennialism and its acceptance among the educated elite in nineteenth-century Britain is remarked upon by Hempton, 'Evangelicalism and Eschatology'. See also Garrett, *Respectable Folly*.

To leave those discussions largely aside, however, Miller is important in the more immediate context of this book for two reasons. First, he is an adequate demonstration of the continuing power of historicist readings of biblical prophecy in the nineteenth century. Millerism also illustrates the extent to which such readings of the books of Daniel and Revelation (as opposed to premillennialism more broadly conceived) gained a firm foothold on American soil: 50,000 Millerites may have been wrong, but they cannot be ignored by anyone researching the history of eisegesis. Second, and here the discussion which follows in the next two chapters is presumed, Millerism is important as the great-grandfather of Branch Davidianism. When David Koresh spoke, he spoke to Seventh-day Adventists, and when he spoke to Seventh-day Adventists, he spoke to members of a tradition which went back to Miller. Not all that Seventh-day Adventists have to say is based upon Miller, and Miller himself never became one. However, the Seventh-day Adventist tradition regarding the proper interpretation of Daniel and the Revelation draws heavily on the basic premillennial-historicist reading of these texts, not just in outline but in any number of countless details, which Miller himself had propagated. But Miller is not the fount of all historicist wisdom. He himself, as has been shown, was heir to a long line of tradition stretching back to those he himself called 'our own standard Protestant writers', namely the interpreters such as Mede, Brightman, Newton, Priestley and Gill. It is only in the context of the broad sweep of this tradition, particularly the Millerite-Adventist branch of it, that Koresh and his followers can be understood. Parents cannot be held entirely responsible for the actions of their children, and Miller cannot be held responsible for the Waco inferno. However, to divorce Koresh and his followers from their tradition is to render them incomprehensible and invest them with an air of cultish novelty that they do not actually deserve.

APPENDIX

This chapter is subheaded: 'Showing when the vision will end, of 2300 days, as given in Daniel 8: 13, 14'. The first part quotes Dan. 8.13, 14, and links it with other texts – 1 Pet. 1.11; Num. 14.34; Ezek. 4.6. It then quotes Dan. 8.15–19, and continues:[47]

---

[47] From Miller's *Evidences of the Second Coming*, chapter 2, pp. 16–18. Spelling, punctuation and italic are reproduced without alteration.

What may we learn from the foregoing texts? We learn first that Daniel was very anxious to understand the vision, and to know its meaning, and that it will not be wrong for us, my kind reader, to understand and know too. In the second place we learn, that Gabriel was commanded to make Daniel understand the vision. We also learn that the vision carries us down to the end, and that in the vision the time when the end of indignation shall be, is appointed. – Thus, far the whole subject appears to be clear and conclusive, but one thing remains yet to clear away all doubts. Daniel did not yet know when the vision began, or was to begin, and although the Angel was sent to instruct him, yet that part was left untold until about 15 years afterwards. In the first year of Darius the Mede, when Daniel made supplication by confession and prayer to his God, the same angel Gabriel was sent to instruct Daniel further into the vision which he was so anxious to understand. Dan 9:21. 'Yea while I was speaking in prayer, even the man Gabriel, whom I had seen in the vision at the beginning, being caused to fly swiftly, touched me about the time of the evening oblation.' 22d verse. 'And he informed me, and talked with me, and said, O Daniel, I am now come forth to give thee skill and understanding.' 23d verse. 'At the beginning of thy supplications the command came forth, and I am come to shew thee; for thou art greatly beloved: therefore understand the matter, and consider the *vision*.' By these verses we learn that Gabriel was commanded to instruct Daniel further in the *vision* concerning the daily sacrifice, and the transgression of dessolation; and here follows his instruction. Dan 9:24. 'Seventy weeks are determined upon thy people, and upon thy holy city, to finish the transgression, and to make an end of sins, and to make reconciliation for iniquity, and to bring in everlasting righteousness, and to seal up the *vision* and prophecy, and to anoint the Most Holy.' In this verse Daniel is informed of the time that was determined in the council of God before the Lamb of God, the great antitype should take away sin by the sacrifice of himself, make reconciliation by his own blood, to declare his righteousness for the remission of sins, to make sure the *vision*, and fulfil the prophecies concerning his first coming, and finally enter into the holy of holies once for all as a priest and advocate for his people. And if the angel had stopped here, and given Daniel no more instruction, still Daniel would have been at a loss whether to have begun the vision at the time he had it, either in the first or third year of Belshazzar, or fifteen years afterwards, in the first year of Darius, as Daniel had undoubtedly supposed, by his being so particular in giving us the exact dates of these events; but no, the wisdom of man is foolishness with God – almost 90 years from the first vision before the 70 weeks would begin to be numbered. And here we are taught one important lesson. That it is perfectly vain for us to calculate unless we have, 'thus saith the Lord'. But let us see what saith the angel. 25th verse. 'Know therefore and understand, that from the going forth of the commandment to restore and to rebuild Jerusalem, unto Messiah the Prince, shall be seven weeks and three score and two weeks; the street shall be built again, and the wall, even in troublous times.' In this verse Daniel is commanded to know and understand, that from a certain event, which event was yet hid in futurity, he might begin to reckon his 70 weeks, or as he reckons here, his seven and sixty-two weeks, making in all 69 weeks. And this event was a commandment to restore and build the streets and walls of Jerusalem in troublous times; but yet who should give the command and how long before this first event should happen, was in the dark with Daniel, and undoubtedly caused much anxiety in his mind; but Daniel must wait with patience, and so must we my dear reader, to receive our instruction from God, by 'here a little and there a little'. 26th verse. 'And after three score and two weeks shall Messiah be cut off, but not for himself: and the people of the prince that shall come, shall destroy the city and the sanctuary; and the end thereof shall be with flood, and to the end of the war desolations are determined.' – Here we have a prophecy of the death of Christ, for his people, the destruction of Jerusalem and the temple, by Titus prince of the Romans, the dispersion and desolation of the Jews, or people of God, until all war shall cease and the kingdom of Christ shall fill the whole earth. 27th verse. 'And he shall confirm the covenant with many for one week: and in the midst of the week he shall cause the sacrifice and the oblation to cease, and for the overspreading of abominations he shall make it desolate, even until the consummation, and that determined shall be poured on the desolate.' The first thing noticed in this verse, is, the preaching of the Gospel one week. John preached three years and a half: and Christ three years and a half, making in all seven years or one week, and this week, with the seven and the sixty-two before mentioned, make up the whole 70 weeks mentioned in the 24th verse. The next thing is, that in the midst, or *last half of the week*, as it might be rendered, the sacrifices and oblation should cease, that is, Christ would fulfil the typical law, and nail to his cross the ceremonies of the Jewish ritual. The third thing noticed is the overspreading of abominations, and the desolation of the city and sanctuary, until the consummation, or end of the 2300 days when the sanctuary will be justified.

We have followed the instruction of the Angel Gabriel to Daniel, thus far, and find he brings us down to the end of sublunary things invariably. He has told us how long the vision shall be, 2300 years, he has shown us that 70 weeks or 490 of those years would be accomplished at the crucifixion of Christ; he has told us when the 490 years would begin at the going forth of the commandment to build the streets and walls of Jerusalem in troublous times; he has given us an exact account of the destruction of Jerusalem, the death of Christ, &c. All may be plain to us, who live after almost all is fulfiled, for we can know when the decree went forth, we know that 490 years afterwards Christ was cut off and not for himself; we know Jerusalem has been destroyed, the Jews scattered, the church trodden underfoot , by the abomination of desolation. We can take 490 years from 2300 years, and find the number of years after Christ's death, before the vision will end, viz. 1810 years – we can add the age of Christ, 33 years, to 1810 and by this calculation find that A. D. 1843 the vision will be accomplished. But Daniel could not do all this for he had no instruction to tell him how much time would elapse before the commandment to build the walls would be given or who would issue that decree; therefore Daniel was not satisfied, and four years afterwards the same Angel Gabriel came to instruct

Daniel in this *one thing*, who should issue this decree. Dan 10.1. 'In the third year of Cyrus King of Persia, a thing was revealed unto Daniel whose name was called Belteshazzar, and the thing was true, but the time appointed was long, and he understood the thing, and had understanding of the vision.' We see in this verse that Daniel lived, and received this visit and instruction under Cyrus the first king in the Persian line of kings, and we further learn, that the thing revealed to Daniel was true, and that it had reference to an appointed time, and that time was long, and that it was concerning this very vision of 2300 years, that being the longest time appointed. In the next place we are informed that Daniel had prayed and mourned three full weeks, and after this he beheld the glory of Christ in the form of a man, and after strengthening him, the Angel Gabriel informs him, that he is come in answer to his prayers, and says 13th, verse, 'But the prince of the kingdom of Persia withstood me one and twenty days: but, lo, Michael one of the chief princes, came to help me; and I remained there with the kings of Persia.' What the angel meant by 'one and twenty days', being withstood by the prince of Persia, is to me as yet in the dark; but we may notice, that it is the same length of time Daniel mourned and prayed, and the angel seems to present this as an excuse why he did not come when Daniel began praying. We may also notice that it was 21 years from the time he had his first vision in the 7th chapter, until he received this last instruction in the last three chapters; and it teaches us that we ought not to give over praying, and searching for truth, although we might be twenty one days, or even as many years, before we obtain. Dan. 10:14. 'Now I am come to make thee understand what shall befall thy people in the latter days: for yet the vision is for many days.' In this verse we learn that the Angel came to make Daniel understand the vision, which would concern the people of God in the last or latter day, for it would be many days yet to come.

CHAPTER 8

'A Lamb-like Beast': Rev. 13.11–18 in the Seventh-day Adventist tradition

It has been demonstrated that a number of biblical texts have a vibrant 'afterlife', that is, they continue to live on beyond their own immediate time and function in altogether foreign cultural contexts. Nowhere, perhaps, is this more clearly seen than in the history of the interpretation of the Apocalypse of St John. Indeed, so colourful and varied is the course of that document's eisegetical trajectory that even the strange symbolism and bizarre imagery of the book itself seem unable to account for it. And of course it cannot. For it is only as the lifeless but suggestive body of the now dead text is imbued with the imaginative spirit of the culturally fashioned reader that the dazzling array of possible meanings arises. Among Christian millennial groups in particular, for whom the Apocalypse of St John is often of central significance, that process is seen clearly enough. This is not a new phenomenon, but goes back perhaps almost as far as the text itself.

Some of the main contours of that eisegetical tradition have been examined. Thus in chapters 2 and 3 the post-Reformation Protestant view relative to the book of Revelation was sketched in. There the predominance of the historicist method of prophetic interpretation, including the almost universal view that the Pope and/or the Roman Catholic Church was Antichrist, was noted and examples of such positions given. In chapter 4 the chief elements of the Catholic response to the Protestant historicist paradigm were noted. Preterism and futurism were particularly significant in that context. In chapters 5 and 6 the trajectory was traced further, into the Methodist tradition, and the views of Charles Wesley in particular were subjected to detailed analysis. Throughout these studies one thing seems plain: the book of Revelation (and together with it several other parts of the scriptures) is capable of almost unlimited and unrestricted manipulation. As has been argued briefly in the previous chapters, and will be argued more fully in this and the following chapter, this is not always a good thing.

In chapter 7 the eisegetical views of William Miller were examined in some detail. In Millerism the older British historicist method of prophetic interpretation found a firm foothold on American soil. From Millerism there arose a number of other groups, some of which maintained the distinctive Millerite hermeneutic relative to Daniel and the Apocalypse. The remainder of this book is concerned to trace through the trajectory of one of those offshoots. In the present chapter the views of the Seventh-day Adventist Church are discussed, attention being paid especially to one particular aspect of the interpretative paradigm adopted by that group, namely the understanding of the Lamb-like (or two-horned) Beast of Revelation 13. The reason for taking particular notice of the views of the Seventh-day Adventist Church regarding this entity will, it is hoped, become clear. In summary it is noted here that the Seventh-day Adventist view of the beast is both distinctive and also, it is suggested, of central significance in the context of what happened at Waco. Finally, the events at Waco, and the significance of the book of Revelation to them, are the subject of the last chapter, as the history of the Branch Davidian understanding of Revelation, particularly Revelation 13, is traced through from Seventh-day Adventism to the Shepherd's Rod (later to be known as the Davidian Seventh-day Adventists) and into the Branch Davidian movement.

The present chapter falls into two parts. The first contains a brief summary of the main contours of the Protestant interpretative paradigm relative to Rev. 13.11ff. which was operative in post-Reformation England. This provides the more immediate context in which Seventh-day Adventist interpretations of the Lamb-like Beast are to be seen. (The broader, fundamentally historicist reading of Revelation which is apparent in the Adventist tradition will by now be clear to the reader.) In the second part particular attention is paid to the identity of the beast in the eisegetical tradition of the early Seventh-day Adventist Church, and a documented summary is given of the continued predominance of that view in present-day Seventh-day Adventist literature.

Before proceeding further, two brief comments are called for. First, the term 'Early Seventh-day Adventist Church' is used here to denote those followers of Miller and others who became convinced that Miller had in fact got the date right, but the event wrong. As we saw in the previous chapter, the number of original Millerites who came to this view was small, but it was from that group that the later Seventh-day Adventist Church was to grow. Some might object that the term is somewhat anachronistic, since as an organisation the Seventh-day Adventist Church did not come officially into existence until 1863. However, as Bull and Lockhart note, though the organisation might have lacked an official structure, even in this early period what was to become the Seventh-day Adventist Church had a definite form and function, defined primarily by its distinctive theology and practice.[1] Second, it should be noted that in the KJV, Rev. 13.11 reads 'And I beheld another beast coming up out of the earth; and he had two horns like a lamb, and he spake as a dragon', a description which is somewhat flexible. There is clearly a considerable potential difference between a beast that has two horns 'like a lamb' and a 'Lamb-like Beast' with two horns. As will be seen, some commentators saw this prophetic symbol as a beast in the same order of satanic magnitude as the beast with seven heads and ten horns described in Rev. 13.1ff. There are no redeeming features to this thoroughly evil entity; it is, and can be seen to be, totally wicked. In the Seventh-day Adventist tradition, however, it was the 'lamb-like' qualities of this symbol that came to be noted in particular. Here, according to early Seventh-day Adventist interpreters, we have a picture of what is actually a beast, but looks like a lamb; a beast in lamb's clothing.[2] To some commentators, for example J. N. Loughborough, whose work is examined in detail below, the lamb-like nature of the beast is an important factor in its claimed identification. The Adventist literature is not consistent on this distinction. No attempt is made here formally to discriminate between the two, but, as has been noted, the distinction is potentially important.

It was observed extensively above that the book of Revelation was seen by almost all Protestant interpreters from the Reformation on as a timetable of world events, spanning the entire course of world and/or Church history during the Christian era and leading up to (and perhaps even a little beyond) the dawn of the millennium. As a part of the attempt to discern the history of the world (past, present and future) from the text of the Apocalypse, Protestant interpreters turned their attention to Revelation 13. In this chapter the career of two beasts is described. On the identity of the first beast there was widespread

---

[1] Bull and Lockhart, *Seeking a Sanctuary*, pp. 37–8.
[2] On the metamorphosis of the 'two-horned beast' into the 'Lamb-like Beast' in the Seventh-day Adventist tradition, as reflected in artistic representations of it, see Ron Graybill, 'America: The Magic Dragon', *Insight* 2 (1971): 6–12; Ron Graybill, 'Picturing the Prophecies', *Adventist Review* (5 July 1984): 11–14. The change is noted also by Jonathan M. Butler, in 'Adventism and the American Experience', in Edwin S. Gaustad (ed.), *The Rise of Adventism: Religion and Society in Mid-Nineteenth-Century America* (New York: Harper & Row, 1974), p. 191.

agreement among Protestant interpreters from the period c. 1550–1800. Here was a prophetic picture of the Roman Catholic Church, that is, Antichrist himself.[3] The only major Protestant alternative to this view was that the first beast was a symbol of pagan Rome and/or its successor the Holy Roman Empire in its civil embodiment. Such a view, while not as common as that which saw the beast from the sea as a symbol of the Roman Catholic Church, is nevertheless reasonably well represented in the literature.[4]

On the interpretation of the second beast of Revelation 13, however, the beast with 'two horns like a lamb', there was much more debate. Three basic positions emerged. First, those Protestant commentators who subscribed to the theory that the first beast was a symbol of pagan Rome and/or the Holy Roman Empire almost invariably went on to argue that this second beast was a symbol of papal Rome, which, they suggested, had taken over the mantle of Antichrist from its pagan/civil predecessor.[5]

A second view, which was more common, was that this 'Lamb-like' or 'two-horned' Beast was a more specific symbol of the Roman Catholic hierarchy and/or the Popes themselves. So, for example, as was noted in chapter 3, the Baptist commentator John Gill is clear on this point. Commenting on Rev. 13.11 he stated that the beast which is there described is

The same with the first beast, only in another form; the same for being and person, but under a different consideration; the same Antichrist, but appearing in another light and view: the first beast is the pope of Rome ... this other beast is the same pope of Rome, with his clergy, cardinals, archbishops, bishops, priests &c.[6]

---

[3] It is perhaps worth re-echoing here the views of Benjamin Keach, discussed more fully in chapter 2. Shortly before the close of the seventeenth century, he wrote that

'tis evident to all who are men of any Reading, that most of our Eminent Protestant Writers, both Ancient and Modern, do affirm without the least doubt, that the Church of *Rome* is the great Whore spoken of [in] *Rev.* 17. (Keach, *Antichrist Stormed*, p. 1)

Not only, argued Keach, was the Roman Catholic Church to be equated with the great whore of Revelation 17; it was also that Church that fulfilled, according to the standard Protestant view of the age, parts of Revelation 13 (Keach makes the identification of the Roman Catholic Church with the beast explicit on p. 41), Daniel 7–8, 2 Thess. 2, Matt. 7.15 and Acts 20.29.

[4] Note, for example, Adam Clarke, *Commentary on the New Testament* (3 vols., 1817) *in loc.* (Clarke's *Commentary* does not have page numbers.)

[5] This view was taken by no less important an interpreter than Joseph Mede, whose work *Clavis Apocalyptica* (1627) was a dominant influence in English Protestant eisegesis for much of the seventeenth and eighteenth centuries.

[6] Gill, *Exposition*, p. 794.

The same basic point is made by Durham,[7] and even earlier by Bale.[8] Bale drew a distinction between the first and second beast of Revelation 13 only in so far as they represented different aspects of Roman Catholicism. He argued that the Lamb-like Beast was a prophetic symbol of the prelates of Antichrist's Church (Rome) whose function it was to promote worship of the first beast, that is, the papal Antichrist itself. In fact the origin of such views could be taken back even further. Similar suggestions to those of Bale had been made by the Lollard expositors Walter Brute (*floruit* c. 1391) and John Purvey (c. 1354–1428).[9] Thus, according to this view, the first beast was a general symbol of Roman Catholicism, while the second beast was a more specific picture of the Roman Catholic Church, or perhaps the ecclesial hierarchy in particular. Some argued that the second beast represented the religious orders of the Roman Catholic Church such as the Jesuits.[10] These orders had arisen in these latter days to enforce worship of the first beast (the papacy).

It has been noted throughout that the historicist paradigm in general has been the subject of continued updating as expositors sought to make the text particularly relevant to their own day. This is certainly true of Rev. 13.11ff., for following the events of the French Revolution the paradigm was fine-tuned once again by some. The first beast, it was argued, was a symbol of the Roman Catholic Church, while the second was a symbol of some specifically end-time enemy such as the French Republic[11] or Napoleon.[12] Hence the text continued to inspire the thoughts of those concerned to match history and prophecy and to see in Revelation 13 a timely warning of the enemies of God who had already, or were about to, come into the world.

From the evidence surveyed above, it is apparent that the identity, function and destiny of the second beast of Rev. 13.11ff. were a matter of particular concern to English Protestant interpreters from the Reformation on, and some slight evidence from the pre-Reformation Church has

---

[7] Durham, *Commentarie*, pp. 542–73.

[8] Bale, *Ymage of Bothe Churches* (Bale's work does not have page numbers).

[9] See further Froom, *Prophetic Faith*, vol. II, pp. 74–87, 92–100.

[10] See, for example, ibid., vol. II, p. 711 (on Johann Albrecht Bengel).

[11] See especially Brady, *Number of the Beast*, pp. 246–8. Froom, *Prophetic Faith*, vol. II, pp. 779–81, notes in particular the work of Joseph Galloway (1730–1803) who made the identification of the two-horned beast with the French Republic explicit.

[12] See especially Brady, *Number of the Beast*, pp. 242–6, who gives several references. One is the work of Lewis Mayer, who, in 1803, published *A Hint to England; or, a Prophetic Mirror; containing an Explanation of Prophecy that Relates to the French Nation, and the Threatened Invasion; proving Bonaparte to be the Beast . . . whose Number is 666*.

also been noted. This interest was a constituent part of the more general concern with Revelation evident in the Protestant literature of the period, a literature that exudes a fundamentally historicist approach to biblical prophecy.

Such an approach to Revelation was not limited to Britain, and in America in particular the methodology flourished.[13] A dramatic expression of this American form of the historicist-interpretative paradigm was that evidenced in the rise and development of Millerism. Miller's prediction that the end of the world would come in 1843/44 has been discussed in chapter 7, together with the thorough-going historicist and, it must be said, somewhat imaginative reading of the book of Daniel which gave rise to it. Miller was novel in some of the details of his historicist scheme. Regarding the Lamb-like Beast, however, he kept within the norms of the eisegetical tradition to which he belonged. This second beast, argued Miller, was a symbol of papal Rome and particularly the orders such as the Jesuits.[14] The first beast he interpreted as pagan Rome.[15]

Some of Miller's followers disagreed. Josiah Litch was among Miller's first followers, and a determined supporter of the Millerite cause. A medical doctor and a clergyman of the Methodist Episcopal Church, Litch turned his hand also to prophetic exposition, a topic on which he was the author of numerous books and pamphlets and the editor of many more.[16] He was one who argued that the second beast was Napoleon.[17] Litch later abandoned this view, arguing instead that the beast was a symbol of some as yet unknown power that would come in the last phase of the world's history to persecute the faithful, a view which was to prove as influential as it was suggestive. However, even if these other views are taken into account, there is relatively little that is distinctive in the early Millerite tradition regarding the interpretation of Rev. 13.11ff., though the views of Hiram Edson and Hiram Case, noted briefly below, do suggest some slight movement in other directions. This was to change, however, with the birth of the

[13] The extent to which the historicist methodology was exported to America from Britain rather than the American expression being a parallel independent example of it is a complex question and is not entered into here in detail. See above, pp. 156–8, and Harrison, *Second Coming*, pp. 163ff. for a brief discussion of the issue.

[14] Froom, *Prophetic Faith*, vol. IV, p. 187.   [15] Ibid., vol. IV, pp. 736–7.

[16] See further ibid., vol. IV, pp. 528ff. for an extensive summary.

[17] Josiah Litch, *Prophetic Expositions; or A Connected View of the Testimony of the Prophets Concerning the Kingdom of God and the Time of its Establishment* (2 vols. [1842], vol. I, pp. 106–7). I owe this reference to P. Gerard Damsteegt, *Foundations of the Seventh-day Adventist Message and Mission* (Grand Rapids, MI: Eerdmans, 1977), p. 196 n. 235.

Seventh-day Adventist Church, arguably Miller's most successful direct descendant.[18]

The history of the Seventh-day Adventist Church, beginning with its emergence from among the scattered Millerite ashes to its position today as one of the more successful, if lesser-known, ecclesial bodies crowded on the margins of Christian orthodoxy, is now well documented.[19] The group survived the great disappointment of 22 October 1844 by means of some imaginative eisegesis. Building upon the suggestion that Miller (and more so S. S. Snow) had made that Christ was the antitype of the Old Testament priesthood, the group which was later to become the Seventh-day Adventists took the view that Miller had been right in thinking that a major event in the history of salvation would occur on 22 October 1844. Miller had thought that the cleansing of the sanctuary referred to in Dan. 8.14 was the return of Christ, but on the morning of 23 October it was revealed to Hiram Edson, whose own description of the event seems to suggest a visionary experience, that in fact Dan. 8.14 spoke of Christ's transfer from the holy to the most holy place of the antitypical sanctuary in heaven, as referred to in Hebrews (Hebrews 8–9). Thus according to this view Christ had entered the last phase of his ministry and his coming was imminent. In relocating the events predicted in Dan. 8.14 and fulfilled on 22 October 1844 to heaven rather than earth, the possibility of testing, and hence disproving, the hypothesis was of course ruled out. This assured the movement's survival. The hope of Christ's coming is always near, but its hour never quite known.[20]

This direct link from Miller to Seventh-day Adventism is clear and undisputed, and there is no need to enter into a fuller discussion of that line of tradition here. As an important and central part of its Millerite legacy, the Seventh-day Adventist Church inherited the historicist method of biblical-prophetic eisegesis, which, as we saw in the previous

---

[18] This is not of course to underestimate the significance of the Jehovah's Witnesses, who similarly followed in Miller's wake; their reinterpretation of Miller's reading of the significance of Daniel 8 was commented on in chapter 7. The line of descent from Miller to the Jehovah's Witnesses is, however, less clear and direct than that from Miller to Seventh-day Adventism, and the former's claim to the Millerite inheritance is somewhat weaker. It is not necessary here to take up this debate in any detail.

[19] Studies are numerous. For a summary see Jonathan M. Butler, 'The Making of a New Order: Millerism and the Origins of Seventh-day Adventism', in Numbers and Butler, *The Disappointed*, pp. 189–208.

[20] See further 'Millerism and the Origins of Seventh-day Adventism', in Numbers and Butler, *The Disappointed*, pp. 189–208; Leon Festinger, H. W. Riecken and S. Schachter, *When Prophecy Fails* (Minneapolis: University of Minnesota Press, 1956).

chapter, Miller himself inherited from the English Protestant historicist
writers of seventeenth and eighteenth centuries. Much of what that
Church had to say on matters prophetic was therefore absolutely standard when seen in its proper context of the history of eisegesis.

However, this is not to say that there was nothing distinctive in early
Seventh-day Adventist eisegesis. The movement did, for example, follow Miller along some of the more obscure eisegetical highways and
found that they led to prophetic-eisegetical territory largely unexplored
in the history of eisegesis, for example that centre-piece of Seventh-day
Adventist theology, the 'sanctuary doctrine'.[21] Nevertheless, in general
one should not overestimate the extent to which the nascent Seventh-
day Adventist Church was distinctive in its general vision of the future or
its prediction that the end was nigh.

On at least one particular issue, however, Seventh-day Adventist
eisegesis was to develop in ways that do seem quite novel, and represent a break with the broader historicist, and even with the more
specifically Millerite, tradition. This issue concerned the identity of the
Lamb-like Beast of Rev. 13.11ff. As has been pointed out, nominations
for potential candidates for the title of this beast were not in short
supply among Protestant interpreters of the prophecies. The early
Seventh-day Adventist Church, however, had a new suggestion, and
one which in the context of mid-nineteenth-century American civil
optimism is startling: the beast, it claimed, was the United States of
America.

The suggestion that the United States of America was predicted in
prophecy was not new with the early Adventists. Indeed, as Boyer and
Tuveson have made abundantly clear, such claims figured prominently
in the prophetic schemes of many American millennialists, though
mainly those of a postmillennial persuasion.[22] However, with the early
Adventists came a dramatic twist. According to them the United States
of America was destined to play not a positive role in the progress of the
kingdom of God, but rather a very negative one. It was not the nation of

[21] See Roy Adams, *The Sanctuary Doctrine: Three Approaches in the Seventh-day Adventist Church* (Berrien
Springs, MI: Andrews University Press, 1981).

[22] See Boyer, *When Time Shall Be No More*, pp. 225–53 and Ernest Lee Tuveson, *Redeemer Nation: The
Idea of America's Millennial Role* (Chicago: University of Chicago Press, 1968). Nathan O. Hatch,
The Sacred Cause of Liberty (New Haven, CT: Yale University Press, 1977); H. Richard Niebuhr, *The
Kingdom of God in America* (New York: Harper & Row, 1937); J. F. Maclear, 'The Republic and the
Millennium', in Elwyn A. Smith (ed.), *The Religion and the Republic* (Philadelphia: Fortress Press,
1971); and Ian S. Markham, *Plurality and Christian Ethics* (Cambridge: Cambridge University
Press, 1994), pp. 91–106 all raise issues pertinent here.

God, but one of his greatest eschatological opponents.[23] This was a startling suggestion in its nineteenth-century context, and one which was and still is largely unparalleled. Indeed, even in the relatively new very negative picture of the United States of America proposed by post-1945 expounders of prophecy (noted extensively by Boyer[24]), it appears to be more the victim of its own moral bankruptcy and religious apathy than an aggressively satanic force.

According to the early Adventists, then, the United States of America was a largely satanic force which was destined to play a key role during the last days. Thus, these early Adventist expositors argued, as their successors still do, it was the United States of America which was to play the role of Antichrist's (that is, Rome's) chief ally in the last days, and which was, with Rome, to form the great eschatological opponent.

Quite when this understanding emerged in early Adventism is not entirely clear, since the view must presumably have predated its written expression. Indeed, Froom has noted that there is some slight evidence in very early Adventist material (and even in pre-Millerite sources) suggestive of the later view, though allowance must be made for Froom's evident bias in this area. In particular his suggestion that the later Seventh-day Adventist view 'was the result of a long and gradual development'[25] does not appear to be supported by the very few sources he himself quotes; one suspects, despite his statement to the contrary, that had he had more evidence it would have been produced. The most significant references Froom makes are to the work of Hiram Edson, the Millerite who, as was noted, played an instrumental role in the eventual emergence of Seventh-day Adventism from the disappointed Millerites. Edson spoke of the Lamb-like Beast as being 'Protestant Rome',[26] though he did not explain his thinking on this point. Hiram S. Case was a little clearer. In 1850 he wrote, referring in the first line to Rev. 14.9–11,

While Bro. Rhodes was showing me the third angel's message, the light in relation to the two horned beast, Rev. xiii, 11, came to my mind all at once, and to me the thing is clear that the two horned beast is the power of Church and State. It is an 'image' of the Papal Beast to whom the dragon gave 'his power, and his seat, and great authority.' The Papal Beast was church and state united. An image must be like the thing imitated; therefore, the image-beast is com-

[23] See further especially Malcolm Bull, 'The Seventh-day Adventists: Heretics of American Civil Religion', *Sociological Analysis* 50 (1989): 177–87; Butler, 'Adventism and the American Experience', pp. 173–206, esp. pp. 180–5; Bull and Lockhart, *Seeking a Sanctuary*, esp. pp. 47–9.
[24] Boyer, *When Time Shall Be No More*, pp. 225–53.   [25] Froom, *Prophetic Faith*, vol. IV, p. 1098.
[26] Hiram Edson, 'An Appeal to the Laodicean Church', *Advent Review* Extra Issue (1850): 9.

posed of church and state united – Protestant churches and Republicanism. The word of the Lord is plain. [27]

Even in these early Millerite sources, then, there is some evidence for a movement away from the traditional (anti-Catholic) reading of Rev. 13.11ff. in favour of a view that included at least 'republicanism' or 'the state', but it is very slight.

In the early Seventh-day Adventist tradition, however, the view that the Lamb-like Beast was the United States of America gained a firm foothold from relatively early in the eisegetical history. Two principal expositors, J. N. Andrews and J. N. Loughborough, seem to have been largely responsible for its initial adoption in the Adventist theological scheme. It was these two who worked out the fairly complex eisegetical scheme relative to Rev. 13.11ff. that was to become standard in Seventh-day Adventism. The subsequent adoption, and thereby divine sanctioning, of the schemes of Andrews and Loughborough by Ellen White (1827–1915), who was and is considered by Seventh-day Adventists to be a prophetess, ensured the long-term survival of this understanding of the beast in the Adventist tradition.

John Nevis Andrews[28] (1829–1883) was early associated, through his parents, with the Millerite movement, and with them went through the traumatic experiences of 1843–44. Like a number of other disappointed Millerites he became persuaded of the necessity of keeping the seventh-day Sabbath, and thus became one of the early sabbatarian Adventists from whom the Seventh-day Adventist Church was later to be formed. He was the first Seventh-day Adventist missionary to continental Europe, an expedition he began in 1874.

Andrews was not the first among the early Seventh-day Adventists to link the United States of America to prophecy[29] (and the views of some Millerites on this issues have been noted already). He was, however, the first to picture it so negatively. In brief, he rejected the view, common among eighteenth-century Protestant expositors, that the Lamb-like Beast described in Rev. 13.11ff. is a further symbol of the papacy. This second beast, he argued, is quite distinct from the first, with which it should not be confused.

---

[27] Letter to J. White, printed in *Present Truth* (November 1850): 85.

[28] On Andrews generally see further Harry L. Leonard (ed.), *J. N. Andrews: The Man and the Mission* (Berrien Springs, MI: Andrews University Press, 1985).

[29] See E. R. Pinney and O. R. Fassett, 'The Vision of the Eagle', *The Voice of Truth, and Glad Tidings of the Kingdom at Hand*, 1 January 1845, pp. 193–4. Here the authors argue that America is predicted in 2 Esdras 12.10ff. See also H. B. Woodcock, 'The True Millennium', *Western Midnight Cry* 30 December 1844, pp. 31–2.

This view can be seen clearly at the beginning of Andrews' comments on Rev. 13.11, for example, where he wrote:

We have already seen that the fourth beast of Daniel, which is the same as the beast whose 'deadly wound was healed', of whom John speaks, does not give his seat to another beast; hence the *location* of the two-horned beast is not in the ten kingdoms of the fourth beast. We cannot take the horns of the fourth beast and constitute another beast, or the horns of another. It is another beast beside the ten-horned beast. It is not the first beast healed of his deadly wound, for the work of the two-horned beast is in the sight of that beast. The first beast was to possess the power and dominion for a period of 1260 years only, at the end of which period its dominion was taken away. Dan vii, 25, 26; Rev. xiii, 5. But if the two-horned beast is but another form of the Papal power, then is the Papacy again to bear sway with all its former authority. Rev. xiii, 12. It would indeed be a surprising change if the ten horns were to be plucked up, and in their stead two other horns should arise. Yet such is a necessary conclusion if the two-horned beast is but another form of the first beast. Hence we conclude that the two-horned beast is another and distinct power.[30]

Andrews then went on to argue that, since this beast arises without war or strife, it must arise in a fundamentally peaceful manner. It is a new kingdom, one that arises without the need to depose another. It comes after the first beast, and so, he concluded, the beast was to arise after 1798. (This was the date given by Andrews to the inflicting of the 'deadly wound' upon the head of the first beast. The common view among early Adventists, and others, was that this 'deadly wound' was that inflicted upon the papacy by the events of the French Revolution and/or the activities of Napoleon Bonaparte.)[31] In this Andrews was building on the ideas of Litch, whose work has already been noted briefly. Litch had originally argued that the second beast of Revelation 13 was Napoleon. However, this is a view that he had changed by 1842, the time of his *Restitution*. Andrews himself quotes Litch as saying that

The two-horned beast is represented as a power existing and performing his part, after the death and revival of the first beast. If asked for my opinion as to what will constitute that beast with two horns, or the false prophet, I must frankly confess I do not know. I think it is a power yet to be developed or made manifest as an accomplice of the Papacy in subjecting the world. It will be a

[30] J. N. Andrews, *The Three Messages of Revelation XIV, 6–12, Particularly the Third Angel's Message and the Two-horned Beast*, 5th edn (1877), p. 82.
[31] See, for example, Uriah Smith, whose work will be discussed in more detail below, who wrote: 'This wounding ... was inflicted when the Pope was taken prisoner by Berthier, the French general, and the papal government was for a time abolished, in 1798' (Uriah Smith, *Daniel and Revelation* (one-volume reprint edition (Watford: The Stanborough Press, 1921)), p. 506).

power which will perform miracles, and deceive the world with them. See Rev. xix, 20.[32]

Thus, according to Andrews, the vision of the Lamb-like Beast is a vision of a 'new' kingdom arising peacefully and coming to prominence in the first years of the nineteenth century, though its birth and preparation for the part it is to play in the eschatological drama will have been prior to its taking centre stage. Andrews wrote:

> The rise of each of the great powers has been gradual. For a series of years they were preparing for the stations which they afterward assumed, but they begin to figure in prophecy, *from the time when they are prepared to act their part in the great drama.*[33]

Andrews buttressed these considerations with others. He argued that the sequence of prophetic 'kingdoms' had been moving towards the west from the first kingdom 'near the garden of Eden', moving through Babylonia, Persia, Greece and Rome into Europe (i.e. the ten-part kingdom into which pagan Rome was divided and the seat of the papacy). Hence this new kingdom would be further to the west again.[34] Furthermore, the United States of America was also suggested by the comparative youth and mild appearance of a lamb.[35]

For all these reasons Andrews could see no candidate for the fulfilment of this prophecy other than the United States of America, and it was this entity that would in the last days play a key role in the eschatological drama. Contrary to the prevailing wind of postmillennial civil optimism, then, the early Seventh-day Adventists argued that the United States of America was the prophetically predicted enemy of God.

Andrews was clear on the identity of the Lamb-like Beast of Rev. 13.11; on its function he was no less certain. The beast, the United States of America, would in the last days seek to destroy truth and replace it with error. In particular, in the guise of Protestantism, it would continue with the age-old Catholic lie of the counterfeit Sabbath. (The early Seventh-day Adventists took the view that the true Sabbath was Saturday and that God required the observance of that day as a mark of submission to the divine law; the Christian Sunday, they argued, was an institution of Satan, who, through the Roman Catholic Church, had set up a counterfeit Sabbath and had thereby deluded humankind and exacted their worship for himself.) Thus, argued Andrews, American

---

[32] Josiah Litch, *The Restitution, Christ's Kingdom on Earth; the Return of Israel, together with their Political Emancipation* [1848], pp. 131, 133.
[33] Andrews, *Revelation*, p. 83 (italic in the original).   [34] Ibid., pp. 82–3.   [35] Ibid., p. 83.

Protestantism (perhaps in all its 666 sects) would join with Rome in an effort to place human laws in the place of those of God. Those who did not conform would suffer persecution. The time between the disappointment of the Millerites and the second coming of Christ was hence a time of trial for the faithful as they struggled in the last days to keep the true Sabbath rather than the one that Protestant America, in conjunction with the Roman Catholic Antichrist, would have imposed. Andrews sketches in the picture:

Here is the 'patience of the saints'. That is, in this period commencing with their disappointment, they are in a day of affliction, a scene of trial and darkness, keeping the word of Christ's patience (Rev. iii. 10) and waiting for redemption at the coming of the Son of man. They are keeping the commandments of God, and in the possession of the faith or testimony of Jesus... We shall indeed need the faith of Jesus that we may stand in that awful hour when the last plagues shall be poured out on the earth.[36]

These three elements, a satanic United States of America, the centrality of the seventh-day Sabbath, and the nearness of the end, were to become even more pronounced and more thoroughly intertwined, in the interpretations of Rev. 13.11ff. in later Seventh-day Adventist sources.

Andrews was followed in what he said regarding the Lamb-like Beast by another early Adventist, John Norton Loughborough (1832–1924). Loughborough was an early follower of the Adventist cause, becoming a Seventh-day Adventist after hearing Andrews on the necessity of observing the seventh-day Sabbath, and was the first Seventh-day Adventist missionary to England, in 1868. He was the author of several books including early histories of the Seventh-day Adventists.[37] In a forty-eight page work devoted to this issue[38] Loughborough took up the question of the identity of the Lamb-like Beast in greater detail than Andrews, and established many of the lines of interpretation relative to Rev. 13.11ff. that were to become and remain standard in the Seventh-day Adventist tradition. Only the briefest outline is given here; the appendix to this chapter contains a substantial extract from the work, to which reference should be made.

[36] Ibid., p. 86.
[37] J. N. Loughborough, *Rise and Progress of Seventh-day Adventists* (1891); *The Great Second Advent Movement* (1905). See Froom, *Prophetic Faith*, vol. iv, pp. 1106–7 for a more substantial summary of Loughborough's life and work.
[38] J. N. Loughborough, *The Two-horned Beast* (1854); *The Two-horned Beast of Revelation XIII, a Symbol of the United States* (1857). References given here are to the 1854 edition.

Loughborough runs through several of the arguments listed by Andrews in support of the view that the second beast in Revelation 13 is the United States of America. The timing is one element; like Andrews, Loughborough quotes Litch in support of the view that the second beast is distinct from the first, after which it comes in chronological sequence (and thus arises after 1798).[39] The location too is significant: the two beasts of Revelation 13 are distinct, and, Loughborough argues, while the two overlap chronologically, they cannot do so geographically. Since, therefore, the kingdom of the first beast (the papal Antichrist) is 'the Eastern continent', i.e. Europe, the kingdom of this Lamb-like Beast must be 'the Western continent', i.e. the United States of America. (Loughborough then goes on to argue that only North America is indicated since South America was at the time when this prophecy was to be fulfilled – 1798 – largely under the control of European powers and hence part of the kingdom of the first beast.)[40] A third element is the nature of the beast's arising. The prophecy says that the beast was to 'come up out of the land', indicating that it would arise in a gradual and peaceful way.[41] Finally, there is the apparent concern for civil and religious freedom. The fact that these horns are 'lamb-like', states Loughborough, indicates 'a mild form of government, probably the mildest that ever existed'. This relates, he argues, to the mild and innocent appearance of the beast, the United States of America, which appears concerned with civil and religious liberty and with equal rights for all, although the reality is far otherwise: the beast like a lamb speaks as a dragon.[42]

According to Loughborough all these factors marked the United States of America out as the fulfilment of this prophecy. It would forge a link with the papacy (the first beast) and seek to compel all to conform to Roman Catholic worship. A key aspect of that plan would be the enactment of a Sunday law which would both enforce worship on the Sunday and prohibit it on the true seventh-day Sabbath. This enforced Sunday worship is the 'mark of the beast' (Rev. 13.16–17), and those who refused to comply would face social exclusion and not be able either to buy or to sell.[43]

These are the key points of an argument that runs throughout the second half of Loughborough's article. Time and again he makes the

---

[39] Loughborough, *Two-horned Beast*, p. 6.   [40] Ibid., p. 7.   [41] Ibid., pp. 8–9.

[42] Ibid., pp. 12–13, 14ff. Cf. the appendix; and note particularly the passionate and emotive polemic against slavery. As pointed out in the previous chapter, many Millerites were convinced abolitionists.

[43] Loughborough, *Two-Horned Beast*, pp. 45–6.

point that the United States of America is the two-horned beast, and
that it is the United States of America which will in the last days enforce
worship of the first beast (the papacy) through the medium of a national
Sunday law. The last days have dawned and hence the work is begun.
The final paragraph reads:

Dear reader, in the foregoing, we have endeavored faithfully to set before you
the work which is being, and is to be performed by this two-horned beast.
These decrees from that power are soon to go forth. The third angel's message
(Rev. xiv, 9, 12) is performing its solemn work of warning us against them, and
shows us that our only hope is in keeping 'the commandments of God and the
faith of Jesus' . . . O keep God's commandments that you may be sheltered in
that fearful day.[44]

However, the awful events which would come upon the people of
God during this final act in the drama of salvation as a result of the
activities of the Lamb-like Beast would nevertheless also be a sign of
great hope. Right at the beginning of the work Loughborough argues
that

While this beast against which we are warned is working, with his decrees out
against his people, Jesus comes, and they are delivered. See Rev. xiii, from the
19th verse, to the 6th verse of chap. xiv. Therefore, when this beast is doing his
work as marked out in the prophecy, the way-worn traveller may rejoice,
knowing that his redemption is nigh.[45]

This, then, according to Loughborough, and in the subsequent thinking of the Seventh-day Adventist movement ever since, is a prophecy for
the end time. Just before the end a great power, the United States of
America, will seek to destroy the last faithful remnant of God's people.
As will be seen, the basic framework of such thinking, even if it supported a rather different outward façade, was in place also at Waco.

While there is no doubt that it was first Andrews and then Loughborough who were largely responsible for forming later Seventh-day
Adventist views regarding the second beast of Revelation 13, it was Ellen
White, considered by Seventh-day Adventists (and Branch Davidians)
to be a prophetess for the last days, who gave the doctrine canonical
status. White's writings are considerable, and no thorough survey is
attempted here. However, at least one clear statement in one of her
more influential books ought to be noted. Speaking of Rev. 13.11ff., she
first runs through several of the arguments already encountered in the
work of Andrews and Loughborough. Like them, for example, she notes

that the beast comes up 'out of the earth' rather than overthrowing some other power, and that it arises some time after 1798. She then comments:

What nation of the New World was in 1798 rising into power, giving promise of strength and greatness, and attracting the attention of the world? The application of the symbols admits of no question. One nation, and only one, meets the specifications of this prophecy; it points unmistakably to the United States of America.[46]

White then goes on to paint a picture of the career of this beast which has the same basic features as that given by Loughborough. The United States of America will, in the last days, join together with Antichrist (the Roman Catholic Church) in a final attempt to stamp out the faithful remnant. This remnant will be flushed out into the open by the passing of a national Sunday law. White writes:

The prophecy of Revelation 13 declares that the power represented by the beast with lamb-like horns shall cause 'the earth and them which dwell therein' to worship the papacy – there symbolized by the beast 'like unto a leopard'. The beast with two horns is also to say 'to them that dwell on the earth, that they should make an image to the beast'; and, furthermore, it is to command all, 'both small and great, rich and poor, free and bond', to receive the mark of the beast. Revelation 13.11–16. It has been shown that the United States is the power represented by the beast with lamb-like horns, and that this prophecy will be fulfilled when the United States shall enforce Sunday observance, which Rome claims as the special acknowledgment of her supremacy.[47]

It is the task of the faithful to hold out against this satanic coalition of Rome and the United States of America, perhaps even to the point of martyrdom.

The endorsement by White of the Andrews–Loughborough line of eisegesis relative to Rev. 13.11ff. is highly important. Her views are not considered by Adventists to be merely her own. She has prophetic status. What she had to say was and is highly influential in Adventism, and this includes her remarks on the Lamb-like Beast. Similarly, her various works are in wide circulation both within and without Adventism, and while it is unlikely that many Adventists have read the works of Andrews or Loughborough, most will have at least a basic knowledge of the writings of Ellen White. This might be especially the case with the five volumes of her work which are known to Adventists as 'The Great

---

[46] Ellen G. White, *The Great Controversy between Christ and Satan* (Mountain View, CA: Pacific Press Publishing Association, 1911), p. 440.

[47] White, *Great Controversy*, pp. 578–9; see also pp. 449, 573, 592.

Controversy' series.[48] (The quotations above are from the one which is itself called *The Great Controversy*.) These remarks are not true only of mainstream Adventism, for there is plenty of evidence to suggest that White was an important source of authority on matters of interpretation to those in the Davidian–Branch Davidian tradition. This will be discussed further in chapter 9.

Little is to be gained by further demonstration of the nineteenth-century Seventh-day Adventist view that the beast of Rev. 13.11ff. is to be identified with the American nation. The view is ubiquitous in the relevant primary sources. It is important, however, that the impression is not given that this line of interpretation was entirely parasitic upon an assumed wider nineteenth-century eisegetical host, for it is clear in more modern Seventh-day Adventist sources that the Church continues to adopt such a position. Indeed, members of the Church employ a variety of media to disseminate its views regarding the role of the United States of America as an eschatological foe during the last days. These include, as will be demonstrated, books,[49] seminars[50] and the World Wide Web.

As regards books, an important source of what is generally considered authoritative teaching by Seventh-day Adventists is the eight-volume set of the *Seventh-day Adventist Bible Commentary*.[51] Commenting upon Rev. 13.11ff. the editors put forward the case that this beast is a prophetic symbol of the United States of America, which will in the last days seek to destroy the remnant (Sabbath-keeping) Church of God by imposing a universal Sunday law.[52] They write:

For the second beast to exercise *all* the authority of the first beast, it will have to enter the field of religion, and seek to dominate religious worship. For the United States to take this step will mean a complete reversal of its present policy of granting full freedom of religion to its citizens. Such a step is here predicted.[53]

More recently Seventh-day Adventists have made extensive use of the WWW to warn the world of the plans of the Lamb-like Beast. Thus,

[48] These are *The Great Controversy* (1911); *The Acts of the Apostles* (1911); *Patriarchs and Prophets* (1913); *Prophets and Kings* (1917); and *The Desire of Ages* (1940). Some of these volumes are also published under alternative titles. See Froom, *Prophetic Faith* vol. IV *passim*.
[49] See, for example, C. Mervyn Maxwell, *God Cares* (2 vols., Boise, ID: Pacific Press Publishing Association, 1981–5), vol. II, pp. 340–9.
[50] See, for example, the evangelistic study pack, accompanied by a series of public lectures, produced by the Seventh-day Adventist Church under the title 'Revelation Seminar'. Copies are available from the British Union of Seventh-day Adventists, Stanborough Park, Watford, Herts., WD2 6JP.
[51] *Seventh-day Adventist Bible Commentary* (8 vols., Washington, DC. Review and Herald Publishing Association, 1953–60).
[52] Ibid., vol. VII, pp. 819–22.   [53] Ibid., vol. VII, p. 820.

for example, at http://ourworld.compuserve.com/homepages/clt4/drrevi.htm,[54] a classic Seventh-day Adventist source on matters of prophetic interpretation, Uriah Smith's *Thoughts Critical and Practical on the Book of Revelation* (1865) and his *Thoughts Critical and Practical on the Book of Daniel* (1873) have been made available. Smith reflects the standard Adventist view in his thoughts on the Lamb-like Beast.[55] At another web site, this one set up by Davenport Seventh-day Adventist Church, further comments are offered on the interpretation of Revelation 13. The United States of America is first clearly identified as fulfilling the description of the beast in Rev. 13.11. The commentator then goes on to note that 'According to John's prophecy, **the United States is to play a central role in Satan's final attempt to destroy God's people** and so to thwart His eternal purpose.'[56] At yet another web-site we read:

The United States (the two horned beast), will cause all to worship the first beast by enforcing the 'mark of the first beast' by law! The word 'cause' in the original Greek means 'force.' A national Sunday law will be enforced in our country. In chapter one we've already seen that it is coming and some of the reasons why.[57]

It is apparent from these sources that the views of Andrews and Loughborough, views endorsed by White, are still matters of great concern in Seventh-day Adventism. There is still an expectation that in the last days the United States of America will play out its divinely predicted role as the ally of Catholic Rome, with whom it will join as part of the great satanic plot to drive truth from the earth. The faithful must be warned and be prepared for the difficult times which are to come. In this general context the activities of the Eternal Gospel Seventh-day Adventist Church based in West Palm Beach, Florida, are also of interest. This Church is not, it seems, located within the General Conference of Seventh-day Adventists, with whom it appears to be in some dispute.[58] However, on the question of the role of America in the last days the group is well within the basic Seventh-day Adventist tradition, though its expression of its views is more dramatic and public.

---

54 This reference is valid at the time of writing, as are all other internet addresses. The reader will be aware, however, of the inherent instability of these addresses. Keyword searches will usually provide a navigation path if the link as given fails.

55 Smith also wrote *The United States in the Light of Prophecy; or an Exposition of Rev. 13:11–17* (1874).

56 http:// www.tagnet.org/davenportsda/revbeast.htm (bold type as in the original).

57 http://www2.andrews.edu/whitt/career/zsu051.html. See also the very extensive material to be found at http://www.sundaylaw.com, a web-site which reflects Seventh-day Adventist thinking on this issue.

58 See the letter published at http://7th-day-adventist.org/gc2perei.htm, and the account of the incident published at http://7th-day-adventist.org/perez—report.html.

On 27 June 1997 the group took out a full broad-sheet advertisement in the *Washington Times* promoting its views on this and related issues. A copy of that advertisement is reproduced as figure 8.

This modern aspect of the belief in the apocalyptic role of the United States of America in Seventh-day Adventist sources, both mainstream and otherwise, it is here suggested, is important and is not just a matter of mild intellectual curiosity. It will be argued in the next chapter that the demonisation of the United States government which is found ubiquitously in such Seventh-day Adventist sources as those surveyed above predisposed members of the Branch-Davidian movement (nearly all of whom, including Koresh himself, were drawn from the Seventh-day Adventist Church) to view the siege of their headquarters by the FBI as being of apocalyptic significance. Thus, it seems, the apparently strange views of Andrews and Loughborough, as endorsed by White and fine-tuned by a host of Adventist interpreters ever since, have proven to be far more than just mildly amusing. Cut free from its historical moorings, the text of Revelation 13 has been placed at the mercy of its interpreters. Andrews and Loughborough saw in that text a picture of a satanic force. Roman Catholicism and the United States of America would combine to extinguish truth. The text, pliable in the extreme because of its extensive use of imagery, serves its interpreters well as they seek to stake out their claim to being 'on God's side' and distance themselves from their godless, indeed worse still satanic, contemporaries. However, unknown to them Andrews and Loughborough had started a line of eisegesis that would not simply run out of steam or change course as it sought to cross new terrain. Neither will it be simply a matter of amusement or theoretical analysis as its developments are observed. Rather they put spark to a fire that would one day burn out of control and consume in its heat the lives of some eighty innocents. That process is the subject of the following chapter.

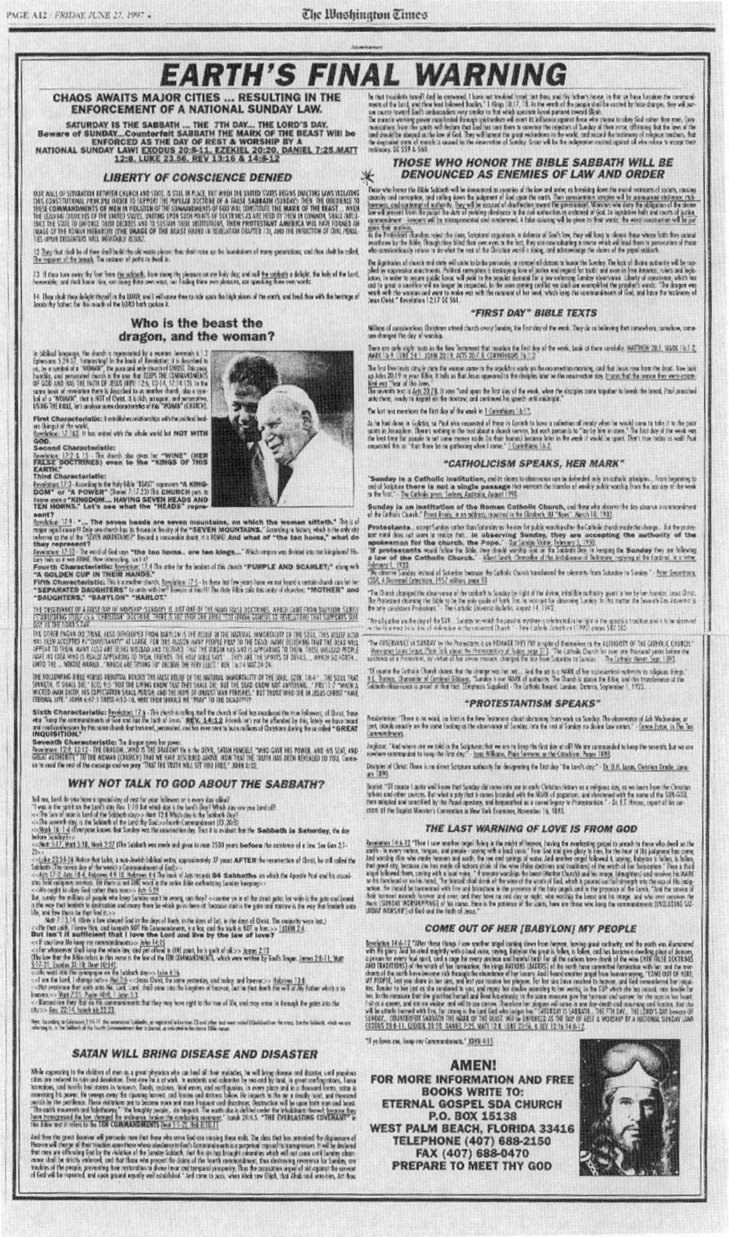

PAGE A12 / FRIDAY, JUNE 27, 1997 · The Washington Times

Advertisement

EARTH'S FINAL WARNING

CHAOS AWAITS MAJOR CITIES ... RESULTING IN THE ENFORCEMENT OF A NATIONAL SUNDAY LAW.

SATURDAY IS THE SABBATH ... THE 7TH DAY... THE LORD'S DAY. Beware of SUNDAY...Counterfeit SABBATH THE MARK OF THE BEAST Will be ENFORCED AS THE DAY OF REST & WORSHIP BY A NATIONAL SUNDAY LAW! EXODUS 20:8-11, EZEKIEL 20:20, DANIEL 7:25,MATT 12:8, LUKE 23.56, REV 13:16 & 14:8-12

LIBERTY OF CONSCIENCE DENIED

Who is the beast the dragon, and the woman?

WHY NOT TALK TO GOD ABOUT THE SABBATH?

SATAN WILL BRING DISEASE AND DISASTER

THOSE WHO HONOR THE BIBLE SABBATH WILL BE DENOUNCED AS ENEMIES OF LAW AND ORDER

"FIRST DAY" BIBLE TEXTS

"CATHOLICISM SPEAKS, HER MARK"

"PROTESTANTISM SPEAKS"

THE LAST WARNING OF LOVE IS FROM GOD

COME OUT OF HER [BABYLON] MY PEOPLE

AMEN!
FOR MORE INFORMATION AND FREE BOOKS WRITE TO:
ETERNAL GOSPEL SDA CHURCH
P.O. BOX 15138
WEST PALM BEACH, FLORIDA 33416
TELEPHONE (407) 688-2150
FAX (407) 688-0470
PREPARE TO MEET THY GOD

Figure 8 Advertisement taken out in the *Washington Times*, 17 June 1997 by the Eternal Gospel Seventh-day Adventist Church

APPENDIX[59]

The Revelator[60] declares, when the first beast went into captivity, 'I beheld another beast coming up out of the earth, and he had two horns like a lamb, and he spake as a dragon.' As we have traced the first beast to this point, we inquire, What power was rising in 1798 answering the description of the two-horned beast? Some tell us it was France. France was one of the horns of the first beast; and the Revelator does not tell us the mystery of one of those horns becoming another two-horned beast. But he gives us the destiny of the first beast, and while contemplating the scene of its overthrow, his mind is caught away by *another* beast presented before him. If it is *another* beast it cannot be a part of the first beast; but France is one of the horns of the first beast. The Franks conquered a portion of the Roman kingdom and settled in France, A. D. 407.

The first beast had the dominion of the eastern continent. It received the power, seat, and great authority of the dragon, whose power extended over the then known world. Proof. First. 'There went out a decree from Caesar Augustus, that all the world should be taxed.' Luke ii, 1. Second. Power was given to the Papal beast 'over all kindreds, and tongues, and nations.' Rev. xiii, 7. The first beast we find covered the eastern continent. The two-horned beast, then, must be located on the western continent for this reason: two governments cannot rule over the same territory at the same time. Our attention shall be turned for a few moments to the western continent. We inquire, Where is the government marked out as the two-horned beast? We look at South America, its history at that time (1798) is summed up in the following. Quite a large portion of it was Spanish Provinces, and so remained until 1816. The remainder of it was under the dominion of other portions of the first beast. We view North America. At that time here was British America, and the Russian Possessions on the North, and to the South West the Spanish dominions of Mexico. Where then was the power? We find no place to locate it except in these United States, which did then exist as an independent republican government, or in the language of the prophecy, '*another beast.*'

The rise and work of these United States, we shall show, fulfill the specifications of the prophecy. 'I beheld another beast coming up *out of the earth.*' The four beasts [Dan. vii,] also the first beast, [Rev. xiii,] are said to rise out of the sea, (sea or 'waters', denoting 'people, nations,' &c. Rev. xvii, 15,) by the striving of the winds. These winds are not the literal winds of heaven but commotions among the people, which caused kingdoms to arise; aggressive wars. Those who are acquainted with the rise of the four kingdoms, [Dan. vii.] know it was thus they arose. A beast, or kingdom, the Revelator saw, 'coming up out of the earth.' The first idea suggested by the expression, is the growth of a plant. The sap, obedient to the laws of the plant, passes into the roots, and

---

59 From J. N. Loughborough, *Two-horned Beast*, pp. 6–9, 11–17. Spelling, punctuation and italic are reproduced without alteration.

60 I.e. St John – Loughborough uses this term throughout.

there extracts from the moist earth around, such particles as are congenial to its nourishment, when it again returns, and as it courses its way through the veins of the plant, deposits that strength and nourishment where it is most needed to cause the plant to grow. So these United States, since 1798, when first noticed in the prophecy, have not risen by wars and conquest, but by means of that which existed within themselves. Their form of government is such, that it attracts other people and states to unite themselves to the federation; and thus cause a growth in numbers, territory, and industry; or cause the beast to 'come up'. Some object, that there has been a bloody war in these United States: the revolution. That war was before the beast occupies a place in the vision. The Revelator introduces his career at the point where the Papal beast is led into captivity, 1798. When first introduced in prophecy, it is a beast with two horns, speaking: which shows that it had already commenced its work, and rise, when presented before him. To show that this power has not arisen by war, but in the manner already presented, I will copy from the Dublin Nation.

[There follows a lengthy extract – about 500 words – pointing out the massive growth of the United States of America over the previous seventy years, supported by figures contrasting the census of 1792 with that of 1852.]

And still year by year they are 'coming up', growing in numbers, power and pride. It is stated that at the recent world's fair, in London, the United States was brought into a position among the nations and obtained a name which far excels all her former reputation. There, as the United States displayed her wonderful improvements, her apartment in the great Palace was thronged with astonished admirers of her ingenuity. So far did the United States come up, that she could come home and enjoy a world's fair in her own dominions.

The rise of this nation, since the time of the settlement of these colonies, just prior to the reformation in the territory of the Papal beast, has not a parallel in human history. And who would dare to say in regard to its spread of dominion, (were it not for the coming of the long-expected and just One,) 'Thus far shalt thou go and no farther.' Some at present are so bold as to state, that should ten or twenty years roll away, United States' boundaries will be *the boundaries of North America*.

Verse 11. 'And he had two horns like a lamb, and he spake like a dragon.' The horns are not explained in connection with this beast, but with an understanding of what has before been said on the subject of horns we may be prepared to understand what the two lamb-like horns represent. From those texts where the symbol has been used and explained, we learn that the two horns of the ram [Dan. viii,] denoted the kings of Media and Persia. The great horn between the eyes of the goat denoted the first king of Grecia. This being broken, and four standing up for it, represents the kingdom divided into Macedon, Thrace, Syria, and Egypt, as ruled over by Alexander's four generals. The ten horns of the fourth beast, [Dan. vii, 23, 25,] denoted the ten kingdoms into which the Roman Empire was to be divided. The little horn which came up after them, denoted the Papal church, to which Justinian gave power over the fourth beast by his decree. A horn then we find to symbolize a ruler, either civil or ecclesiastical. The little horn (church of Rome) is called definitely, a horn, before the three are plucked up and dominion given to it over the fourth beast.

No power previous to this two-horned beast, has been in prophecy symbolized by lamb-like horns. They must symbolize a power in its embryo state, with a mild form of government, probably the mildest that ever existed. They cannot symbolize a despotic or a Papal government, but true to the character of the symbol, they must represent a mild appearing, innocent power. The lamb is the symbol of innocence. Where is a government to be found more lamb-like in its appearance than this our own nation, with its Republican and Protestant rulers? We shall then call the two horns, Protestant ecclesiastical power and Republican civil power. Do they not each sustain a lamb-like appearance? Mark the language of the Declaration of Independence of these United States. 'We hold these truths to be self-evident, that all men are created free and equal, that they are endowed with certain inalienable rights, among these are life, *liberty*, and the pursuit of happiness. Where ever appeared a government with a declaration more lamb-like? In a place where the people are pledged to carry out such a declaration, we should expect to find a God-like class, carrying out the principle of the Bible to which it is so nearly allied – 'Love thy neighbour as thyself.' Here is a government placing men, as persons on an equal footing, lamb-like in appearance – yea, Christ-like. Jesus is called 'the Lamb of God, which taketh away the sin of the world.' John i, 29. But we pass to notice the horn called Protestantism. They declare that freedom of conscience is for all, that the Bible is the only standard of faith for Protestants; believe whatever is found in the Bible. Against the professions of Protestants and Republicans we have nothing to offer: their profession is right. We might expect a millennium indeed, were their profession lived out. But as presented by the Revelator, the scene is sadly degenerate when the beast begins to act. Instead of carrying out his lamb-like profession, '*he speaks as a dragon.*' Yes, that very national executive body, who have before them this declaration of Independence, and profess to be carrying out its principles, can pass laws by which 3,500,000 slaves can be held in bondage. Slaves, what are they! men like ourselves, except perhaps in their complexion. The Declaration of Independence should have a clause supplied, and should read, All men are created *free* and *equal* except 3,500,000.

Again: the constitution professing to be based on that declaration, pledges that all men shall be protected in worshiping God according to the dictates of their own consciences. Well, I as Christian profess to have my conscience in accordance with the Bible, which says, 'Thou shalt not deliver unto his master, the servant which is escaped from his master unto thee.' Deut. xxiii, 15. Now, that is my conscience on that point. Will they regard my conscience as sacred? Let us see. We will say that, by some means, a poor slave at the south has heard the clause in the declaration, that 'all men are created free.' A new idea springs up in his mind, that he ought to be free; but where can he go to be free? is the question. The world is naught to him, his knowledge is confined to his master's plantation. He is surrounded with slave-dealers who would not let him enjoy freedom. Just then the proclamation of Queen Victoria (as represented in the fugitive slave songs) salutes his ear.

> 'I heard that Queen Victoria said, if we would all forsake
> Our native land of slavery and come across the lake,
> That she was standing on the shore, with arms extended wide,
> To give us all a peaceful home beyond the rolling tide.'

If he was only there, he might enjoy his liberty. He views the dangers attendant on the way, but concludes that liberty is sweeter than life. He starts – for what? A country in which he can enjoy freedom. Yea, and he starts for that very lion power, from whose grasp, less than one century since, our own nation extricated itself because of oppression. He plods his way, faint and fatigued, by day and night, until he reaches the northern boundary of the United States. He is about to take passage for the dominion of the Queen. He turns to give one long, last look at the boasted land of freedom, but whose soil he has found to be cursed with the damning sin of slavery. There perhaps he has left a companion or children – now he is laying plans by which he may perform the generous act of *purchasing* their freedom, and again enjoy their friendly society. While he is taking his last view of that weary road over which he has passed, a tear trickles down his cheek, and he bids slavery good bye for ever. Just then a ruthless hand taps him on the shoulder, and a gruff voice says, You are mine. Half bewildered he beholds that long-hated and much dreaded man, his master. Slavery with all its galling pains again stares him in the face. Again it occurs to him, liberty is sweeter than life. Every energy of his being is stirred. He gives a leap, and is beyond the reach of that cruel master. Perhaps *you*, Christian, are standing by, and behold this scene, desirous that the fugitive should escape. You now hear the call for, Help! Help! What? *Help catch that slave!* You are almost benumbed at the thought of aiding that cruel master. You see the slave step aboard of a steamer which quickly leaves the shore, and bears the happy fugitive away from the land of slavery. You have seen the slave get his freedom – all is over. Is it? The next day you find yourself pursued, summoned to appear before the bar and answer for your transgression. What have you done? Stood still, and seen a slave get just what the Declaration of Independence of these United States says all men are entitled to – '*Liberty.*' And now for the offence you must pay $1000 fine. You plead, The constitution pledges me protection in matters of conscience; but it is of no avail. The fine is made out against you, you cannot pay it, and into prison you must go, and there lie until the claims of the law are satisfied. This, reader, is not a fancy sketch, but a real echo of the dragon-voice. But, says the reader, this is only the work of Republicans; Protestants do not, and would not, act thus. If Protestants are one horn of this beast, then *they* will act as marked out in the Word; speak like a dragon. The great red dragon, [Rev. xii,] according to its profession, had no more right to condemn an innocent man than these United States; yet when

Christ was tried, Pilate said, 'I have found no cause of death in him; [Luke xxiii] and with the next breath says, 'Crucify him.' The Protestant says, The Bible is the only standard of faith for Protestants; and yet hundreds have been expelled from their fellowship for no other cause than believing, and talking to others of the Bible doctrine of the near, personal return of the Saviour. Protestants and Republicans, both unitedly and separately, speak as a dragon.

CHAPTER 9

Waco Apocalypse: the book of Revelation in the Branch Davidian tradition[1]

We saw in chapter 7 that William Miller, and more particularly his followers, took the view that Jesus was to return to this earth on 22 October 1844. The Millerites arrived at this date through their understanding of Dan. 8.14. From the disappointment which followed Miller's failed predictions there arose a number of different groups, one of which was later to become the Seventh-day Adventist Church. In chapter 8 that story was taken up further. In particular we saw that the Seventh-day Adventist Church continued to work within the basic historicist, premillennial, anti-Catholic interpretative paradigm that Miller had himself adopted. However, while Dan. 8.14 remained, and indeed remains, central to the Seventh-day Adventist Church's understanding of itself and its role in these latter days, a radically different understanding of that text was introduced to that taken by Miller. According to the early Seventh-day Adventists, Miller had misunderstood the nature of 'the sanctuary' spoken of in Dan. 8.14. Miller had understood 'the sanctuary' as this earth; the early Seventh-day Adventists disagreed and as an alternative put forward the view that the text relates rather to Christ's entry into the heavenly (antitypical) sanctuary, that is, 'the most holy place', where he then began to conduct the ceremonies befitting the heavenly (antitypical) Day of Atonement. This view became absolutely central to the Seventh-day Adventist understanding of the purposes of God and to their understanding of the role of 'remnant' Church (themselves) in these latter days. This 'sanctuary doctrine' and its constituent eschatological imperative remains an important part of the Seventh-day Adventist theological

---

[1] Since the events at Waco a great deal of academic work has been conducted on the origins and social-scientific significance of this group, and on the events leading up to the fire. See, for example, Lewis, *From the Ashes*; Wright, *Armageddon in Waco*; Tabor and Gallagher, *Why Waco?*; Reavis, *The Ashes of Waco*. Relatively little, however, has been done on the theological views of Koresh and his followers.

scheme.² Once Christ has completed his antitypical ministry in the heavenly most holy place, he will return to this earth. In Seventh-day Adventism, then, Christ's coming is always imminent, but its precise date and time ever unknown. This chronological imprecision ensures the viability of the movement in the longer term. No precise date is set and so there is always a little longer to go.³

The basic historicist paradigm adopted by the Seventh-day Adventist Church is seen in their reading of Revelation 13. As was argued and documented in the previous chapter, from a very early stage in the Seventh-day Adventist eisegetical tradition, the view was accepted that the great Antichrist of that chapter was the Roman Catholic Church. As has been shown in chapters 2–3, this view is standard in Protestant historicism and came to the early Seventh-day Adventists via Miller. However, to this much older view, the early Seventh-day Adventists added a new dimension. The second beast of Revelation 13 (the beast with two horns), Andrews and others argued, was none other than the United States of America. America, then, as Antichrist's chief ally in the latter days, is destined to play out the part that has been written for it in the eschatological drama. Such views are still easily identifiable in the literature and other media generated by the Seventh-day Adventist Church; evidence to support this claim has been given in the previous chapter.

Here this eisegetical trajectory is traced a little further. In particular the prophetic-interpretative views of one of the offshoot trajectories of the Seventh-day Adventist Church are examined. (The number of such offshoots is surprisingly small – the Church has had remarkable success in avoiding wholesale fragmentation.⁴) The trajectory in view begins with the rise within Seventh-day Adventism of a group known as the 'Shepherd's Rod' movement, later the 'Davidian Seventh-day Advent-

² See, for example, *Seventh-day Adventists Believe... A Biblical Exposition of 27 Fundamental Doctrines* (Washington, DC: The Ministerial Association of the Seventh-day Adventist Church 1988), p. 152, where the twelfth fundamental belief of the Church is stated as follows:

The universal church is composed of all who truly believe in Christ, but in the last days, a time of widespread apostasy, a remnant has been called out to keep the commandments of God and the faith of Jesus. This remnant announces the arrival of the judgment hour, proclaims salvation through Christ, and heralds the approach of His second advent. This proclamation is symbolized by the three angels of Revelation 14; it coincides with the work of judgment in heaven and results in a work of repentance and reform on earth. Every believer is called to have a personal part in this worldwide witness.

³ On survival strategies of disappointed groups see further Festinger et al., *When Prophecy Fails*.
⁴ See further Lowell Tarling, *The Edges of Seventh-day Adventism* (Barragga Bay, New South Wales: Galilee, 1981).

ists'. It was from this group that there came the Branch Davidians, whose headquarters at Mount Carmel, Waco was the scene of the dramatic events in February to April 1993. It is argued and documented here that the view that the United States of America is the 'Lamb-like Beast' of Rev. 13.11ff., a fundamentally satanic entity which will take part in the last great battle between the forces of good and evil, was one which was to influence the minds of the vast majority, probably all, of those inside the Mount Carmel Centre during the siege. As will be shown, Koresh certainly fine-tuned the paradigm relative to the Lamb-like Beast, and his views may have developed in the early 1990s in ways that have not been adequately documented in the surviving primary material. However, it is clear from those materials that do exist that Koresh remained convinced that America was to play a significant part in the eschatological show-down. Further, in the one unambiguous source that relates directly to Revelation 13, a tape recording of a Bible study which Koresh gave in 1987,[5] his views on the issue are expressed very clearly indeed: America is the Lamb-like Beast which will make war on the faithful. Koresh's statements to this effect can be pinned down precisely. That tape is fully discussed below and a substantial extract from it is presented in the first appendix to this chapter, together with a short summary of the remainder. The siege of the headquarters by the FBI did not in any way disabuse the Branch Davidians of the traditional Seventh-day Adventist-Davidian view on the Lamb-like Beast; indeed, if anything, it further entrenched it. Finally in this chapter, developments in Branch Davidian eisegesis since Waco are briefly discussed.[6] These post-Waco developments make an informative study as the process of adapting the interpretation to fit recent events is seen in action. The eisegesis continues, and so, in all probability, does the danger of some further flare-up.

This is not a idle study, or one that is designed only for the satisfaction of the curious mind. The eighty or so charred bodies at Waco are an unwelcome and sobering reminder of the fact that when placed in the hands of certain readers, certain texts can and do become volatile and

[5] The original tape is held by Mark Swett at the Waco Never Again! Archive and Research Centre. It is a pleasure to acknowledge my indebtedness to Mr Swett for supplying a copy of the tape and for permission to print a transcription of that material.
[6] It was only after completing this chapter that I became aware of a paper on this topic by Eugene Gallagher entitled 'The Persistence of the Millennium: Branch Davidian Expectations of the End after "Waco"'. The paper is unpublished at the time of writing. Gallagher discusses both Fagan and the 'Seven Seals' group and offers remarks on the way in which the two groups continue in and yet adapt and expand the original message of Koresh.

potentially explosive. The scholarly community has a duty to understand this chemistry; so also, perhaps, do those involved in stand-offs with millennial groups.

The history of the Branch Davidian movement is complex, and this is not the place to enter into a full discussion of it.[7] However, the basic line from William Miller to David Koresh is relatively easy to trace. We saw above that it was from among the ranks of the disappointed Millerites that the early Seventh-day Adventists emerged. It was from them in turn that, in the 1930s, the movement came which was known originally as the 'Shepherd's Rod', later the 'Davidian Seventh-day Adventists', forerunners of the Branch Davidians. The most significant person in the emergence of this group and sub-group from their Seventh-day Adventist mother faith was Victor T. Houteff, who was born in Raikovo, Bulgaria, on 2 March 1885 and died in Waco on 5 February 1955. He emigrated to the United States of America in 1907. His early years in America brought prosperity to the point where he owned a hotel, but his good fortune was not to last and by 1923 he had lost the hotel and was working as a washing machine salesman. He was a convert to the Seventh-day Adventist Church in 1919, being baptised on 10 May at Rockford, Illinois.[8] During the 1920s Houteff became increasingly convinced that he had been called by God to reform the Seventh-day Adventist Church from within. The Church had, he argued, erred on several fundamental doctrinal points, especially those that relate to the interpretation and fulfilment of biblical prophecy. Thus the opening words of volume I of Houteff's two-volume work *The Shepherd's Rod* read:

It is the intention of this book to reveal the truth of the 144,000 mentioned in Revelation 7 but the chief object of this publication is to bring about a reformation among God's people. The truth herein contained is divided into seven sections, giving proof from seven different angles, to prevent any doubt or confusion. This subject is made clear by the use of the Bible and the writings given by the Spirit of Prophecy.[9]

The truth revealed here is of great importance to the church just now because of the foretold danger which God's people are soon to meet. It calls for decided action on the part of the believers to separate themselves from all worldlings

---

[7] See especially William L. Pitts Jnr, 'Davidians and Branch Davidians 1929–1987', in Wright, *Armageddon in Waco*, pp. 20–42.

[8] Committee on Defense Literature of the General Conference of Seventh-day Adventists, *The History and Teachings of 'The Shepherd's Rod'* (2 vols. [Washington, DC], 1930–2), vol. I, p. 3.

[9] The phrase 'the Spirit of Prophecy' is from Rev. 19.10. Seventh-day Adventists in general use this phrase to refer to the prophetic ministry of Ellen G. White (see, for example, *Seventh-day Adventist Bible Commentary*, vol. VII, pp. 876–7; *Seventh-day Adventists Believe . . .*, pp. 216–29).

and worldliness; to anchor themselves on the Solid Rock by obedience to all the truth known to this denomination, if we must escape the great ruin. 'The Lord's voice crieth unto the city, and the man of wisdom shall see thy name: Hear ye the rod, and who hath appointed it.' Micah 6:9.[10]

It was with this call that Houteff launched his mission to reform Seventh-day Adventism. He had little concern about Christians in general, and less still about non-believers. His mission, as he understood it, was to the Seventh-day Adventist Church, which he believed to be the true Church, but one that had in the latter days slipped from the purity of the faith. It is of fundamental importance here that this direct link between the Shepherd's Rod and the older Seventh-day Adventist Church is noted. Houteff was not starting a new movement, but rather reforming an older one from within. Allowing for the fact that, sociologically speaking, it is often precisely this kind of 'movement from within' that provides the germ from which another movement altogether will eventually grow,[11] it is likely that that 'germ' will share at least some of the major characteristics of its parent body. In the case of the Shepherd's Rod this is certainly so, for much of what is found in the Shepherd's Rod tradition, including the historicist, premillennial, anti-Catholic reading of Daniel and Revelation, is simply a continuation, with some further fine-tuning, of the older paradigm.

Houteff's acceptance of the role of Ellen G. White (the 'Spirit of Prophecy') is also important to note. This again ties him to the Adventist tradition, and the fact that he leans upon Ellen White for 'proof text' support makes it clear that his message is designed for Adventist ears. As we saw in the previous chapter, Ellen White, considered by Seventh-day Adventists to be a prophetess for the last days, endorsed the views of Uriah Smith regarding the book of Revelation, including his understanding of the Lamb-like Beast. Indeed, White puts forward the standard Seventh-day Adventist view on the identity of the Beast throughout her own work.[12] This is not the voice of just another Adventist. These are the inspired words of the prophetess.

Houteff's voice, or, as he would have said, 'The Rod's' (cf. Micah 6.9, 'The Lord's voice crieth unto the city, and the man of wisdom shall see thy name: hear ye the rod, and who hath appointed it'), fell on deaf ears and he was eventually forced to leave the ranks of the group he was

---

[10] Victor T. Houteff, *The Shepherd's Rod* (2 vols., Los Angeles, CA: Universal Publishing Association, 1930–2), vol. I, p. 4.
[11] Stark and Bainbridge, *The Future of Religion*, argue this case throughout.
[12] See chapter 8.

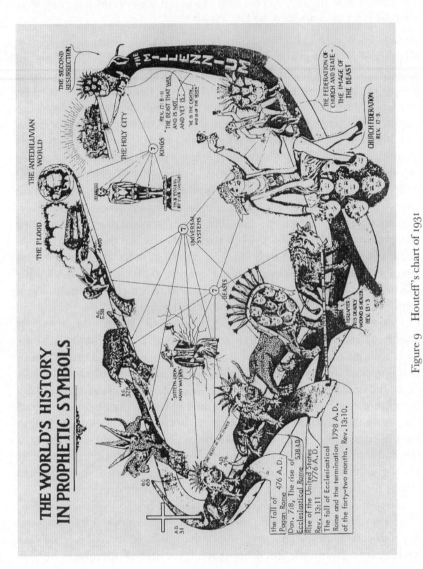

Figure 9   Houteff's chart of 1931

seeking to reform. On 20 November 1930 a motion was passed by the Olympic Exposition Park Seventh-day Adventist Church in Los Angeles disfellowshipping him.[13] He did not give up easily. Now from the sidelines rather than as a active participant in the game, he continued to shout advice and warnings to his former team-mates. Over the course of the next years his output was prodigious, the most important statement of his views by far coming in the completed 559-page work *The Shepherd's Rod*, and he was successful in gaining a modest following. In 1935 the group took up residence at the Mount Carmel Centre in Waco, Texas, where it and its most prominent successor,[14] the Branch Davidian movement, were to remain until April 1993. In 1942 the pressures of conscription made it necessary for the group to take on a name formally. To this point it had been operating under the title of the chief publication of its founder, namely *The Shepherd's Rod*. It chose 'The Davidian Seventh-day Adventists' in recognition of the fact that Houteff and his followers saw themselves first and foremost as Seventh-day Adventists whose tradition they claimed as their own. However, the word 'Davidian' was added in an attempt to identify the movement as one that looked forward to the restoration of the kingdom of David prior to the premillennial coming of Christ. This 'kingdom of David', which would be based in Jerusalem, would be ruled over by an antitypical David.[15]

Houteff continued the leadership of the movement until his death, at which point leadership was taken up by his wife, Florence. Her rule was disastrous for the movement and it reached the point of near collapse, especially after the failure of her prophecy that the world would end on

[13] Committee on Defense Literature of the General Conference of Seventh-day Adventists, *History and Teachings of the 'Shepherd's Rod'*, vol. 1, pp. 4–6.

[14] Other Davidian groups which came from the fragmentation of the Houteffs' Davidian Seventh-day Adventists include those which Tarling refers to as the Davidian Seventh-day Adventist Association – The Bashan Movement, and the Eleventh Hour Adventist Remnant Church – The Isaac Branch. See Tarling, *The Edges of Seventh-day Adventism*, pp. 136–7. Pitts, 'Davidians and Branch Davidians', pp. 31–2 refers to eight Davidian splinter groups that grew up following the collapse of the original movement under Florence Houteff.

[15] Thus on p. 2 of *The Leviticus of the Davidian Seventh-day Adventists* (1943) Houteff wrote

The name, Davidian, deriving from the name of the king of Ancient Israel, accrues to this Association by reason of its following aspects: First, it is dedicated to the work of announcing and bringing forth the restoration (as predicted in Hosea 1:11; 3:5) of David's kingdom in antitype, upon the throne of which Christ, 'the son of David', is to sit. Second, it purports itself to be the first of the first fruits of the living, the vanguard from among the present-day descendants of those Jews who composed the Early Christian Church. With the emergence of this vanguard and its army, the first fruits, from which are elected the 12,000 out of each of the twelve tribes of Jacob, 'the 144,000' (Rev. 14:1; 7:2–8) who stand on Mount Zion with the Lamb (Rev. 14:1; 7:2–8), the reign of antitypical David begins.

22 April 1959.[16] During this time the General Conference of Seventh-day Adventists sought to bring the Davidians back into the fold; the attempt failed.[17]

Florence Houteff's role as leader of the Davidians did not go unchallenged, and after some dispute and failure to reach agreement on the leadership issue there emerged a second 'Davidian' group, namely the 'Branch' Davidians. The word 'Branch' was added to the name 'Davidians' since it had been Houteff's view that in addition to being ruled over by the antitypical King David, the 'Kingdom of David' would be ruled over also by 'the Branch', that is, Christ himself. As it says in Jer. 23.5,

Behold, the days come, saith the Lord, that I will raise unto David a righteous Branch, and a King shall reign and prosper, and shall execute judgment and justice in the earth.

This premillennial rule of Christ would be non-physical, but nevertheless very real. Following Houteff's original lead, the Branch Davidians developed this understanding of 'the Branch'. According to them one should consider also Isa. 11.1: 'And there shall come forth a rod out of the stem of Jesse, and a Branch shall grow out of his roots.' According to Ruth 4.17 Jesse was the father of David. This, as Pitts has noted,[18] made the link with the Davidians while allowing the movement to argue for its own special status in the sequence of remnant communities.

This 'Branch Davidian' trajectory of Davidianism began under the leadership of Ben Roden (1902–78).[19] He felt that he had been called by God to bring order to the increasing chaos of the Davidians following the death of Houteff, and saw the action of God in the history of salvation as coming to a head in the three final stages. The first of these was the Seventh-day Adventist Church and the establishment of the Sabbath truth, the second was the Davidians and the gathering of the remnant people, and the third was the 'Branch' Davidians. This latter

[16] See further Pitts, 'Davidians and Branch Davidians', pp. 30–1.
[17] Between 24 June and 7 July 1959 a series of sixteen public meetings was held between the two parties. These led to a further forum, held between 27 July and 7 August of the same year. See Tarling, *The Edges of Seventh-day Adventism*, p. 128.
[18] Pitts, 'Davidians and Branch Davidians', p. 32.
[19] The biographical information on all the Branch Davidian leaders is sketchy, and has been compiled with difficulty. It therefore appears useful to record that information more fully than usual, although its accuracy cannot be guaranteed. To avoid disrupting the analysis of Branch Davidian thought, the information has been placed in the second appendix to this chapter. It is a pleasure to acknowledge the assistance of Mark Swett in compiling the information. See that appendix for information on Ben Roden.

movement had the seal of the name of Christ ('the Branch') and constituted the hub of the 144,000 of Rev. 7.4; 14.1, 3. These 144,000 were to be formed perfectly into the image of Christ prior to the coming of Christ in glory.

After Ben's death the leadership was taken by his wife, Lois,[20] whose claim to the office had first been made even before her husband's death. Her energies were largely given to seeking to establish the doctrine of the femininity of the Holy Spirit, and also the view that the second appearance of the Messiah would see him (her) in feminine form. Lois was not, however, the only relative of Ben Roden to stake a claim to the leadership of the movement. Their son George[21] was particularly clear that God had called him to this role, and sought to wrest control from his mother.[22] Her choice of successor, however, was not her own son but the younger man named Vernon Howell, later to be known as David Koresh.[23] After a complex series of events, sketched out briefly in appendix 2, Howell and his followers took possession of the Centre on 23 March 1988,[24] and remained there until the fire in April 1993. Despite the events in Waco, the Branch Davidian movement continues, though the extent of its membership cannot be easily ascertained.

This is a book about the eisegetical process and not the history of religious groups. The story of the emergence of the Branch Davidians has been outlined in this detail, however, in order that the direct line of descent from Miller to Koresh may be made clear. For obvious and quite understandable reasons the Seventh-day Adventist Church has sought, very successfully, it must be said, to distance itself from the events at Waco and to create the impression that the Church was simply descended upon by a wholly extraneous cult.[25] However, this suggestion of absolute dissimilarity between the movements, while clearly in the interests of the Seventh-day Adventist Church, is unhelpful to anyone studying Branch Davidian views on biblical prophecy, particularly as they relate to the interpretation of Daniel and Revelation. There can be no disputing the fact that Branch Davidianism and Seventh-day Adventism are very closely tied in at least three major ways. First, because

---

[20] See appendix 2 for biographical information.
[21] See appendix 2 for biographical information.
[22] See further Pitts, 'Davidians and Branch Davidians', pp. 36–8.
[23] See appendix 2 for biographical information.
[24] Pitts, 'Davidians and Branch Davidians', p. 38.
[25] See further Ronald Lawson, 'Seventh-day Adventist Responses to Branch Davidian Notoriety: Patterns of Diversity within a Sect Reducing Tension with Society', *Journal for the Scientific Study of Religion* 34 (1995): 323–41; 'Adventists Disavow Waco Cult', *Christian Century* 110 (1993): 285–6.

of the historical roots of Branch Davidianism; second, because almost all Branch Davidians were former mainstream Seventh-day Adventists; and third, as a result of the other two, because of the substantial overlap in theological outlook, especially as it relates to end-time events. Branch Davidianism is more of a grandchild than a second cousin of Seventh-day Adventism, albeit a grandchild that has been largely disinherited. Traditional Seventh-day Adventist views on Revelation will therefore need to be taken into account when dealing with the theology and beliefs of this movement. Clearly Houteff, Roden and Koresh took the theology of Seventh-day Adventism in a different direction, but this does not mean that they departed from it altogether.[26]

With these general remarks in mind, we can now turn our attention to detail. In view of the mass of material relating to the book of Revelation that is found among the Davidian/Branch Davidian sources, it will be both necessary and helpful to limit this study to one particular passage. The one that has been chosen is Revelation 13, for two reasons. First, because it allows the study of the previous chapter to continue into this one and hence a more rounded and extended eisegetical history can be brought into view. Second, because, it is argued here, the understanding of Revelation 13 in the Davidian-Branch Davidian tradition was an important element at Waco, and the negative afterlife of this section of the biblical text can hence be seen very clearly.

The views of Victor T. Houteff himself have not to date been the subject of much in the way of detailed examination.[27] This may partly be because of difficulty in accessing the relevant documents, a difficulty now largely overcome through the creation of the Shepherd's Rod web-site and the production of a CD containing a large quantity of Houteff's material.[28]

It is not necessary here to enter into a full investigation of Houteff's

---

[26] Houteff and his followers up to and including Koresh continued to see their primary mission as being to Seventh-day Adventists and not to the world at large. There are major overlaps between Branch Davidian theology and that of the official Seventh-day Adventist Church, including, importantly, the acceptance of Ellen G. White as a prophetess. Note, for example, the statement made by Koresh in his 'Study on Joel and Daniel 11', p. 1 (http://home.maine.rr.com/waco/joel.html), where he appeals to Mrs White's prophetic authority in support of a claim he is about to make; and note also statements such as those in 'Judge What I Say' (http://home.maine.rr.com/waco/judge.html), which several times includes such statements as 'Ellen G. White tells us' and 'Sister White tells us' in support of arguments. See further generally Pitts, 'Davidians and Branch Davidians'.

[27] The most substantial study is that contained in Tarling, *The Edges of Adventism*, pp. 113–24.

[28] http://www.shepherds-rod.org (operated by Bread of Life Ministries, Route 3, Box 404, Fletcher, NC 28732). A printed scriptural index of Houteff's writings was compiled by Don Adair: *A Complete Scriptural Index to the Original Writings of V. T. Houteff* (Salem, SC: General Association of Davidian Seventh-day Adventists, 1993).

overall eisegetical paradigm, except to note that it is substantially the same as that of the Seventh-day Adventist tradition to which he belonged. A basic historicism runs throughout, though on numerous points of detail Houteff differed from his Adventist heritage. One obvious and extreme case is that of Ezekiel 9. This passage speaks of a slaughter of terrible proportions, a time when all who do not have a particular mark written upon them will be slain ('Slay utterly old and young, both maids, and little children, and women: but come not near any man upon whom is the mark' – Ezek. 9.6). This is a passage that Seventh-day Adventists in general have understood as being a prophecy relating to the end of time, when the wicked in general will be slaughtered. 'The mark' here is understood to be the seal of God, that is, Sabbath observance, the antithesis of the mark of the beast in Rev. 13.17.[29] Houteff took a different view. The slaughter of that chapter was not, he argued, part of a general slaughter of the wicked, but rather of unbelieving Seventh-day Adventists, particularly ministers, shortly before the coming of Christ.[30] 'The mark' of that chapter, he argued, was not the Sabbath (although only Sabbath keepers were eligible for it), but rather a mark or 'seal' placed upon those who sought to root out all error in the Church. He wrote:

The only ones who can have the seal are those who sigh and cry for all the abominations (sins) that are done in the church. But if any take part and try to throw a cloak over the existing evil in the church, then they are left without the seal.[31]

On numerous other key points, however, Houteff keeps well inside the standard Seventh-day Adventist (and indeed more often than not the Millerite and general Protestant-historicist) eisegetical pathways. The Pope is the 'man of sin' predicted in 2 Thess. 2,[32] the 1,260 days of Rev. 12.6 are so many years and lasted from AD 538 to 1798,[33] the 'two witnesses' of Rev. 11.3 are the Old and the New Testaments[34] and the 'little book' of Rev. 10.2, 8–10 is the book of Daniel.[35]

---

[29] See *Seventh-day Adventist Bible Commentary*, vol. IV, pp. 605–7; here the editors argue that the slaughter is in part a reference to the slaughter which came during the destruction of Jerusalem by Nebuchadnezzar, but also a prophecy for the end time when those who do not have the seal (Sabbath observance) will be slain. Like Houteff, the editors of the *Seventh-day Adventist Bible Commentary* argue that it is the professed spiritual leaders of the people who will be slain first; naturally they would have differed on the question of who these leaders would actually be.

[30] Committee on Defense Literature of the General Conference of Seventh-day Adventists, *History and Teachings of the Shepherd's Rod*, pp. 22–3.

[31] Houteff, *Shepherd's Rod*, vol. I, p. 8.   [32] Ibid., vol. II, p. 152.   [33] Ibid., vol. II, p. 227.

[34] Ibid., vol. II, p. 283; cf. White, *Great Controversy*, p. 267; *Seventh-day Adventist Bible Commentary*, vol. VII, p. 801.

[35] Houteff, *Shepherd's Rod*, vol. I, p. 16.

On Revelation 13 Houteff had some interesting, and, in the context of later events at Waco, potentially significant things to say. On the first beast of Rev. 13.1–10 he differed from his mainstream Seventh-day Adventist forebears on a number of important details. Seventh-day Adventists understand this beast as a symbol of papal Rome and papal Rome only.[36] Houteff, however, argued that the beast of Rev. 13.1–10 represents 'the world, but more particularly the entire western civilisation, with their civil and religious systems'.[37] The seven heads of the beast represent the specifically religious bodies of 'western civilisation', one of which, the one that had the deadly wound that was healed, was a symbol of the papacy. That deadly wound was inflicted upon the papacy by the reforms of Martin Luther and by the imprisonment of Pius VI in 1798.[38] This latter point is standard Seventh-day Adventism.[39] The other six heads represent Protestantism in the form of six groups from which, according to Houteff, all Protestant denominations ultimately spring. These six are Lutherans, Presbyterians, Methodists, 'Christians' (this appears to be a slip for 'Baptists'),[40] First-day Adventists and Seventh-day Adventists. These six, together with Catholicism, make up the totality of the apostate Church and are all alike destined for destruction. Clearly there are differences here from the older Seventh-day Adventist view, and the reason for those differences is not difficult to imagine. Houteff had been rejected by those whom he felt called to reform. He now finds the reason for that rejection: the Seventh-day Adventist Church, like all other Protestants and Rome itself, is presently the instrument of Satan.

Houteff, then, differed from his denominational forebears on the question of the identity of the first beast of Revelation 13, though the difference is one of reference rather than meaning; they agree that it is a symbol of an antichristian power which was, from John's perspective, yet to arrive, but differ on the question of the precise identity of that power. Houteff's interpretation of the 'Lamb-like' or 'two-horned' beast, however, ran along the standard Seventh-day Adventist lines. He had no doubt that the beast there described is none other than the

---

[36] *Seventh-day Adventist Bible Commentary*, vol. VIII, p. 817.   [37] Houteff, *Shepherd's Rod*, vol. II, p. 88.

[38] Ibid., p. 95.   [39] See, for example, *Seventh-day Adventist Bible Commentary*, vol. VII, p. 817.

[40] See further *Timely Greetings* 2 (39): 14, where in another context Houteff lists Lutherans, Presbyterians, Methodist, Baptists, First-day Adventists and Seventh-day Adventists and then states that 'other sects with their additions, omissions, and deductions, have obviously branched from these six denominations'. A full run of the Shepherd's Rod publication *Timely Greetings* is available at the Shepherd's Rod web-site (http://www.shepherds-rod.org).

United States of America. After outlining the chief characteristics of the Lamb-like Beast, he wrote:

The United States of America is the only government in the world that answers to all these specifications. It originated in a new world ('the earth'), not in the territories of the ancient world ('the sea'). It is the only government which is lamb-like – youthful and Christian, established upon the innocent principles of peace and liberty, having two non-royalist ruling parties (crownless horns), the Republican and the Democratic.[41]

Houteff also argues that it is America which will, in the last days, in keeping with the standard Seventh-day Adventist view, seek to destroy the people of God by enacting a Sunday observance law and enforcing it with the most severe penalties. He comments on the beast's decree that

[t]his drastic decree of the two-horned beast shall be adopted by the nations of the world, and the image of the beast, which will demand obedience to an ecclesiastical form of worship, will be internationally set up. The mark of the beast is Sunday observance. Under one pretext or another, the careless and indifferent will worship the image of the beast, and receive the mark.[42]

What Houteff says in *The Shepherd's Rod* on this issue is thus entirely in keeping with the broader Seventh-day Adventist tradition from which he came.[43] The United States of America, predicted in prophecy as the Lamb-like Beast of Rev. 13.11ff., will play a key eschatological role in the great cosmic struggle between good and evil. This role is on the side of Satan, as under his influence and at his prompting the United States government establishes a law to enforce the observance of the Roman Catholic (counterfeit) Sabbath.

No more need be said regarding Houteff's interpretation of this section of Revelation 13, for already the continuity is seen. The early Seventh-day Adventists argued that America was the Lamb-like Beast of Revelation 13 and, as we saw in the previous chapter, this understanding of Rev. 13.11ff. continues to be put forward in standard Seventh-day Adventist sources today. Houteff, founder of the Shepherd's Rod (later the Davidian Seventh-day Adventists), agreed. But such views outlived him and continued to be operative in one of the Davidians' denominational offspring, the Branch Davidians.

As we saw above, the key figure in the emergence of the Branch Davidians from the Davidian Seventh-day Adventists was Ben Roden.

---

[41] Houteff, *The World Yesterday, Today, Tomorrow*, p. 39. This source is a tract published by Houteff in 1941. It is available at http://www.shepherds-rod.org/Tracts/trac012.html.

[42] *Shepherd's Rod*, vol. II, p. 109.   [43] See ibid., vol II, pp. 107–9.

He saw himself as a reformer of the Davidians, who, he felt, had fallen into disarray. There is some evidence that he saw himself as the antitypical King David, who would rule over the premillennial (and pre-second coming) kingdom of Christ.[44]

Little is known directly of Ben Roden's views regarding the Lamb-like Beast, but there is nothing to suggest that either he or his wife Lois departed from the standard Adventist-Davidian line on this issue. What we do know is that as they emerged from the period under Houteff the Davidians held to an eisegetical line relative to the Lamb-like Beast which was substantially the same as that which had been taken by the early and later Seventh-day Adventists. We also know that Koresh too held a view on Revelation 13 that overlapped very significantly with that of the older Seventh-day Adventists. This suggests that the Rodens did not substantially shift the paradigm at any point during their leadership, although it is not possible to demonstrate this conclusively from the available primary material.

It seems, then, that the early Seventh-day Adventist understanding of the Lamb-like Beast as a symbol of a satanic America went with Houteff into the Davidian tradition and then with Roden into the Branch Davidians. There is a trajectoral continuity on this eisegetical point that should not be missed. Just as important, however, is the fact that the Davidian and Branch Davidian understanding of its own mission is entirely built upon the existence of the mainstream Seventh-day Adventist Church. There is little or no evidence to suggest that Davidians or Branch Davidians had any interest in 'converting' ('correcting', as they would have seen it) anyone who was not already a Seventh-day Adventist. Those they addressed, therefore, as a result of that allegiance already had on board a substantial part of the Davidian-Branch Davidian eisegetical baggage. Indeed, Houteff's original view of the three final stages of truth, the acceptance of which would lead to the formation of an ever more narrowly defined 'remnant' community, would logically preclude extended missionary activity to any who were not already Sabbath keepers. It is a simple and telling fact that almost all Branch Davidians, including of course David Koresh himself, had been Seventh-day Adventists and continued to see themselves as such after accepting the Branch Davidian message.[45] In fact Livingstone Fagan, to

---

[44] See further Pitts, 'Davidians and Branch Davidians', p. 35.
[45] Thus speaking on Rev. 10.5–6, Koresh states: 'Now we as Seventh-day Adventists understand this to refer to prophetic time . . .', 'Study on Joel and Daniel 11' (http://home.maine.rr.com/waco/joel.html), p. 1.

whom further reference will be made below, worked for a short while as a Seventh-day Adventist pastor in Britain prior to his departure for Waco. For two obvious reasons, then, it must be at least a possibility that the kind of eisegetical paradigm relative to Rev. 13.11ff. traced above was operative also at Waco as a result first of the continuing influence of the parent body's eisegesis directly upon the theology adopted by the movement and second of the fact that almost all Branch Davidians had been Seventh-day Adventists and so were well acquainted with the paradigm already. Further investigation suggests that that possibility was in fact a reality.

Seeking to understand the theology of the Branch Davidians after the Rodens, and in particular the constituent task of exploring the eisegetical labyrinth Koresh constructed, is not easy. However, while the outward form of this later development of Branch Davidian theology may have the appearance of chaos, it contains what appears to be an elaborate and reasonably self-consistent core. Indeed, it is apparent in the sources that have survived from Koresh, and particularly from those of his associate Steve Schneider, that the Branch Davidian leaders and spokespersons absolutely rejected any charge that what they had to say was inconsistent or not open to rational analysis. Schneider, for example, often speaks very negatively about 'feelings' as a guide to the religious life. He is concerned to prove from scripture all he has to say.[46] The rationale and method of biblical interpretation employed is not that which most modern critical scholars would accept. However, if it is seen in its own context there is a level of consistency and a certain internal logic operative in the Branch Davidian paradigm. That context is one of extreme biblical fundamentalism, mixed with a now largely anachronistic historicism relative to the prophetic books. Sitting alongside this is a traditions history going back to Miller and the almost endless supply of extra-canonical writ from the pen of Ellen White. This is a complex, interwoven system. Fortunately there is no need to explore that complexity in any great detail here. However, this wider context should not be forgotten when an attempt is made to extract one single element from the mass.

Koresh understood the book of Revelation as a summary of all biblical prophecies that had gone before. It was a key, or rather a 'code

[46] This remark is made on the basis of listening to a series of nine tapes made of Branch Davidian recruitment meetings held in Manchester, England in the early part of the 1990s. These tapes are in my own private possession, but copies have been lodged with the archive collected by Mark Swett to which reference has already been made above.

breaker', by which one might unlock all other parts of scripture. He states as much very clearly in an early study dated 4 February 1985:

The book of Revelation contains all the books of the bible. All the books of the bible meet and end there. This is what we have learned over the years.[47]

It is this basic assumption that drives much of what Koresh has to say on the book of Revelation; unless one fully appreciates this, much of Koresh's thinking on matters prophetic will appear as simply bizarre. What this understanding of Revelation entails in practice is that Koresh will read Revelation looking all the time for the verbal clues, the 'stitch-words', as scholars would call them in another setting, that relate the passage under consideration to its (generally Old Testament) context. The clues Koresh discovers are often very subtle. Thus, for example, he notes that Rev. 10.3 states that the angel there depicted 'cried ... as a lion roars'. For Koresh this is part of the code; lions 'roar' but eagles 'cry'; therefore the one who wants to interpret this part of Revelation will need to look for another place in scripture where a lion and an eagle are linked in one symbol. The only one, says Koresh (and he is as usual correct on this biblical detail), is the symbol used to depict Babylon or Nebuchadnezzar. He clearly has Dan. 7.4 in mind. By this somewhat circuitous route he arrives at the conclusion that the angel of Rev. 10.3 will lift up his voice against 'Babylon' (understood as a symbol of the apostate Church).[48] For Koresh, then, the book of Revelation is very much the tip of the prophetic iceberg; its bulk lies beneath the surface in places like Zechariah, Amos, Joel, Daniel and especially the book of Psalms. Indeed, this latter source Koresh referred to as the 'key of David'[49] (cf. Rev. 3.7) in that it was there that one found means by which the secrets of Revelation might be unlocked. This approach makes reading Koresh hard work, particularly as most of what is available takes the form of transcriptions from poorly recorded tapes. However, despite first appearances, he is not simply ranting: there is an order to his thought, though not one that can be immediately recognised.

This view of the relationship between the book of Revelation and the rest of the Bible is one which few even of the more conservative wing of the Christian Church would share. In critical scholarship it is now

---

[47] 'Judge What I Say', p. 1.   [48] Ibid., p. 1.
[49] Koresh is clearly heard to say this in a tape which was widely broadcast on 3 March 1993. A copy of that tape is held at the Waco Never Again! Archive. A substantial section is given over to Koresh's attempt to show, using such stitch-words, that the First Seal (the rider on the white horse) is to be understood in the context of Psalm 45 and Revelation 19.

widely recognised that each book of the Bible has its own author or authors, who were working independently of each other. If the books have a common strand, it is not the direct verbal inspiration or dictation of the Holy Spirit. However, Koresh must be seen in his own more immediate context and not in one in which he simply did not operate. In fact, the difference between Koresh and mainstream Seventh-day Adventism on this point is one of degree more than kind. In general terms Seventh-day Adventists advise students of the scriptures to treat the Bible as having a fundamental unity. According to the Seventh-day Adventist view the Bible must be taken as a whole, for in it God has revealed himself 'little by little'.[50] Further, the Old and New Testaments interlock: 'The Old Testament serves as foundation for the New. It provides the key to unlock the New while the New explains the mysteries of the Old.'[51] In order to interpret correctly, then, scripture must be compared with scripture; the Bible is its own interpreter.[52] This attempt to allow scripture to interpret itself was what Koresh himself did, although the parts he compared would not have been those that mainstream Seventh-day Adventists would have chosen.

More specifically, Adventists do approach the book of Revelation in particular on the assumption that it is a coming together, better a 'revealing', of other parts of the Bible. Such a view is clearly set forth in volume VII of the *Seventh-day Adventist Bible Commentary*, where Ellen White is quoted approvingly on the matter: 'The book of Daniel is unsealed in the revelation to John',[53] and elsewhere 'In the Revelation all the books of the Bible meet and end.'[54] The latter statement is picked up by Koresh in the quotation above, where he states of Revelation 'All the books of the bible meet and end there.' Seventh-day Adventist recruits to Koresh's form of Branch Davidianism, then, would not have found his methodology particularly problematic, and the comment made above seems fair: the difference between Koresh and mainstream Seventh-day Adventism on this point is more one of degree than of kind.

This understanding by Koresh and his followers of the relationship between various parts of the Bible leads to another area where again the roots of Koresh's thinking in Seventh-day Adventism must be taken into proper account. As has been seen, from its inception with Miller

[50] *Seventh-day Adventists Believe...*, p. 14.   [51] Ibid., p. 14.   [52] Ibid., p. 18.
[53] *Seventh-day Adventist Bible Commentary*, vol. VII, p. 731; the reference to Ellen White is to *Testimonies to Ministers and Gospel Workers* (Mountain View, CA: Pacific Press Publishing Association, 1923), p. 115.
[54] *Seventh-day Adventist Bible Commentary*, vol. VII, p. 724; the reference to Ellen White is to *Acts of the Apostles* (Mountain View, CA: Pacific Press Publishing Association, 1911), p. 585.

(and more particularly S. S. Snow), the movement which became Seventh-day Adventism placed an emphasis upon the use of 'types' and 'antitypes' in the interpretation of scripture. This method of interpretation is of course much older than Miller, and it would be wrong to classify this approach as distinctively 'Millerite' or 'Adventist'.[55] However, in Seventh-day Adventism this typology was to take on particular significance, and lies at the heart of its truly distinctive theological vision: the 'Sanctuary Doctrine'. As we saw in the last two chapters, according to Seventh-day Adventism much of the Old Testament cult system is to be understood as a 'type' of things to come. For example, the Aaronic high-priestly ministry is a type of the ministry of Christ, its antitype. Similarly, the temple on earth is a type of the true sanctuary in heaven and the Day of Atonement was a type of the events of 22 October 1844 when Christ concluded his 'daily' ministry and entered into the heavenly (antitypical) most holy place.[56] The basic thrust (though not the details) of this kind of thinking is not at all uncommon in Christian history, or even for that matter in the New Testament itself.[57] However, in Seventh-day Adventism it has a particular focus and is brought very much to the fore. It is in its unpacking of the typology inherent in the Old Testament cultus that Adventism makes its claim to theological originality, and indeed denominational legitimacy. The Adventist Church was raised up by God to proclaim the three angels' messages during this last phase of Christ's antitypical heavenly ministry. Adventists are, then, fully acquainted with the importance of typology and Koresh could assume this basic knowledge in presenting his extension of it. As with the basic approach to scripture as a unity and its own interpreter, then, the typological method of biblical interpretation espoused by Koresh would not have sounded odd to Seventh-day Adventist ears. The content was novel, the method well-worn.

It was on the basis of such typology that Koresh changed his name from 'Howell' to 'Koresh'. He was, he claimed, the antitypical Cyrus (which in Hebrew is written 'כּוֹרֶשׁ', that is, 'Koresh'); his 'type' was

---

[55] See further 'Typology', in R. J. Coggins and J. L. Houlden (eds.), *A Dictionary of Biblical Interpretation* (London: SCM Press, 1990), pp. 713–14.

[56] For a statement of the Seventh-day Adventist view see further *Seventh-day Adventists Believe...*, pp. 312–31.

[57] Probably the best example is the book of Hebrews, from which Seventh-day Adventists draw much. Paul uses the word 'allegory' (ἀλληγορούμενα) to describe the two covenants symbolised by Hagar and Sarah in Gal. 4.24, and Jonah's abdominal sojourn is seen as a type of Christ's burial and subsequent resurrection in the Q tradition (Matt. 12.39–41; Luke 11.29–32).

the Cyrus of Isaiah 44 and 45 etc., who had come to destroy Babylon.[58] The Babylon in question was the antitypical one, namely apostate religion; the equation of latter-day Babylon with apostate religion, both Protestant and Roman Catholic, is a commonplace in Seventh-day Adventist literature.[59]

Koresh's general understanding of his own broader role in the eschatological events is not of immediate concern here. However, one particular part of it is of direct relevance, namely his view that he was the seventh angel of Rev. 10.7. It was partly upon this text that he staked his claim to authority. While such statements might sound to the outsider as nothing short of insane, Koresh's potential and actual Seventh-day Adventist converts would surely have been able at least to understand the claim, even if they did not agree with it. Angels are very frequently mentioned in the book of Revelation, and in general Seventh-day Adventists have understood some at least of these angels as messages and/or messengers – the two of course overlap. There are, for example, the angels to the seven churches in Revelation 2–3. These seven churches are understood by Adventists as seven periods in Church history, a view to which Koresh also subscribed.[60] The messages to the seven angels are hence messages to the seven periods of the Church and the angels to whom the message is originally given (who may be human beings)[61] in turn relay the message to the people.[62] There are two further sequences of angels in Revelation, one of seven (Rev. 8.7, 8, 10, 12; 9.1, 13;11.15) and one of three (14.6, 8, 9). Seventh-day Adventists understand the first of these sequences, the seven trumpet-blowing angels, in the standard historicist way, as marking a chronological sequence of events in the history of the Church and the world.[63] The second sequence, however, may be of particular significance here. These 'three angels',

58 See Koresh's 'Letter to the Seventh-day Adventist Church' (http://home.maine.rr.com/waco/son.html), where he states (capitals as in the web-page) 'My Name is Cyrus, and I Am here to destroy Babylon (Rev. 9:14).'
59 See, for example, *Seventh-day Adventist Bible Commentary*, vol. VII, pp. 828–30, which provides an extended note on the meaning of the term 'Babylon' in Rev. 14.8.
60 In 'Judge What I Say', p. 2, for example, Koresh speaks of Miller's message being to the church of Philadelphia. This is not the actual city of Philadelphia, but the period of Church history from about 1789 to 1844; see further *Seventh-day Adventist Bible Commentary*, vol. VII, pp. 725, 758.
61 See ibid., vol. VII, p. 741.
62 See further ibid., vol. VII, p. 741, where the argument is presented that the 'angels' here are the 'leaders of the [seven] churches'. This statement, combined with the oft-repeated view that the Churches are themselves periods in the history of the Church in general, implies (it is not spelt out) that the 'angels' here are human messengers who have a particular message appropriate to the time in which it is spoken.
63 Ibid., vol. VII, p. 788.

and particularly their messages, are very much a central part of the Seventh-day Adventist Church's understanding of its own role in the latter days. The angels hold the messages that are to go out to the world during this countdown to Christ's return: the gospel and the Sabbath (angel one), the identification of Roman Catholicism and apostate Protestantism as Babylon (angel two) and the final warning against the mark of the beast, that is, Sunday observance (angel three).[64] Thus in the Adventist tradition some at least of Revelation's angels are taken as representing particular messengers and/or messages, each message relating directly either to the Church (i.e. period in Church history) to which it is spoken or to the Church's function during the end times.

Koresh appears to take this understanding a little further. The sources available are incomplete, with the result that the full picture is obscured. However, it appears that he found another sequence of angels in Revelation, namely the 'messages' of the seven thunders of Rev. 10.3–4. These, states Koresh, are so many 'messages' or 'angels'. The first angel was William Miller,[65] the second is not identified (and who Koresh thought it was is not at all easy to guess), but the third, fourth, fifth and sixth are identified as respectively Ellen White, Victor Houteff, Ben Roden and Lois Roden.[66] These individuals had begun the work; they had given the messages of truth for the final phase of history. They had not, however, gathered the 144,000 of Revelation 7. This would be the work of the seventh angel/thunder. The seventh angel would also reveal the content of the seven thunders of Revelation 10 itself (this is a master-stroke; like the Johannine Christ, Koresh reveals that he is the revealer). Koresh thought that he and perhaps to a lesser extent the entire latter-day Branch Davidian movement under his leadership was that angel.[67]

As we have seen, Koresh's views on Revelation are complex, and it is clear that he did diverge from the standard Seventh-day Adventist line

---

[64] Ibid., vol. VII, pp. 827–33. It is perhaps also worth noting that until recently an outline of three calling angels was the logo of the Seventh-day Adventist Church in the UK and is clearly seen on stationery from the British Seventh-day Adventist Church prior to that date, as well as being on the side of the headquarters building at 119 St Peter's Street, Watford, Hertfordshire, UK. In November 1997, in conformity with the rest of the Seventh-day Adventist Church worldwide, this three angels logo was changed to a picture of an open Bible with a flame coming out from the centre.

[65] 'Judge What I Say', p. 11.   [66] Ibid., p. 11.

[67] See ibid., p. 1 and *passim*, and also 'Letter to the Seventh-day Adventist Church', where Koresh states 'I Am here on earth to give you the Seventh Angel's Message (Rev. 10:7).' Koresh's views on the angel sequences appear to have been even more complex than has been outlined, for he also thought that the four angels which hold back the winds (Rev. 7.1ff.) were White, Houteff, Ben Roden and Lois Roden ('Judge What I Say', p. 9).

on numerous points. In fact, the sources suggest that that divergence increased as the movement became increasingly insular and distant from the wider (but still primarily Seventh-day Adventist) world to which it belonged. However, this is not to say that an Adventist listening to Koresh, even the Koresh of the early nineties, would have found what he had to say altogether new or incomprehensible. There are major points of overlap. It may be helpful at this point to summarise some of what has already been stated.

Koresh appears to have taken a basically historicist line on Revelation. This is seen in his understanding of the seven churches of Revelation 2–3, and it will be noted below that this was his view also on Revelation 13. Similarly, his suggestion that certain parts of the Old Testament are to be interpreted typologically would have had a familiar ring about it, even if his specific claim that he was the antitypical Cyrus would have been strange the first time it was encountered. His view that in the book of Revelation angels are used as symbols for messages and/or messengers would also have found support, especially when he linked Ellen G. White with one of the angels of Rev. 14.3 (and one of the thunders of Rev. 10.3–4) and spoke so positively about the centrality of the Sabbath in her message and in the wider and eschatological purposes of God.[68] His claim that he could now reveal the content of the seven thunders of Revelation 10 would have aroused more interest than ridicule. After all, even Ellen White herself had once said that the messages of these thunders 'relate to future events which will be disclosed in their order',[69] a thought reproduced in substance in the *Bible Commentary*, which says that

[t]he messages of the seven thunders obviously were not a revelation for the people of John's day. They doubtless revealed details of the messages that were to be proclaimed at 'the end of time'.[70]

Thus, despite first appearances, appearances which the Seventh-day Adventist Church, for good reasons, has been keen to stress, it simply will not do to describe the success of Koresh (and Schneider) in recruiting Seventh-day Adventists to the Branch Davidian cause as an act of unfathomable (if not satanic) intellectual deception. The Seventh-day Adventist ground provided fertile soil for the Branch Davidian seed. In

[68] See, for example, 'Judge What I Say', p. 10.
[69] See *Seventh-day Adventist Bible Commentary*, vol. viiA, p. 971; right at the beginning of the tape on Revelation 13 Koresh can be heard to say 'but she [Ellen White] herself speaks of another angel to come'.
[70] Ibid., vol. vii, p. 797–8.

any case, as Eileen Barker has shown in the case of the Unification Church, it is quite possible for perfectly rational individuals to believe of their own free will what others might consider to be insane things without the need for brainwashing.[71] One does not need to be duped, misled or even downright stupid before one can accept as truth what may appear to some others to be outrageously bizarre claims. And if a Methodist can become a Moonie, a Seventh-day Adventist can surely become a Branch Davidian. Indeed, in the latter case the wheels of the recruitment process turn easily, being oiled with a common tradition and running along a substantially parallel track.

With these more general remarks in mind, we may now turn to the question of Koresh's interpretation of Revelation 13. On numerous details Koresh differed from the interpretation which was (and is) standard in Seventh-day Adventism, but in general approach there is considerable overlap. We have seen already in chapter 8 that according to Adventist interpreters Revelation 13 gives a prophetic picture in the two beasts of two worldly agencies opposed to the people of God, namely the papacy and the United States of America. Koresh too read Revelation 13 in this same basic way. Here, he argued, was a warning given by God to the faithful concerning worldly and ecclesiastical powers.

Koresh's precise views on the beasts of Revelation 13 are not entirely obvious from the sources so far available,[72] but there is certainly enough material from which to gain at least a basic outline. This material comes in three forms. First, there are the general hints and suggestions relating to Koresh's views of Revelation 13 as they can be pieced together from the numerous sources that do not deal directly with the issue. These are largely transcriptions of audio tapes. Second, there are the often much clearer expositions of Livingstone Fagan, one of Koresh's closest followers. The extent to which Fagan accurately relates Koresh's own views must remain open to question, but his work should not be overlooked. Third, and most important, is a tape of a Bible study Koresh gave on Revelation 13 itself. The quality of this recording is

---

[71] See Eileen Barker, *The Making of a Moonie: Choice or Brainwashing?* (Oxford: Basil Blackwell, 1984).

[72] Here I have been dependent almost exclusively on materials that have been made available on the WWW primarily through the work of Mark Swett (http://home.maine.rr.com/waco), and private correspondence sent to me by members of the Branch Davidian movement, principally Livingstone Fagan. There is much more primary material available than has so far become accessible. Mark Swett's list of holdings, for example, contains many sources that have not been utilised here (http://home.maine.rr.com/waco/archive.html). However, while the manuscript base upon which this chapter is founded is far from exhaustive, the results which have emerged seem reasonably stable and secure.

poor, and in particular the words spoken by Koresh's audience are often unrecoverable. This is unfortunate, for Koresh's mode of teaching was often to ask questions of his audience and then correct what came back. Only a part of that process can be heard on the tape. It is unfortunate also that Koresh wanders from the actual text of Revelation 13 fairly frequently and does not give simply a verse-by-verse account of what he thought the chapter was about. It must also be borne in mind that the tape is relatively early, and it may be that Koresh's views on the issue changed somewhat prior to the siege itself.[73] Despite these limitations, however, this is a uniquely important source in an attempt to reconstruct Koresh's views on Revelation 13, and the impact this may have had on the minds of those inside the compound before and during the siege. It is therefore properly discussed here in some detail. My transcription of part of this tape is included as appendix 1 to this chapter, and might usefully be referred to at this point.

These three sources together provide an interesting and important insight into Koresh's own broad acceptance, but also development of, the traditional Seventh-day Adventist/Davidian/Branch Davidian paradigm relative to Revelation 13. In the tape the situation is spelt out clearly. Koresh states that the first beast is to be understood as a composite symbol of worldly and religious powers. The worldly powers are represented by the seven heads of the beast and are in order Babylon, Medo-Persia, Greece, Rome, Ecclesiastical Rome, Europe and America. This view is expressed more than once on the tape. Seventh-day Adventists hearing this for the first time might have been a little surprised, for they had traditionally been taught to understand this beast as a symbol of papal Rome only. However, the sequence of world powers was familiar ground, for the same sequence, America excluded and 'Rome' and 'ecclesiastical Rome' combined, is thought by Seventh-day Adventists to be symbolised in the statue of Daniel 2.[74]

---

[73] In this context the words of Livingstone Fagan must be noted. According to him, Koresh did not make the direct equation of the United States of America with the Lamb-like Beast (Letter of Livingstone Fagan to Kenneth Newport, 10 September 1997, p. 1). However, allowance must be made for the fact that Fagan is writing from a later perspective and in the context of his own developing views in the light of the events of Waco itself. It is true, of course, that Koresh may have developed his thinking in the period leading up to the siege and perhaps even during the siege itself. We simply do not have the documentary evidence illustrative of this later period. Fagan may be right. All the other evidence that does exist, however, points in another direction.

[74] See further Roy Allan Anderson, *Unfolding Daniel's Prophecies* (Pacific Press Publishing Association, 1975), pp. 41–53. The sequence put forward there is Babylon (head), Medo-Persia (chest and arms), Greece (abdomen), Rome (legs) and Europe (feet). The book is written by a Seventh-day Adventist author and published by an Adventist press.

America hence appears in Koresh's understanding of Revelation 13, symbolised as one of the heads of the first beast, and following on from the other world powers in chronological sequence. Moving on to the second beast, Koresh reflects, though the image is somewhat distorted in the process, the traditional Seventh-day Adventist view. Here, he states, is a symbol of America in another guise, namely an America which is supporting an apostate religious system. It is specifically a latter-day America which is in league with apostate religion to stamp out the last vestiges of truth upon earth. This is merely a fine-tuning of the position put forward long before by Andrews and Loughborough. The Lamb-like Beast is no longer a symbol of America in general, that being given by the seventh head of the first beast. The Lamb-like Beast is rather a specific symbol of an America which has become the bearer of apostate religion – a latter-day America as it gears up to do Satan's work.

At this point it is necessary to follow Koresh in what appears at first to be a rather irrational leap from Revelation 13 to Revelation 17. It is central to his understanding of the Lamb-like Beast that the reality behind this symbol is portrayed also in Revelation 17, in the vision of the Whore of Babylon and the Scarlet Beast. The whole of Revelation 17 will need to be kept in mind at this point if Koresh's reasoning is to be followed. It is rather tortuous, though not incomprehensible to someone willing to put in the effort to unpack it. The most relevant section of the chapter reads:

I saw a woman sit upon a scarlet coloured beast, full of names of blasphemy, having seven heads and ten horns. And the woman was arrayed in purple and scarlet colour, and decked with gold and precious stones and pearls, having a golden cup in her hand full of abominations and filthiness of her fornication: And upon her forehead was a name written, MYSTERY, BABYLON THE GREAT, THE MOTHER OF HARLOTS AND ABOMINATIONS OF THE EARTH. And I saw the woman drunken with the blood of the saints, and with the blood of the martyrs of Jesus: and when I saw her, I wondered with great admiration. And the angel said unto me, Wherefore didst thou marvel? I will tell thee the mystery of the woman, and of the beast that carrieth her, which hath the seven heads and ten horns. The beast that thou sawest was, and is not; and shall ascend out of the bottomless pit, and go into perdition: and they that dwell on the earth shall wonder, whose names were not written in the book of life from the foundation of the world, when they behold the beast that was, and is not, and yet is. And here is the mind which hath wisdom. The seven heads are seven mountains, on which the woman sitteth. And there are seven kings: five are fallen, and one is, and the other is not yet come; and when he cometh, he must continue a short space. And the beast that was, and is not, even he is the eighth, and is of the seven, and goeth into perdition. And the ten horns which thou sawest are ten kings, which have received no kingdom as yet; but receive power as kings one hour with the beast. These have one mind, and shall give their power and strength unto the beast. These shall make war with the Lamb, and the Lamb shall overcome them: for he is Lord of lords, and King of kings: and they that are with him are called, and chosen, and faithful. And he saith unto me, The waters which thou sawest, where the whore sitteth, are peoples, and multitudes, and nations, and tongues. And the ten horns which thou sawest upon the beast, these shall hate the whore, and shall make her desolate and naked, and shall eat her flesh, and burn her with fire. For God hath put in their hearts to fulfil his will, and to agree, and give their kingdom unto the beast, until the words of God shall be fulfilled. And the woman which thou sawest is that great city, which reigneth over the kings of the earth.

Koresh argues that this composite picture of the woman riding upon the scarlet beast is a further illustration of part of what is portrayed in Revelation 13. The scarlet beast is America, supporting the Whore of Babylon, that is, the consummation of all religious error. It is this phase of America that is symbolised in the beast of Rev. 13.11ff. The symbol of America as the seventh head of the first beast of Rev. 13.1ff. is simply a statement concerning the transition of world powers. For Koresh, then, the Lamb-like Beast both is a part of the first beast and follows on from it, in that America as a secular world power develops into America as the supporter of the Whore of Babylon, apostate religion.

Six of the seven 'heads' or 'mountains' upon which the woman of Revelation 17 sits are, says Koresh, Luther, Knox, Wesley, Campbell, Miller and White. The other is Rome. It is unlikely, given Koresh's continued respect for the prophetic office of Ellen White, that he thought that she was personally part of the satanic conspiracy. Rather, as Houteff had also reasoned with some slight differences in detail, these seven individuals have given rise to religious communities which, despite at times promising beginnings, have gone on to reject truth and accept error. Thus the Whore of Babylon is, according to Koresh, a picture of a supremely blasphemous religious system that takes in all the errors of Roman Catholicism and apostate Protestantism. The blasphemous conspiracy needs a host as the woman needs a beast upon which to ride, and that host, says Koresh, is latter-day America. This is all fairly clear on the tape and is found also in the transcription of the tape 'Judge What I Say'. Like mainstream Seventh-day Adventism,

Koresh expected America to take on a very negative role in the last days. It was one half of a satanic conspiracy, and would provide the physical means by which 'apostate religion' would exercise its influence.

From this point the Revelation 13 tape becomes less clear, and no claim can be made to complete accuracy. Koresh jumps back and forth between the passage in Revelation 17, Revelation 13 and also Revelation 10. The 'seven kings' mentioned in chapter 17 are, he says, the same as the 'seven heads' of the beast in Rev. 13.1–10, i.e. the seven worldly powers. Jumping back quickly to Revelation 17 he points out that 'five are fallen, and one is, and the other is not yet come'. The five that are fallen are Babylon, Medo-Persia, Greece, Rome and Ecclesiastical Rome; the one that is is Europe and the one that has not yet come is America. The 'eighth' king which is 'of the seven' is also America, but it is America in conjunction with and in the role of the supporter of 'Whore of Babylon' – America in a different phase of its existence, an eschatological America which will support religious error and make war on 'the Lamb'.

This latter point is particularly interesting. Koresh seems to have thought of himself as the 'Lamb' of Revelation 5 who has the power to unseal the seven seals. He plays on this use of the word 'Lamb' here and the use of the same word as part of the description of the beast of Rev. 13.11ff. This latter '*Lamb*-like Beast' makes war on the true 'Lamb' of Revelation 5. It is in that sense the anti-lamb.

From what is at times a frustratingly incomplete body of evidence, then, a number of things seem relatively clear regarding Koresh's overall understanding of Revelation 13, though still some confusion remains. He viewed America as an eschatological enemy of God predicted in that chapter. America's role was to play out its part in the eschatological drama, supporting the Whore of Babylon, apostate religion, in the latter's attempt to suppress truth. This is clearly in keeping with the broad expectations of Seventh-day Adventists in general, though it must be said that there are major differences in detail and in the way in which the paradigm is constructed.

Having outlined what appear to have been Koresh's views on the Lamb-like Beast as far as they can be reconstructed from the one relatively clear source that has survived, we may turn now to survey the remaining relevant material. This is slight and very incomplete, a fact that has almost certainly led to some distortion here. However, the general thrust of this other material appears to support the basic outline of Koresh's thinking as outlined so far.

A potentially significant reference to the view of America as an eschatological foe comes from a study Koresh gave on 24 August 1987. Here he attributes to America a key negative role in the last days. It is America that will launch an offensive against Israel and in so doing bring about a crisis.[75] This centring of the Apocalypse upon Israel was central to the Branch Davidian understanding of things, as indeed it was in the Davidian. America towards the end of time will seek to destroy the people of God, who will by this time be gathered in Israel. This message

[75] The study is difficult to disentangle and Koresh's thoughts are not entirely clear. Some allowance must therefore be made for the potential for error in summarising the contents. However, what Koresh appears to be suggesting is that America, which has funded the restoration of Israel, will become frustrated at the Jews' failure to convert to Christianity, a precursor to the establishment of the millennial kingdom (a theme which is of course well represented in earlier millennial thinking: see especially Christopher Hill, 'Till the Conversion of the Jews' in Popkin, *Millenarianism and Messianism*). Finally America will resort to violence in an effort to achieve the desired end. The transcriber (Mark Swett) warns of transcription errors, and obvious spelling mistakes have been corrected here. However, as they currently stand the key passages read:

So therefore, when they [who 'they' are is not clear because of gaps in the text] get into the political sector of – of – of politics then they're gonna make laws, and make a religious America. And they're the ones who want to reform the Jews even if it's at gunpoint. They realize the necessity of gaining Israel because they believe that they are a modern Israel. They think that they are fulfilling the prophecies, and Zechariah foretells this in prophecy. They're the ones who have funded the restoration of the Jews in Palestine. You see? America sends millions of dollars yearly to Israel in the name of religion to fund the Jews; because they think that the fleshy Jews are gonna go back and inherit the land. ('Shower Head Tape', p. 1)

And further:

But what we're stating is that this was – that takes place [*sic*]. America is going to bring the offensive to police up the area, and in so doing overtake countries in Palestine. They're gonna like the taste of blood, and so doing they're gonna finally take Jerusalem of which time this message begins. Only for those who know of it ahead of time. To stand in the day of trouble – the day of trouble eliminates the righteous from the wicked. But God is not gonna judge the world at this time. Remember, Babylon the great comes into existence and the message is come out of her my people. You must be a part of the 144,000 who are with him or otherwise you're lost. ('Shower Head Tape', pp. 1–2)

And further in the same context:

You see? I mean these American troops, you know their good old American boys. I mean, they're over there cussin, and stuff you know. It's all a religious war. Girls, boys, you know. Mom's apple pie, and Budweiser, and a little religion, you know, and praise to the Lord and all that kind of stuff. . . Just like Joel 1 says. You see? So in other words, the American troops come in and totally devastate Jerusalem take all their food. Joel 1 tells us. ('Shower Head Tape', p. 4)

It appears that at this time Koresh had already begun to have doubts regarding the place of the final battle. It was a standard view in Davidian-Branch Davidian thinking that it would be in Israel. However, immediately before the second passage quoted above, a question is heard on the tape: 'So the world ends in Jerusalem?', to which, somewhat surprisingly, Koresh answers 'well, no', but he does not expand on that ('Shower Head Tape, p. 1). What he appears to be saying, however, is that America will invade Israel in an attempt to gain control of Jerusalem. This will bring about the final crisis, but the great eschaton itself will not occur in Jerusalem.

of an eschatologically belligerent America would have had a very familiar ring in Seventh-day Adventist ears.[76]

In another study, dated 4 February 1985, the beast of Rev. 13.11 is clearly linked with 'earthly governments'.[77] Which government Koresh does not say here. However, at this point the statements of Livingstone Fagan, one of Koresh's most able defenders, clarify matters significantly. On 18 June 1997 he wrote:

This second beast [of Revelation 13] will be the final power prior to the inauguration of the Messianic Kingdom, and will try to oppose it. Consider Rev. 19:19–21; 20:1–10. Theologically this is a detailed subject going right back to Daniel and other O. T. prophets. David spoke on this. It was the subject of a personal conversation I had with him the morning of March 22nd, prior to leaving the center. Looking back I can see why that was. He anticipated their intent to kill him. Those of us who remained would be living through the closing scenes of Rev. 13, and the opening of Rev. 14 when the kingdom is set up.[78]

Here there is evidence of significant development of the older Seventh-day Adventist paradigm, though the negative role played by America and the central eschatological significance of the Lamb-like Beast remain intact.

What Fagan says here is elaborated upon elsewhere. In outline he says that the second beast of Revelation is an end-time foe that will seek to prevent the establishment of the messianic kingdom; Koresh interpreted Rev. 13.11 in this way. This 'Lamb-like Beast' is not, contrary to the Seventh-day Adventist view, to be equated with America alone, but rather is seen as another kingdom altogether. Going back to the Revelation 13 tape we might conjecture (and conjecture it is) that what Koresh meant was that America in its second phase, that is, America in the phase represented by the Scarlet Beast of Revelation 17, would be the final power. Perhaps America would draw in some other worldly powers to take some of the strain, but America was central (as it is in the United Nations, for example). It is perhaps in this context also that one is to

---

[76] Also suggestive is the letter addressed to his lawyer just before the end of the siege, though again the meaning is far from clear. Towards to the end of the letter Koresh indicates that it is his intention to come out of the centre once the task of writing his explanation of the seven seals is completed. 'Then', he writes, 'you can do your thing with this Beast' (David Koresh to Dick DeGuerin, 14 April 1993 (now available at http://home.maine.rr.com/waco/letter414.gif)). Who 'this Beast' is is not clear in the letter. It is possible, however, that Koresh is referring to the governmental forces.

[77] Koresh is commenting on Rev. 15.2, but the reference to the 'beast and his image' clearly links the statement to Rev. 13.11ff. also (see http://home.maine.rr.com/waco/judge.html p. 8).

[78] Letter of Livingstone Fagan to Kenneth G. C. Newport, 18 June 1997, p. 2.

understand a statement made by Koresh on 2 March 1993 in the taped message aired in America to which reference was made above. By this point the siege was well under way. On the tape Koresh is heard to say, and indeed he ends his message on this note, that according to Revelation 13 a beast will arise after which the world will wonder (cf. Rev. 13.3). This is said immediately after a reference to the BATF and in the context of the siege of Mount Carmel in general. These last few sentences on the tape leave no room for doubt that Koresh thought of the forces outside the compound as of prophetic significance.

It seems, then, that Koresh kept in place the central role of America in the eschatological showdown contained in the traditional Seventh-day Adventist paradigm on the question of the identity of the Lamb-like Beast, though he may have fine-tuned it somewhat. For Koresh America *is* clearly predicted in prophecy and has a *negative* role to play in the great eschatological drama. The government forces outside the Mount Carmel gates were hence of potential eschatological significance; here perhaps was the fulfilment of John's prophecy, though the fact that this was occurring in Waco rather than Israel must presumably have thrown the issue into some doubt. Here, possibly, were the forces portrayed as the seventh head of the first beast of Rev. 13.1ff., and, in substantial part, the Lamb-like Beast of Rev. 13.11ff. and the Scarlet Beast of Revelation 17, which, in keeping with the prophecies, were making a satanic attempt to stamp out truth.

How much of this had actually filtered through to the rank and file in Mount Carmel cannot be ascertained. It may well have been that some of these details were lost upon them. However, as Seventh-day Adventists they were well acquainted with the basic paradigm and to some extent the details mattered little. The facts were plain. America was laying siege to Mount Carmel. The eschaton had come.

It was originally believed by the movement, though not very widely publicised, that David Koresh would return to this earth 1,335 days after his death, that is, on 13 December 1996. The date is arrived at, of course, on the basis of Dan. 12.12, taking the days there as literal days. On this day the Davidians expected Koresh to return as the rider on the white horse of Rev. 19.11–15 to engage, with his followers, in the mass slaughter of the wicked. When Koresh did not return, Fagan at least saw this as one final act of God to test the faith of the righteous. He drew attention to 1 Cor. 13.8, which predicts that prophecies will fail. The fact that David Koresh did not return was hence a fulfilment of the prophecy that prophecies will fail. Like Noah in the ark, the Davidians had done what

God had required and now had to wait for God to fulfil his part. After all, Noah was in the ark several days before it started raining (Gen. 7.10). So too, this is a time of patient expectation.[79]

It is apparent, then, that the death of Koresh did not mean the death of the movement or the abandonment of prophetic speculation. Rather the members of the group see themselves as living in a time of particular crisis and eschatological significance. Naturally they look to Revelation for support as they seek to integrate these new developments, especially the death of Koresh, into the paradigm. One significant wing of this post-Waco Davidian community is that which is represented by Livingstone Fagan himself. He continues, from prison, in what he clearly sees as the ever-necessary task of taking recent developments into account and fitting them into the paradigm. Each time this is done, of course, the paradigm shifts slightly, but to date there has been no wholesale abandoning of it.

In addition to Fagan, however, there is at least one other obvious successor to Koresh, namely Renos Avraam, a Branch Davidian from London.[80] He was one of the survivors of the Waco siege, escaping from the buildings as they burnt out of control on 19 April. The followers of Avraam go by the name of the Students of the Seven Seals and at the time of writing are active in putting forward their views over the Internet. The most significant exposition of the views of this group is a substantial (c. 600-page) document entitled *Seven Seals*,[81] but the 'Questions and Answers' section of the web-site is also highly informative.[82]

In outline this group thinks of Avraam as 'the chosen vessel' who is to carry on the prophetic-revelatory work of Koresh. Avraam completes the revelation of the seven seals and the work of collecting the faithful few. Probably the most important of the views put forward by this group is that the 2,300 days of Dan. 8.14 are literal days and are the number of days that there will be between the wounding of the head of the first beast of Revelation 13 and the 'cleansing of the sanctuary', that is, the end of the world. This end of the world will see the death of the rest of the faithful, the first contingent having been slaughtered with Koresh in

---

[79] Open letter of Livingstone Fagan, n.d. A copy of this letter is in my possession.

[80] Avraam, a former businessman, was born on 26 February 1964. He is currently serving a ten-year sentence in a federal prison. See http://home.maine.rr.com/waco/renos.html for a few more details.

[81] See http://www.sevenseals.com for book one and http://www.BranchDavidian.com for book. Also available on CD and in hard copy from Hidden Manna, PO Box 2166, London, KY 40741, USA.

[82] See http://www.sevenseals.com/QandA.html. Also available on CD and in hard copy from Hidden Manna, PO Box 2166, London, KY 40741, USA.

Waco, prior to their return to this earth with the rest of the 200,000,000 martyrs of Rev. 9.16 to carry out the eschatological slaughter.[83] Hence, we may conjecture, on 6 August 1999[84] this group expected to be killed by the beast-whose-wound-was-healed, i.e. the beast of Rev. 13.1ff. This is the beast that slew Koresh, the Lamb, and part of his bride on 19 April 1993, that is, 'the Great Christian Nation', also symbolised by the Lamb-like Beast of Rev. 13.11ff.

However, according to the material produced by the Students of the Seven Seals, that beast was wounded by the testimony of the Lamb, and his days are numbered. Further, since the Lamb-like Beast is also one of the heads of the first beast of Rev. 13.1ff., that earlier beast participates in the effects of the wounding. Religious-political governments as a whole are coming to an end. The wound heals (Rev. 13.3, 12), but the relief is only a temporary stay of the inevitable final execution.

The Students of the Seven Seals have, it must be said, introduced some radically new thinking into the tradition. However, it is clear from the material presented above that the eisegetical traditions relative to the book of Revelation to which the earlier Davidians and Branch Davidians were heir continued to exercise an influence upon the group in the latter part of the 1980s and into the 1990s. From Houteff on, Davidians and Branch Davidians continued to look to the book for information regarding present and future events. Houteff was working within a firmly Seventh-day Adventist context, but introduced new elements (for example the nature of the beast with seven heads in Rev. 13.1ff.). Roden appears to have maintained the status quo on this issue, but with Koresh came some fairly radical innovations. Even he, however, was working within the confines of an accepted paradigm. He did not, for example, take a wholly futurist line, though he begins to veer towards it, and neither did he see the book as a symbolic portrayal of universal truths. His method was basically historicist, though on many details of that historicism he broke with his tradition. His followers were not, however, being asked to shift eisegetical house; it was more a matter of rearranging the furniture in the one in which they were already firmly ensconced. The thinking of the 'chosen vessel' (= Renos Avraam), on the other hand, seems much more radical.

---

[83] Such views are, with difficulty, disentangled from the Seven Seals MS itself, but see especially 'Chronology of Last Day Events', located at http://www.sevenseals.com/chron.html, which gives a summary of the key points.

[84] This chapter was completed in June 1999.

In a modern critical context (though the criticism would be unfair in a pre-critical one) it would be easy to dismiss such speculations as of no real consequence. Here in the case of the Adventist tradition we have the somewhat outdated views of a group trajectory who seem unable to cut loose from the now anachronistic moorings to which their tradition has tied them. In the Davidian-Branch Davidian, and now the Students of the Seven Seals, trajectories we have further development of the paradigm to the point where, in the latter case, it has shifted in an effort to take into account the events that the group have collectively witnessed. At best, we might say, such views are to be seen in the broader context of modern-day prophecy belief in America of the kind outlined so clearly by Paul Boyer.[85] They are interesting and give an indication of how the millennial mind works.

However, it would be negligent of the scholarly guild to leave the matter there. Such beliefs, even if they strike the average academic as rather odd, can and do have real consequences. We have noted one. Indeed, it is the suggestion here that had those responsible for the negotiations with Koresh been more familiar with this, or indeed any, aspect of the thought world of the Branch Davidians, a less catastrophic outcome to the siege might well have resulted. It is possible that those inside the centre did not expect the end to occur immediately, and it may be that Koresh did intend to keep his promises to 'come out'. One should not underestimate the extent to which the arrival of government forces would have enforced upon the minds of the Branch Davidians the view that the eschatological dawn had broken. As Seventh-day Adventists they listened for the dragon-like voice of the Lamb-like Beast, and as Seventh-day Adventists they expected that eschatological roar to come from America. When on 28 February 1993 the BATF arrived and laid siege to Mount Carmel, it must surely have seemed to those inside that those days had now come.

In the event, 6 August 1999 came and went without incident, though the potential for another major incident was certainly in place. Precisely how the group will adjust its views remains to be seen. One thing is certain; whatever happens to this group, there will be others arising with no less dramatic a message for these last times. The book of Revelation will continue to exert an influence. And, to quote what are probably authentic words of the one the author of Revelation sought to present to his first-century audience, the text might say of itself 'Think not that I

[85] Boyer, *When Time Shall Be No More.*

am come to send peace on earth: I came not to send peace, but a sword.'[86]

APPENDIX I[87] TRANSCRIPTION OF TAPE ON
REVELATION 13 BY DAVID KORESH

The tape begins with a general statement by Koresh on the question of the way in which one might know the truth today. God has been at work in the past, but none have remained true to his word. The followers of Luther, Knox, Wesley, Campbell, Miller and White have all fallen into error and the whole world, including Adventists, are in darkness and all teach much the same, bland message, 'Jesus loves you . . . do a good deed' and the like. However, Ellen White herself said that there would be another angel who would bring the truth.

The discussion later turns to the question of the identity of the first beast. This beast, says Koresh, is a composite picture of present cultures of the earth. However, there arises another Lamb-like Beast which is 'modern-day Rome'. This Koresh equates with 'Christianity', that is 'apostate Protestantism'. However, it becomes clear immediately after this statement that what he has in mind at this point is not Christianity in general but rather its American form, and in showing how this second beast enforces worship of the first Koresh refers to the activities of 'this Christian nation America'.

Later Koresh jumps to Revelation 17 and talks about the great harlot who is riding on the back of the beast with seven heads and ten horns. The seven heads/kings are, says Koresh, seven churches; presumably the usual line-up of Catholics, Lutherans, Presbyterians, Methodists, Baptists, Millerites (First-day Adventists) and Seventh-day Adventists. But the beast itself is an eighth king which is both of the seven and also a unity of them which goes beyond the sum of the parts. This eighth beast is a conglomeration of blasphemy and Koresh links it to 'the Evangelical Association of America' of which, he says, the Seventh-day Adventists are a part. This in fact is the 'Lamb-like' part of the Lamb-like Beast. America looks 'Lamb-like'; it is outwardly Christian, but that is not the reality. In truth this beast is 'the dragon, the devil himself'. Koresh then argues that the great blasphemous conglomeration of error symbolised in the eighth head of the beast of Revelation 17 (which is of the seven) currently awaits a sponsor who will give support and space to its satanic agenda. This sponsor comes in the form of the 'beast' of Rev. 13.11ff. The tape continues:[88]

---

[86] Matt. 10.34.
[87] The following transcription is of a tape recording of a Bible study given by David Koresh some time in 1987. The original tape recording is held by Mark Swett at the Waco Never Again! Research Centre and is used here with permission. Some words have been added for the sake of clarity; these are enclosed in square brackets.
[88] Words in roman type are those spoken by David Koresh. Words in italics are those spoken by members of the audience.

This beast is what beast?

Indecipherable response

The lamb; the beast shall make war with the lamb. Now you have the lamb fighting the what?

[Pause]

The lamb; there's a lamb of God, isn't there? Standing on Mount Zion; now when this is being done, Revelation 14 says the same thing. Let's count the number of the beast – 666. Well, and I looked during this time, Revelation 14 says, and this is all taking place, and Lo a lamb stood on Mount Zion and with him 144,000, having his Father's name written in their foreheads, and I heard a voice from heaven as the voice of many waters and the voice of great thunders or the voice of harpers harping with their harps, and [one word undecipherable] the one you saw, the voice of heaven, right? Before the throne and before the four beasts and the elders, and no man can learn that song but who?

Indecipherable response

But the redeemed [three words undecipherable] ... So the Lamb-like Beast makes [one word undecipherable] ... at a time when the false prophet appears, because God has already sealed a group of people, who are standing where at this time?

Indecipherable response

On Mount Zion. It's a mystery to John who this Babylon is. Well, Sister White says the greatest persecutor against God's people will be what? Adventists. These have one mind to give their power and strength to the beast. The beast shall make war with the lamb, the lamb shall overcome them for he is the Lord of Lords and King of Kings and they that are with him are called chosen and faithful. Who is with him on Mount Zion?

Indecipherable response

They are called, they are chosen and they are faithful. And he said to me 'these waters which thou sawest where the whore sitteth' on the seven heads, right? – the sea 'are peoples, multitudes and nations and tongues'. So the earth is the earth. America is going to put its dogmas, its so-called Jesus Christ doctrine, on everybody in the world. And they are not based in the word of truth or the prophecies so therefore all the world will worship the beast and his image, Jesus Christ.[89] Daniel chapter 11 states that the man of sin, king of the north, honours

---

[89] The point here seems to be that America will promote the worship of a false Jesus, a Jesus who does not require a knowledge of the truth.

the God of [one word undecipherable] ... of which [one word undecipherable] ... of them were saying that they should build up armaments against poor Russia, who never even knew about it. [Four or five words undecipherable] upon the beast, these shall hate the whore and shall make her desolate and naked and shall eat her flesh and burn her with fire, because they find out that they have been deceived after a while, don't they? They find out America is the dragon, don't they, when it is too late, right? For God has put it into their hearts to fulfil his will and to agree to give their kingdom to the beast until the words of God shall be fulfilled. And where are those words at?

Prophecies

Prophecies; and the woman which thou sawest is that great city which reigneth over the kings of the earth. And what city is that?

Largely indecipherable response ending with the word 'Washington'

Washington DC – Washington DC[90] – it's America, the two horns of the lamb [two or three words undecipherable] ... is power of the beast which is the lamb, a counterfeit of the true lamb, the lamb on Mount Zion. And that's when this mighty angel comes down with this light and glory and [says] Babylon is fallen, the great is fallen, is fallen. It can't fall till you learn about it first, can it?

So now, we learned about Edom, didn't we? When does this take place? Well, let's go back to Revelation, chapter 10, and we'll go back over the three previous chapters we just learned, and we're going to find out even more clearly how clear they are. Revelation does say in the seventeenth chapter that the seven heads are what?

Indecipherable response

So the mountains symbolise what?

Indecipherable response

So therefore the seven heads that unite into nine are on the beast, but the beast had been revealed – must have been churches that were in existence and all had the names of blasphemy. But if someone might continue with that point of doctrine we at least say this much: if seven symbolises complete it means that all the religions [one word undecipherable] ... blasphemies. No matter which way we go the story still [one word undecipherable] ... doesn't it? If you don't want to agree that they are Luther, Knox, Wesley, Campbell, Miller and White along with the Papacy, then you at least might have to admit that seven means complete, meaning all religions on the face of the earth, all mountains,

---

[90] These words are spoken slowly with an apparent concern for clarity and emphasis.

all ways of thinking were false. That makes you feel a little better, wouldn't it?

Excuse me, what about the 666, what if ... [Tape breaks off at this point]

[Several indecipherable words] ... describe it because it had so many facets, right? You had Babylon, Medo-Persians, Greece, Rome – pagan Rome[91] – and then we had ecclesiastical Rome, church-state Rome, as a political power that ruled over the nations, right? And then we had another form of government, we had Rome split up which ruled as Europe, no ecclesiastical power and it ruled for a long time, didn't it? And what nation began to come into being while Europe ruled?

America

Which makes America the Lamb-like Beast, number seven, right?

Hm-hm

In other words we see that America being seven, complete, makes an image that becomes the eighth which is of the seven, and goes into perdition. We repeat it one more time? Repeat it again? Start again. Count the beast; Babylon, still in existence right?

Hm-hm

The first beast recorded in prophecy was Babylon, wasn't it? Medo-Persia, Greece, Rome, ecclesiastical Rome, Europe – ecclesiastical Rome fell, right? It did not have the crowns upon the heads, the crowns went to the horns, it was a different form of government, was it not?

Hm-hm

And then we have America the seventh. Babylon one, Medo-Persia two, Greece three, Rome four, ecclesiastical Rome five, Europe six, the Lamb-like Beast seven. These empires, all with the religion involved in them had – what?

Blasphemy

Blasphemy; their religions amongst them were all blasphemous. The eighth that rises up out of the bottomless pit is of the seven, meaning that the eighth government will be a coalition of all the errors of the seven. It rises up with the sole purpose of – what?

[Pause]

[91] Koresh says simply 'Rome' and then 'pagan Rome', but it is clear that the latter is a finer definition of what he meant by the former rather than two separate entities.

Going into perdition; [two words undecipherable] . . . the story is with America, apostate Protestantism, brings about church-state, they are going to hell. Because America will make war with the Lamb. OK? Now we know that five are fallen – Babylon, Medo-Persia, Greece, Rome, ecclesiastical Rome, are fallen, right? One *is* – modern Europe which was in existence in 1929 when they gave back the Vatican power its city – Vatican city its power.

And yet the Lamb-like Beast which speaks as a dragon has not yet come; but when it comes America with its church-state education/application (?) will continue to [one word undecipherable] . . . and when he does the miracles and causes all both small and great, rich, poor, free and bond, then he goes to perdition. None shall help him. Babylon is fallen. See how *clear*[92] it is. But only he who has wisdom is to count the number of the beast. It is the number of [a] man, what man? King David was the eighth son of Jesse. David was a priest-king, a ruler who had divine vision, eyes. Whereas in Daniel's prophecy there are ten horns three are plucked up, which makes what? Seven; and the little horn makes eight. A theocratic form of government of which the papacy tried to obtain a counterfeit King David. Though the prophecies all talk about David will arise and rule in the last days as a priest king. So what do you think America wants to do? Counterfeit that. A false king-priesthood. [one word undecipherable] . . . the eighth is of the seven, all blasphemies, and will rise up and go to perdition. Isn't that simple?

Hm-hm

Simple isn't it? And there's still a lot more to learn about this, because who knows the mind of God? It can only get brighter and brighter when we have the present truth.

Koresh then turns his attention to Revelation 10 and the vision of the mighty angel. This he says is a vision of an end-time messenger who will reveal the 'little book'. This angel reveals complete truth through the seven thunders. Koresh then calls the group to faith in the content of this message, which he clearly thinks it is his job to explain. The weak and the uneducated of the earth will listen to the message, and by it be transformed into the people of God. But there is opposition in the form of the beast from Daniel 12, the same beast as that in Revelation 17, which is 'America with its religio political'. This beast will make war on the two witnesses and slay them (in Jerusalem) and they will lie dead for three-and-a-half days. At this point Koresh appears to refer also to the necessity of his own death in the words 'what do you think that they are going to do to me, Cyrus, the angel from the east?' Later he says clearly that he will be 'delivered' from the hour of temptation and will be in heaven while the others remain on earth during the last times.

[92] Koresh emphasises this word in the text by, apparently, banging his hand down on the open page of the Bible.

APPENDIX 2 BIOGRAPHICAL INFORMATION ON
THE LEADERS OF THE BRANCH DAVIDIANS

Ben and Lois Roden

Little biographical information is available, and what there is is often patchy, particularly for Lois, and very poorly documented. Much is in the form of tapes, including one of Ben's funeral eulogy, popular-level (sometimes sensationalist) books and other such media.

Ben Roden was born in a small town in the State of Oklahoma on 5 January 1902, one of the six children of James Buchanan and Hattie Roden. He trained and worked as a teacher in Oklahoma and married Lois I. Scott on 12 February 1937. Both Ben and Lois joined the Seventh-day Adventist Church in Kilgore, Texas, being baptised in 1940. They later moved to the Seventh-day Adventist Church in Odessa, Texas, where Ben became a head elder. They had six children: Jane, Kathleen, George, Ben II, John and Samuel.

In 1946 Ben accepted the message of Victor Houteff, and in 1953 moved with his family to the Mount Carmel Centre, where he became head gardener. Following Houteff's unexpected death in 1955 and the chaos that ensued under the leadership of Florence, Ben felt himself called to the prophetic ministry. His chief concern at this time was the announcement of the restoration of God's kingdom in Israel; he also sought to restore many of the Old Testament religious feasts. In 1958 he moved his family to Israel and settled in a small communal village in the Golan Heights. His plan was to establish an arm of the 'Branch' Davidians that would eventually be populated by his followers from the United States of America and would be the nucleus of the coming kingdom of God. Both he and Lois moved between this community in Israel and America for the next several years. In 1965, Ben Roden received a vision concerning Waco, Texas, and it was there that he established the new Mount Carmel Centre. In 1977 while on the Mount of Olives Roden had been told by God to build the temple of Ezek. 40–5; the next year the Rodens met President Jimmy Carter and sought his assistance in building the new temple of the Lord. Carter's response is unknown.

During the last year of Ben's life his wife Lois had a vision concerning the femininity of the Holy Spirit, a message that was eventually accepted by the movement as a whole. (This appears to be Lois' only divergence from teaching the standard views of the Davidian-Branch Davidian tradition to which she belonged.) Lois' message is referred to by Branch Davidians, including Koresh, as the 'Branch-She' message while Ben's is referred to as the 'Branch-He'. Ben took the Branch-She and Branch-He messages to the General Conference of the Seventh-day Adventist Church in Washington in autumn 1978. On 22 October 1978, after returning from the Washington Conference, Ben died. In 1982 Lois persuaded the Israeli authorities to allow him to be buried in Israel, and he was finally laid to rest on the Mount of Olives in the land that he thought he would rule in God's theocratic kingdom.

In June 1981 the young Vernon Howell first arrived at Mount Carmel. It appears from the surviving materials and eye-witness accounts that Lois had a particular regard for him: she was impressed with his ability as a handyman and also with his knowledge of the Bible. When he left the Centre a short time after his initial arrival, Lois tracked him down and persuaded him to return. It is generally reported that the relationship between them was a good deal more than platonic. One account reports how Howell went to Lois and on the basis of Isa. 8.3 ('I went to the prophetess, and she conceived') suggested that they begin a physical relationship. In October 1981, Lois and Vernon travelled to Israel together. She died on 10 October 1986 and was apparently transported to Jerusalem for burial alongside her husband Ben.

George Roden

As with his parents, little documented biographical information on George Roden is available. However, it appears that he was born in c. 1938, the year after his parents' marriage; he is widely reported as being sixty at the time of his death in December 1998. He went with his parents to the Mount Carmel Centre in 1945. He was seriously involved with at least two women, putting away his legal wife Carmen in favour of another woman, Amo Bishop.

Following his unsuccessful attempt to wrest control of the Branch Davidians from his mother in 1979, George continued to bide his time, convinced that he was the rightful heir to his father's leadership and prophetic roles. There is some suggestion that he thought of himself as the reincarnation of (or perhaps the antitypical?) King Solomon. He is rumoured to have ended prayers with the words 'in the name of George B. Roden'. He mounted a presidential campaign in 1984.

George managed to gain control of the Mount Carmel Centre in 1985, the year before his mother died, and proceeded to evict Howell and his supporters. The Centre itself was renamed Rodenville. Although he had succeeded in physically evicting Howell, he was not as yet satisfied that he had managed to exorcise his influence or leadership pretensions. To put the matter beyond dispute, he challenged Howell to a resurrection contest, in preparation for which he dug up the remains of Anna Hughes, a Davidian who had died some twenty years earlier. Howell did not oblige, but instead reported the illegal exhumation and claimed corpse abuse. The authorities asked for proof, which Howell and a few followers sought to provide by making a nocturnal visit to the Centre to take the necessary photographs. George met them and a gun battle ensued, following which all participants were arrested. There were no convictions, but George was jailed for six months for contempt of court after threatening the judge with plagues and herpes.

After his release George later killed a former Branch Davidian acquaintance with an axe. He was found innocent of the crime by reason of insanity and sent to the Vernon State Hospital, and later to the Big Spring State Hospital, where he resided until the time of his death in December 1998. He escaped twice, once in June 1993 and again in September 1995, and when he was reported missing from the hospital in December 1998 it was at first assumed that he had made another escape. However, his body was found inside the grounds, and it was established that he had died of a heart attack.

Vernon Howell / David Koresh

Vernon Howell was born the illegitimate son of Bonnie Clark and Bobby Howell on 17 August 1959. His mother had been raised a Seventh-day Adventist and he was initially sent to the Dallas Seventh-day Adventist academy, but transferred to state school in subsequent years. His poor results led to his dropping out of school altogether in the eleventh grade. At nine years of age he was attending the Seventh-day Adventist church in Richardson, Texas. In 1979 he attended a Seventh-day Adventist church in Tyler, Texas, where he was baptised, but later disfellowshipped for inappropriate behaviour. He was married to Rachel Jones and had several children by her and by others; the children include Cyrus, Star, Bobbie Lane, Dayland, Paige, Serenity, Chica, Latwan, Chanel, Startle, Mayanah and Hollywood.

When George Roden was jailed in 1988, Howell and his followers took possession of the Mount Carmel Centre, where they remained until the fire in April 1993. Howell was buried on 4 June 1993 in a quiet ceremony in Texas.

Bibliography

Adair, Don, *A Complete Scriptural Index to the Original Writings of V. T. Houteff*, Salem, SC: General Association of Davidian Seventh-day Adventists, 1993

Adams, Roy, *The Sanctuary Doctrine: Three Approaches in the Seventh-day Adventist Church*, Berrien Springs, MI: Andrews University Press, 1981

Addis, William E., Arnold, Thomas and Scannell, T. B. (eds.), *A Catholic Dictionary*, 9th edn, London: Kegan Paul, Trench, Trubner & Co., 1917

Albin, Thomas R., 'Charles Wesley's Other Prose Writings', in ST Kimbrough (ed.), *Charles Wesley: Poet and Theologian*, Nashville, TN: Kingswood Books, 1992

Andrews, J. N., *The Three Messages of Revelation XIV, 6–12, Particularly the Third Angel's Message and the Two-horned Beast*, 5th edition, 1877

Arasola, Kai, *The End of Historicism: Millerite Hermeneutic of Time Prophecies in the Old Testament*, University of Uppsala, 1990

Armogathe, Jean-Robert, 'Interpretations of the Revelation of John: 1500–1800', in Collins et al., *The Encyclopedia of Apocalypticism*

Bachmair, J., *The Revelation of St. John Historically Explained*, 1778

Baker, Frank, *William Grimshaw 1708–1763*, London: Epworth Press 1963

Bale, John, *The Ymage of Both Churches after the Moste Wonderful and Heavenly Revelacion Of Saincte John the Evangelist*, 1550

Barker, Eileen, *The Making of a Moonie: Choice or Brainwashing?*, Oxford: Basil Blackwell, 1984

Bauckham, Richard, *Tudor Apocalypse*, Abingdon, Oxford: The Sutton Courtenay Press, 1978

Bebbington, D. W., *Evangelicalism in Modern Britain: A History from the 1730's to the 1980's*, London: Unwin Hyman, 1989

Beckerlegge, Oliver A. and Albin, Thomas R., *Charles Wesley's Earliest Evangelical Sermons: Six Shorthand Manuscript Sermons Now for the First Time Transcribed from the Original*, Ilford: Wesley Historical Society, 1987

Benson, Joseph, *Four Sermons on the Second Coming of Christ and the Future Misery of the Wicked*, 1781

Beverly, Thomas, *The Command of God to His People to Come out of Babylon, Revel. 18.4. Demonstrated to Mean the Coming Out of the Present Papal Rome*, 1688

Bible and Culture Collective, The, *The Postmodern Bible*, New Haven, CT: Yale University Press, 1995

Blayney, B., *A Dissertation by Way of an Inquiry into the True Import and Application of the Vision Related in Dan IX verse 20 to the End, usually Called Daniel's Prophecy of the 70 Weeks*, 1775

Bliss, Sylvester, *Memoirs of William Miller*, 1853

Blom, F. et al., *English Catholic Books, 1701–1801*, Aldershot, Hants: Scolar Press, 1996

Bossuet, Jacques Bénigne, *L'Apocalypse avec une Explication*, 1689

Bowmer, John C., *The Sacrament of the Lord's Supper in Early Methodism*, London: Adam and Charles Black, 1951

Boyer, Paul, *When Time Shall Be No More: Prophecy Belief in American Culture*, Cambridge, MA: The Belknap Press of Harvard University Press, 1992

Brady, David, 'The Number of the Beast in Seventeenth- and Eighteenth-Century England', *Evangelical Quarterly* 45 (1973)

'1666: The Year of the Beast', *Bulletin of the John Rylands University Library of Manchester* 61 (1979)

The Contribution of British Writers between 1560 and 1830 to the Interpretation of Revelation 13:16–18 (The Number of the Beast): A Study in the History of Exegesis, Tübingen: J. C. B. Mohr (Paul Siebeck), 1983

Brightman, Thomas, *A Revelation of the Apocalyps*, 1611

Brooks, J. W., *A Dictionary of Writers on the Prophecies*, London, 1835

Brown, J., *Harmony of Scripture Prophecies, and the History of Their Fulfillment*, 1784

Brown, Kenneth O., 'John Wesley – Post or Premillennialist?', *Methodist History* 28 (1989)

Bull, Malcolm, 'The Seventh-day Adventists: Heretics of American Civil Religion', *Sociological Analysis* 50 (1989)

Bull, Malcolm and Lockhart, Keith, *Seeking a Sanctuary: Seventh-day Adventism and the American Dream*, San Francisco: Harper & Row, 1989

Bullinger, J. H., *A Hundred Sermons on the Apocalips of Jesus Christ*, 1557/1561

Burdon, Christopher, *The Apocalypse in England: Revelation Unravelling, 1700–1834*, London: Macmillan, 1997

Butler, David, *Methodists and Papists: John Wesley and the Catholic Church in the Eighteenth Century*, London: Darton, Longman and Todd, 1995

Butler, Jonathan M., 'The Making of a New Order: Millerism and the Origins of Seventh-day Adventism', in Numbers and Butler, *The Disappointed*

Caird, G. B., *The Revelation of St John the Divine*, London: A. & C. Black, 1984

Calmet, Augustin, *Commentaire Littéral*, 1707–16

Dictionnaire Historique, Critique, Chronologique, Geographique et Littéral de la Bible, rev. edn, 4 vols., 1730

Capp, Bernard, *The Fifth Monarchy Men: A Study in Seventeenth-Century English Millenarianism*, London: Faber, 1972

Case, Hiram, *Present Truth*, November 1850

Christianson, Paul, *Reformers and Babylon: English Apocalyptic Visions from the*

Reformation to the Eve of the Civil War, Toronto: University of Toronto Press, 1978

Clark, R., *A Warning to the World; or the Prophetical Numbers of Daniel and John Calculated*, 1759

Clarke, Adam, *Commentary on the New Testament*, 3 vols., 1817

Clayton, R., *A Dissertation on Prophecy, wherein the Coherence and Connexion of the Prophecies in both the Old and New Testament are Fully Considered; together with an Explanation of the Revelation of St. John*, 1749

Coggins, R. J. and Houlden, J. L. (eds.), *A Dictionary of Biblical Interpretation*, London: SCM Press, 1990

Cohn, Norman, *The Pursuit of the Millennium: Revolutionary Millenarians and Mystical Anarchists of the Middle Ages*, London: Paladin, 1970

Coke, Thomas, *A Commentary on the Holy Bible*, 4 vols., London: 1803

Collins, John J., McGinn, Bernard and Stein, Stephen J. (eds.), *The Encyclopedia of Apocalypticism*, 3 vols., New York: Continuum, 1998

Committee on Defense Literature of the General Conference of Seventh-day Adventists, *The History and Teachings of 'The Shepherd's Rod'*, 2 vols. [Washington, DC], 1930–2

Cowper, William, *The Workes of Mr William Cowper Late Bishop of Galloway. Now Newly Collected into one Volume. Whereunto is added a Commentary on the Revelation Never before Published*, 1623

Cross, F. L. and Livingstone, E. A. (eds.), *The Oxford Dictionary of the Christian Church*, Oxford: Oxford University Press, revised edn, 1997

Curnock, Nehemiah (ed.), *The Journal of the Rev. John Wesley, A.M.*, 8 vols., London: Charles H. Kelly, 1909–16

Damsteegt, P. Gerard, *Foundations of the Seventh-day Adventist Message and Mission*, Grand Rapids, MI: Eerdmans, 1977

Davies, Rupert, George, A. Raymond and Rupp, Gordon (eds.), *The History of the Methodist Church in Great Britain*, 4 vols., London: Epworth Press, 1965–88

Delaney, John J. and Tobin, James Edward (eds.), *Dictionary of Catholic Biography*, London: Robert Hale, 1961

Doddridge, Philip, *The Family Expositor; or a Paraphrase and Version of the New Testament; with Critical Notes*, 6 vols., 1739–56

Douie, Decima L., *The Nature and the Effect of the Heresy of the Fraticelli*, Manchester: Manchester University Press, 1932

Dowley, T. E., 'The History of the English Baptists During the Great Persecution, 1660–1688', Ph.D. thesis, University of Manchester 1976

Downes, James Cyril, 'Eschatological Doctrines in the Writings of John and Charles Wesley', Ph.D. thesis, University of Edinburgh 1960

Durham, Thomas, *A Commentarie Upon the Book of the Revelation*, 1658

Edson, Hiram, 'An Appeal to the Laodicean Church', *Advent Review* Extra Issue (1850)

Elliott, E. B., *Horae Apocalypticae; or, A Commentary on the Apocalypse, Critical and Historical*, 4th edn, 4 vols., London: Seeley, 1851

Emmerson, Richard Kenneth, *Antichrist in the Middle Ages: A Study of Medieval Apocalypticism, Art, and Literature*, Seattle: University of Washington Press, 1984

Encyclopaedia Judaica, 17 vols., Jerusalem: Keter Publishing House, 1972–82

Fagan, Livingstone, Open letter, n.d.
    Letter to Kenneth G. C. Newport, 18 June 1997
    Letter to Kenneth G. C. Newport, 10 September 1997

Family Bible; or, Christian's Best Treasure. Containing, the Sacred Text of the Old and New Testament, With Annotations from Grotius, Boyle, Prideaux, Pearson, Tillotson, Poole, Whitby, Henry, Burkitt, Doddridge, &c. &c., 1771

Family Expositor; Containing the Sacred Text of the Old and New Testament; Illustrated with a Commentary and Notes, Historical, Geographical and Critical, Taken from the Most Eminent Commentators Ancient and Modern ... Wherein the Text is Explained, Doubts Resolved, Scriptures Paralleled, and Various Readings Observed, 1763

Festinger, Leon, Riecken, H. W. and Schachter, S., *When Prophecy Fails*, Minneapolis: University of Minnesota Press, 1956

Firth, Katherine, *The Apocalyptic Tradition in Reformation Britain 1530–1645*, Oxford: Oxford University Press, 1979

Fish, Stanley, *Is There a Text in this Class? The Authority of Interpretive Communities*, Cambridge, MA: Harvard University Press, 1980

Force, James E., *William Whiston, Honest Newtonian*, Cambridge: Cambridge University Press, 1985

Ford, J. Massyngberde, *Revelation*, Garden City, NY: Doubleday, 1975

Froom, Le Roy Edwin, *The Prophetic Faith of Our Fathers*, 4 vols., Washington, DC: Review and Herald Publishing Association, 1946–54

Fuller, Reginald, Jonston, Leonard and Kearns, Conleth (eds.), *A New Catholic Commentary on Holy Scripture*, London: Thomas Nelson & Sons, 1969

Garnham, Robert Edward, 'An Enquiry into the Time, at which the Kingdom of Heaven will commence', in Priestley, Joseph (ed.), *Theological Repository*, 6 vols., 1769–88, vol. VI, pp. 244–84

Garrett, Clarke, *Respectable Folly: Millenarians and the French Revolution in England and France*, Baltimore: The Johns Hopkins University Press, 1975

Gaustad, Edwin S. (ed.), *The Rise of Adventism: Religion and Society in Mid-Nineteenth-Century America*, New York: Harper & Row, 1974

Gill, John, *Exposition of the Bible*, NT, 3 vols., 1748; OT, 6 vols., 1766

Gillow, Joseph, *A Literary and Biographical History, or Bibliographical Dictionary of the English Catholics: From the Breach with Rome, in 1534, to the Present Time*, 5 vols., n.d. [1885–1902]

Goodwin, Thomas, *Exposition upon the Book of the Revelation*, 1683

Graybill, Ron, 'America: The Magic Dragon', *Insight* 2 (1971)
    'Picturing the Prophecies', *Adventist Review* (5 July 1984)

Hammond, Henry, *A Paraphrase and Annotations upon all the Books of the New Testament*, 1653; 4th edn, 1675

Hardy, Richard, *A Letter from a Clergyman to one of his Parishioners who was Inclined to Turn Methodist*, 1753

Harmon, Nolan B. (ed.), *Encyclopedia of World Methodism*, 2 vols., Nashville: United Methodist Publishing House, 1974

Harrison, J. C. F., *The Second Coming: Popular Millenarianism 1780–1850*, London: Routledge & Kegan Paul, 1979

Hartmann, Louis F. and di Lella, Alexander A., *The Book of Daniel*, Anchor Bible, vol. 23, New York: Doubleday & Co., 1977

Hatch, Nathan O., *The Sacred Cause of Liberty*, New Haven, CT: Yale University Press, 1977

Haydon, Colin, *Anti-Catholicism in Eighteenth-Century England c. 1740–80: A Political and Social Study*, Manchester: Manchester University Press, 1993

Heitzenrater, Richard P., 'John Wesley's Earliest Sermons', *Proceedings of the Wesley Historical Society* 37 (1969–70)

Hempton, D. N., 'Evangelicalism and Eschatology', *Journal of Ecclesiastical History* 31 (1980)

Methodism and Politics in British Society 1750–1850, London, Hutchinson, 1984

Hill, Christopher, *Antichrist in Seventeenth-Century England*, rev. edn, London: Verso, 1990

Houteff, Victor T., *The Shepherd's Rod*, 2 vols., Los Angeles, CA: Universal Publishing Association, 1930–2

The World Yesterday, Today, Tomorrow, 1941

The Leviticus of the Davidian Seventh-day Adventists, 1943

Ivimey, Joseph, *A History of the English Baptists*, 4 vols., 1811–30

Jackson, Thomas, *The Life of the Rev. Charles Wesley, M.A.*, 2 vols. 1841

(ed.), *The Journal of the Rev. Charles Wesley, M.A.* 2 vols. [London: John Mason, 1849]

K[nollys], H[anserd], *An Exposition of the whole Book of the Revelation. Wherein the Visions and Prophecies of Christ are opened and Expounded: Shewing the Great Conquests of our Lord Jesus Christ for his Church over all His and Her Adversaries, Pagan, Arian and Papal; and the Glorious State of the Church of God in the New Heavens and New Earth, in these Latter Days*, 1689

Keach, Benjamin, *Antichrist Stormed*, 1689

Distressed Sion Relieved, 1689

Kimbrough ST (ed.), *Charles Wesley: Poet and Theologian*, Nashville, TN: Kingswood Books, 1992

Kimbrough, ST and Beckerlegge, O. (eds.), *The Unpublished Poetry of Charles Wesley*, 3 vols., Nashville, TN: Kingswood Books, 1988–92

Knox, R. A., *Enthusiasm: A Chapter in the History of Religion*, Oxford: Clarendon Press, 1950

Lawson, Ronald, 'Adventists Disavow Waco Cult', *Christian Century* 110 (1993): 285–6

'Seventh-day Adventist Responses to Branch Davidian Notoriety: Patterns of Diversity within a Sect Reducing Tension with Society', *Journal for the Scientific Study of Religion* 34 (1995)

Leonard, Harry L. (ed.), *J. N. Andrews: The Man and the Mission*, Berrien Springs, MI: Andrews University Press, 1985

Lewis, James R. (ed.), *From the Ashes: Making Sense of Waco*, Lanham, MD: Rowman & Littlefield, 1994

Litch, Josiah, *Prophetic Expositions; or A Connected View of the Testimony of the Prophets Concerning the Kingdom of God and the Time of its Establishment*, 2 vols. [1842]

　The Restitution, Christ's Kingdom on Earth; the Return of Israel, together with their Political Emancipation, [1848]

Loughborough, J. N., *The Two-horned Beast of Revelation XIII, a Symbol of the United States*, 1857

McGinn, Bernard, *The Calabrian Abbot: Joachim of Fiore in the History of Western Thought*, New York: Macmillan, 1985

　Antichrist: Two Thousand Years of the Human Fascination with Evil, San Francisco: HarperCollins, 1994

Markham, Ian S., *Plurality and Christian Ethics*, Cambridge: Cambridge University Press, 1994

Maxwell, C. Mervyn, *God Cares*, 2 vols., Boise, ID: Pacific Press Publishing Association, 1981–5

Mayor, S. H., 'James II and the Dissenters', *Baptist Quarterly* 34 (1991)

Mede, Joseph, *Clavis Apocalyptica*, 1627

Miller, J., *Popery and Politics in England 1660–88*, Cambridge: Cambridge University Press, 1973

Miller, William, *William Miller's Apology and Defence*, Boston, MA, 1848

More, Henry, *The Theological Works of the Most Pious and Learned Henry More, D.D.*, 1708

　The Theological and Miscellaneous Works of Joseph Priestley, 25 vols., 1817–31

Morgan, Robert with Barton, John, *Biblical Interpretation*, Oxford: Oxford University Press, 1988

Mounce, Robert H., *The Book of Revelation*, rev. edn, Grand Rapids, MI: Eerdman's, 1998

Mumford, James, *The Catholike Scripturist, or, the Plea of the Roman Catholikes Shewing the Scriptures to Hold forth the Roman Faith in above Forty of the Chief Controversies now under Debate*, 2nd edn, 1662

　The New Catholic Encyclopedia, 14 vols., Washington, DC: McGraw-Hill, 1967

Newport, Kenneth G. C., 'Benjamin Keach, William of Orange and the Book of Revelation: A Study in English Prophetical Interpretation', *The Baptist Quarterly* 35 (1995): 43–51

　'Charles Wesley's Interpretation of Some Biblical Prophecies according to a Previously Unpublished Letter Dated 25 April, 1754', *Bulletin of the John Rylands University Library of Manchester* 77 (1995): 31–52

　'Methodists and the Millennium: Eschatological Belief and the Interpretation of Biblical Prophecy in Early British Methodism', *Bulletin of the John Rylands University Library of Manchester* 78 (1996): 103–22

　'The French Prophets and Early Methodism: Some New Evidence', *Proceedings of the Wesley Historical Society* 50 (1996): 127–40

　'George Bell, Prophet and Enthusiast', *Methodist History* 35 (1997): 95–105

'Premillennialism in the Early Writings of Charles Wesley', *Wesleyan Theological Journal* 32 (1997): 85–103

'Revelation 13 and the Papal Antichrist in Eighteenth-Century England: A Study in New Testament *Eisegesis*', *Bulletin of the John Rylands University Library of Manchester* 79 (1997): 91–103

Newport, Kenneth G. C. and Lloyd, Gareth, 'George Bell and Early Methodist Enthusiasm: A New Source from the Manchester Archives', *BJRULM* 80(1) (Spring 1998): 879–101

Newton, Sir Isaac, *Observations upon the Prophecies of Daniel and the Apocalypse of St John*, 1733

Newton, Thomas, *Dissertation on the Prophecies*, 18th edn, 1834

Nichol, Francis D., *The Midnight Cry: A Defense of William Miller and the Millerites*, Washington, DC: Review and Herald Publishing Association, 1944

Niebuhr, H. Richard, *The Kingdom of God in America*, New York: Harper & Row, 1937

Numbers, Ronald L. and Butler, Jonathan M. (eds.), *The Disappointed: Millerism and Millenarianism in the Nineteenth Century*, Bloomington and Indianapolis: Indiana University Press, 1987

Numbers, Ronald L. and Numbers, Janet S., 'Millerism and Madness: A Study of "Religious Insanity" in Nineteenth-Century America', in Numbers and Butler, *The Disappointed*

Oddy, John A., 'Eschatological Prophecy in the English Theological Tradition, c. 1700–c. 1840', Ph.D. thesis, University of London, 1982

'Bicheno and Tyso on the Prophecies: A Baptist Generation Gap', *Baptist Quarterly* 35 (1993): 81–9

Osborn, George (ed.), *The Poetical Works of John and Charles Wesley*, 13 vols., London: Epworth Press, 1868–72

Outler, Albert C. (ed.), *The Works of John Wesley*, vols. I–IV, Nashville, TN: Abingdon, 1984–7

Pastorini, Signor: *see* Walmesley

Patrides, C. A. and Wittreich, J. (eds.), *The Apocalypse in English Renaissance Thought and Literature*, Manchester: Manchester University Press, 1984

Pelikan, Jaroslav and Lehman, Helmut T. (eds.), *Luther's Works*, 55 vols., Philadelphia: Fortress Press, 1958–86

Penton, M. James, *Apocalypse Delayed: The Story of the Jehovah's Witnesses*, Toronto: University of Toronto Press, 1985

Petto, Samuel, *The Revelation Unvailed: Or, an Essay Towards the Discovering I. When Many Scripture Prophecies had their Accomplishment and Turneth into History II. What are Now Fulfilling III. What Rest Still to be Fulfilled, with a Guess at the Time of Them. With an Appendix, Proving, that Pagan Rome Was not Babylon, Rev. 17, and that the Jews Shall be Converted*, 1693

Pinney, E. R. and Fassett, O. R., 'The Vision of the Eagle', *The Voice of Truth, and Glad Tidings of the Kingdom at Hand*, 1 January 1845

Pitts, William L., Jnr, 'Davidians and Branch Davidians 1929–1987', in Wright, *Armageddon in Waco*

Popkin, Richard H. (ed.), *Millenarianism and Messianism in English Literature and Thought 1650–1800*, Leiden: E. J. Brill, 1988

Potter, Francis, *An Interpretation of the Number '666' or 'The Number of the Beast'*, 1642

Priestley, Joseph, *The Present State of Europe Compared with Ancient Prophecies*, 1794 (ed.), *Theological Repository*, 6 vols., 1769–88

Rack, Henry, *Reasonable Enthusiast: John Wesley and the Rise of Methodism*, London: Epworth Press, 1989

Rainbow: A Magazine of Christian Literature, with Special Reference to the Revealed Future of the Church and the World, 24 vols., 1864–87

Räisänen, Heikki, 'The Effective "History" of the Bible: A Challenge to Biblical Scholarship?', *Scottish Journal of Theology* 45 (1992)

Rall, Harris Franklin, 'Methodism and Premillennialism', *Methodist Review*, fifth series, 36 (1920)
   Modern Premillennialism and the Christian Hope, New York: Abingdon, 1920

Rasmussen, Steen Raabjerg, 'Roots of the Prophetic Hermeneutic of William Miller', MA thesis, Newbold College, Bracknell, Berkshire, 1983

Reavis, Dick J., *The Ashes of Waco: An Investigation*, New York: Simon & Schuster, 1995

Reeves, Marjorie, *The Influence of Prophecy in the Later Middle Ages: A Study in Joachimism*, Oxford: Clarendon Press, 1969

Rogers, Philip George, *The Fifth Monarchy Men*, London: Oxford University Press, 1966

[Rollock, M. Robert,] *Lectures upon the First and Second Epistles of Paul to the Thessalonians: Preached by that Faithfull Servant of God M. Robert Rollock, Some-tyme Minister of the Evangell of Iesus Christ, and Rector of the College in Edinburgh*, 1606

Rowe, David L., *Thunder and Trumpets: Millerites and Religious Dissent in Upstate New York, 1800–1850*, Chico, CA: Scholars Press, 1985

Rudd, Sayer, *An Essay Towards a New Explication of the Doctrines of the Resurrection, Millennium, and Judgement*, 1734

Russell, William R., 'Martin Luther's Understanding of the Pope as the Antichrist', *Archiv für Reformationsgeschichte* 85 (1994)

Schüssler Fiorenza, Elisabeth, *Revelation: Vision of a Just World*, Edinburgh: T. & T. Clark, 1991

Schwartz, Hillel, *The French Prophets: The History of a Millenarian Group in Eight-eenth-Century England*, Berkeley: University of California Press, 1980

Scott, Geoffrey, '"The Times are Fast Approaching": Bishop Charles Walmesley OSB (1722–1797) as Prophet', *Journal of Ecclesiastical History* 36 (1985)

Sears, Jeanette, 'The Interpretation of Prophecy and Expectations of the End in Britain, 1845–1883', Ph.D. thesis, University of Manchester, 1984

Sermons by the Late Rev. Charles Wesley, A.M. Student of Christ-Church, Oxford. With a Memoir of the Author, by the Editor, London, 1816

Seventh-day Adventist Bible Commentary, 8 vols., Washington, DC: Review and Herald Publishing Association, 1953–60

*Seventh-day Adventists Believe... A Biblical Exposition of 27 Fundamental Doctrines,*Washington, DC: The Ministerial Association of the Seventh-day Adventist Church, 1988

Shea, William H., *Selected Studies on Prophetic Interpretation,* [Washington, DC:] General Conference of Seventh-day Adventists, 1982

Shelford, Robert, *Five Pious and Learned Discourses,*1635

Simmons, Thomas, *The Sure Side: or, God and the Church. A Sermon Preached on the Fifth of November, 1714 in the Parish of St. John Wapping,*1714

Simpson, David, *A Key to the Prophecies, or a Concise View of the Predictions Contained in the Old and New Testaments, which have been Fulfilled, are now Fulfilling, or are yet to be Fulfilled in the Latter Ages of the World,* 1839

Smith, Benjamin, *Methodism in Macclesfield,* 1875

Smith, Elwyn A. (ed.), *The Religion and the Republic,* Philadelphia: Fortress Press, 1971

Smith, Uriah, *Thoughts Critical and Practical on the Book of Revelation* [1865]
Thoughts Critical and Practical on the Book of Daniel [1873]
The United States in the Light of Prophecy; or an Exposition of Rev. 13:11–17, 1874
Daniel and Revelation, one-volume reprint edition, Watford: The Stanborough Press, 1921

Stackhouse, Thomas, *A New History of the Holy Bible, from the Beginning of the World to the Establishment of Christianity,* 2nd edn, 2 vols. 1742–4

Stark, Rodney and Bainbridge, William Sims, *The Future of Religion: Secularization, Revival, Cult Formation,* Stanford: University of California Press, 1985

Tabor, James D. and Gallagher, Eugene V., *Why Waco? Cults and the Battle for Religious Freedom in America,* Berkeley: University of California Press, 1995

Tarling, Lowell, *The Edges of Seventh-day Adventism,* Barragga Bay, New South Wales: Galilee, 1981

Telford, John (ed.), *Wesley's Veterans,* 7 vols., London: Charles H. Kelly, 1912

Tillinghast, John, *Knowledge of the Times,* 1654

Tumbleson, Raymond D., *Catholicism in the English Protestant Imagination,* Cambridge: Cambridge University Press, 1998

Tuveson, Ernest Lee, *Redeemer Nation: The Idea of America's Millennial Role,* Chicago: University of Chicago Press, 1968

Tyconius: The Book of Rules, translated with an introduction and notes by William S. Babcock, Atlanta, GA: Scholars Press, 1989

Tyerman, Luke, *The Life and Times of the Rev. John Wesley, M.A,* 3 vols., London: Hodder & Stoughton, 1870–1

Tyrrell, George, *Christianity at the Cross-Roads,* London: Longman's, Green & Co., 1910

Tyso, Joseph, *Elucidation of the Prophecies,* 1838

Wainwright, Arthur W., *Mysterious Apocalypse,* Nashville: Abingdon Press, 1993

[Walmesley, Charles,] *The General History of the Christian Church, from her Birth to her Final Triumph and State in Heaven, Chiefly Deduced from the Apocalypse of St. John the Apostle,* 1771

Ward, W. Reginald and Heitzenrater, Richard P. (eds.), *Works of John Wesley*, vols. XVIII–XXIII, Nashville, TN: Abingdon, 1988–95

Weber, Timothy P., *Living in the Shadow of the Second Coming: American Premillennialism, 1875–1982*, University of Chicago Press, 1987

Wesley, John, *Explanatory Notes upon the New Testament*, 1754
 The Works of John Wesley, 14 vols., London: Wesleyan Conference Office, 1872; reprint, Grand Rapids, MI: Zondervan, n.d.

White, B. R., *Hanserd Knollys and Radical Dissent in the Seventeenth Century*, London: Dr Williams's Trust, 1977
 The English Baptists of the Seventeenth Century, London: Baptist Historical Society, 1983

White, Ellen G., *The Great Controversy between Christ and Satan*, Mountain View, CA: Pacific Press Publishing Association, 1911
 Testimonies to Ministers and Gospel Workers, Mountain View, CA: Pacific Press Publishing Association, 1923

Woodcock, H. B., 'The True Millennium', *Western Midnight Cry*, 30 December 1844

Wright, Stuart A. (ed.), *Armageddon in Waco: Critical Perspectives on the Branch Davidian Conflict*, Chicago: University of Chicago Press, 1995

Index of names

Index of scripture references

OLD TESTAMENT

NEW TESTAMENT